In God's Image

THE ANTHROPOLOGY OF CHRISTIANITY

Edited by Joel Robbins

In God's Image

The Metaculture of Fijian Christianity

Matt Tomlinson

UNIVERSITY OF CALIFORNIA PRESS

Berkeley / Los Angeles / London

University of California Press, one of the most distinguished university presses in the United States, enriches lives around the world by advancing scholarship in the humanities, social sciences, and natural sciences. Its activities are supported by the UC Press Foundation and by philanthropic contributions from individuals and institutions. For more information, visit www.ucpress.edu.

University of California Press
Berkeley and Los Angeles, California

University of California Press, Ltd.
London, England

Library of Congress Cataloging-in-Publication Data

Tomlinson, Matt, 1970–
    In God's image : the metaculture of Fijian Christianity / Matt Tomlinson.
        p.   cm. — (The anthropology of Christianity ; 5)
    Includes bibliographical references and index.
    ISBN 978-0-520-25777-1 (cloth : alk. paper) — ISBN 978-0-520-25778-8 (pbk. : alk. paper)
    1. Methodist Church—Fiji—History.   2. Christianity—Fiji.   3. Fiji—Religion.   4. Fiji—Church history.   5. Fiji—Social conditions.   I. Title.

    BX8328.F55T66   2009
    287.099611—dc22   2008031254

Manufactured in the United States of America

18   17   16   15   14   13   12   11   10   09
10   9   8   7   6   5   4   3   2   1

This book is printed on Cascades Enviro 100, a 100% post consumer waste, recycled, de-inked fiber. FSC recycled certified and processed chlorine free. It is acid free, Ecologo certified, and manufactured by BioGas energy.

Contents

Illustrations

Figures

Maps

Tables

Preface and Acknowledgments

Many of the texts analyzed in this book—sermons, prayers, and other speech events—were recorded in Tavuki's Methodist church with the permission of the superintendent ministers serving in 1998–1999 and 2003, Revs. Isikeli Serewai and Setareki Tuilovoni. As I argue in the introduction, verbal performance is central to the efficacy of Fijian Methodist ritual, so I am especially grateful that these men allowed me to bring my tape recorder and microphone to church. Besides recording church services, I gathered data for this book at kava-drinking sessions. At nightly sessions, people are joined together for several hours, relaxed, and in a talkative mood, so I have asked many questions in these contexts on a wide range of subjects, writing my notes up later.

Day by day I took part in village life and wrote field notes on what I saw and heard. I tried to play the role appropriate to a young, unmarried Fijian man by working in gardens, joining communal projects, taking local trips, and joining friends to drink kava each night—making sure to sit down low, where the other unmarried men were, and helping with the preparation and serving. On several occasions I traveled with ministers and government officials around Kadavu to get a sense of how the villages of Tavuki Bay compare with villages elsewhere in Kadavu.

Language, Names, and Images

The indigenous languages of Fiji are divided into two main groups, western and eastern, but placing Kadavu within east or west is complicated because of different degrees of influence in different parts of the island. The variety of Fijian spoken in Tavuki shows uniquely local elements as well as influence from both of the two major branches of Fijian (see Pawley 1980: 1–2).

I am using the standard Fijian orthography devised by the missionary-linguist David Cargill, along with the use of *j* to reflect distinctive Kadavuan pronunciations:

b is pronounced /mb/ as in nu*mb*er

c is pronounced /th/ as in *th*is

d is pronounced /nd/ as in la*nd*ing

g is pronounced /ng/ as in si*ng*er

q is pronounced /ngg/ as in fi*ng*er

j is pronounced /ch/ as in *ch*eek

When quoting Bible verses in English I always use the King James Version. As I discuss in chapter 1, the Fijian Bible is a somewhat awkward translation, with its foreign elements and grammatical quirks. The King James Version's complex and anachronistic phrases give present-day English speakers a reasonable feeling of the Fijian Bible's awkwardness. (The Bible Society in the South Pacific produced a new, idiomatic Fijian New Testament in 1987, but it was not in wide circulation in Kadavu during my fieldwork.)

Ellipses indicate a deleted word or passage. In most translations I have aimed to be precisely accurate, replicating such speech idiosyncrasies as half-finished sentences, stammers, and repetitions, to convey speech's slippery dynamism. An exception to this approach is in chapter 7, where, because of the length of the narrative, I have used a freer translation style in the service of readability.

Throughout the book, I use pseudonyms when discussing sensitive events, and note this fact. Otherwise, all names are accurate. This decision was arrived at in consultation with the Rev. Isikeli Serewai and the Roko Tui Kadavu, Ratu Sela D. Nanovo. I use the adjective and collective noun *Fijian* to designate indigenous Fijians. When discussing citizens of Indian descent, I usually use the term *Indo-Fijian*. Finally, throughout the text, I capitalize *Church* to mean the institution and lowercase *church* to indicate a building.

All photographs were taken by me during fieldwork between 1998 and 2006. They have been cropped, digitally color-corrected, and cleansed of dust and scratches. Stuart Lees provided invaluable advice and assistance in preparing them for publication. The maps were prepared by Kara Rasmanis.

Acknowledgments

Grants for this research came from several organizations. The Department of Anthropology at the University of Pennsylvania supported two months of preliminary work in 1996, and an International Dissertation Research Fellowship from the Social Science Research Council funded research for one year, from September 1998 to August 1999. In 2003 I was able to spend three more months in Fiji thanks to a faculty research grant from Bowdoin College; in 2005–2006 I returned for two more months courtesy of the Faculty of Arts at Monash University.

Material in several of the chapters has been previously published. Much of chapter 4 appeared as "Perpetual Lament: Christianity and Sensations of Historical Decline in Fiji" in the *Journal of the Royal Anthropological Institute* 10, no. 3 (2004): 653–673. Some additional material in chapter 4 was published as "Speaking of Coups before They Happen: Kadavu, May–June 1999," in *Pacific Studies* 25, no. 4 (2002): 9–28. Chapter 5 incorporates material from "Sacred Soil in Kadavu, Fiji," published in *Oceania* 72, no. 4 (2002): 237–257, and "Ritual, Risk and Danger: Chain Prayers in Fiji," published in *American Anthropologist* 106, no. 1 (2004): 6–16. My sincere thanks to Wiley-Blackwell Publishing, the Pacific Institute at Brigham Young University–Hawai'i, and Oceania Publications at the University of Sydney for permission to use this work.

Personally and professionally, I owe a great debt of appreciation to the chiefs and people of the vanua of Tavuki, Kadavu. Since my first visit in 1996, I have been shown kindness, generosity, hospitality, and patience beyond imagination. The work would not have been possible without the permission and guidance of the Turaga Bale na Vunisa Levu, the Tui Tavuki, Ratu I. W. Narokete; the Tu Dau, Ratu Wata Druma; the late Roko Tui Kadavu, Ratu Sela D. Nanovo, and his successor, Osepati Tuicakau, with their staff at the Kadavu Provincial Office; and the superintendent ministers of the Methodist Church in Kadavu, Rev. Isikeli Serewai, in whose house I lived in 1996 and 1998–1999, and his successors, Revs. Setareki Tuilovoni (who hosted me in 2003) and Inoke Bota.

Along with these men and their families, several others have been especially kind and instructive. Ratu Josaia Veibataki, the assistant Roko Tui Kadavu, not only wrote out many of the transcriptions in this study, but has also opened his home to me since the beginning (and hosted me in 2005–2006) and taught me many distinctions of Kadavuan language and culture. In my travels around the island with Ratu Jo—and in story-telling at convivial kava sessions with him at his "blue house" on the lagoon's shore—I have learned a great deal, and also realized how much more I have to learn. The Methodist catechists Tomasi Laveasiga and Sevanaia F. Takotavuki explained many Church issues to me, and they, along with my good friends Viliame Uqe, Ratu Laisiasa Cadri, Maikali Tuvoli, Baleiwai Susu, and Luke Rawalai (bula, tavale) and their fami-lies showed me what daily life in a traditional vanua is like. Finally, the chiefs of Nadurusolo were especially kind to me in their role supporting the household of the superintendent minister. I apologize for not nam-ing all of the people in the villages of Tavuki, Nagonedau, Baidamu-damu, Solodamu, Waisomo, Natumua, and Nukunuku who have been so caring. Au lokali ni sauma rawa na nomu ivakarau ni vikauwaitaki kei na nomu dau vukei au. Au nuitakina ni na bu yaga vei kemu na ivola ka.

At the very beginning of my explorations, Monika Sauriva O'Brien in Philadelphia tutored me in Fijian language and culture. Since then, Paul Geraghty, Sekove Bigitibau, and Albert J. Schütz have provided valuable advice on linguistic matters. Venina Kaloumaira, Margaret Patel, Mosese Uluicicia, Vijay Naidu, Michael Monsell Davis, and Nii-K Plange were all generous with guidance and assistance when I began arranging my research plans and permissions in Suva. During my time in Kadavu, I have had the privilege of interacting with other researchers who have found it an especially hospitable and fascinating place, includ-ing Martin Olsen and Mark Calamia. Shane Aporosa has untiringly shared his expertise and insights based on his work at Rijimodi, and we have continued conversations begun in Fiji over good bowls of kava in New Zealand and Australia. Moreover, his regular kava circle in Hamil-ton has assisted me with some thorny translation questions.

Four individuals have decisively shaped my thinking about language, culture, and religion: Greg Urban and Webb Keane, who were my pri-mary advisors at the University of Pennsylvania; Joel Robbins, without whose sharp advice and sympathetic guidance this book would not have come together; and Susan Gal, whose undergraduate classes in lan-guage and culture at Rutgers University inspired me to pursue anthro-pology as a major, then a postgraduate degree and a career. Ward Good-enough had retired before I arrived at Penn, but has such energy (far more energy in his seventies and eighties than any graduate student could muster) that he supervised my independent studies in the ethnography of Oceania and served on my dissertation committee with Igor Kopytoff and Susan Blum, to all of whom I am immensely grateful.

Over the years that this book has taken shape, many people have discussed the central issues with me and read and commented on drafts of various parts. For their help in many ways at different stages, I thank David Akin, Kristin Cahn von Seelen, Hilary Dick, Matthew Engelke, Rod Ewins, Michael Hesson, Martha Kaplan, Michael Lempert, Debra McDougall, Ellen Moodie, Jeff Oaks, Sabina Perrino, Guido Pigliasco, Deborah Pope, Gerry Schramm, Rev. Jill Small, Tarisi Sorovi Vunidilo, Thomas Strong, Andrew Thornley, Christina Toren, Susanna Trnka, and Jeremy Wallach. Extra special thanks go to Andrew Arno, Ilana Gershon, Hiro Miyazaki, Trevor Stack, and Kristina Wirtz, who have read most or all of the manuscript and provided invaluable comments and criticisms that have improved the final product. I also owe a debt of gratitude to Reed Malcolm, Kalicia Pivirotto, and Jacqueline Volin at the University of California Press, and the Press's three anonymous reviewers.

Finally, I must thank my wife, Sharon Littlefield Tomlinson, for her wisdom, good humor, and support—and for bringing our son, Andrew Cayo, into the world. But I must conclude on a note of sadness, for four men who I wished would see this book have passed away in the past several years. My father, Gerald Tomlinson, passed away in 2006, shortly before my uncle Francis Price and five years after my maternal grandfather, S. John Usakowski. One of the first and kindest men I met in Tavuki, the Roko Tui Kadavu and then senator, Ratu Sela D. Nanovo, passed away in 2003. I miss all of them every day, and dedicate this book to their memories.

PART ONE

Situation

Like all global religions, Christianity is forged in distinct local forms. Compared cross-culturally, these forms differ extensively in the ritual practices they motivate and the visions of the spiritual world they inspire. Fijian Methodism, the subject of this book, is a "land-centered Christianity," in the fitting phrase of Martha Kaplan (1990b: 16): land is considered sacred and sometimes dangerous, given to Fijians by God but haunted by local spirits.

Fijian Methodist discourse rings with the theme of loss; decline, entropy, and disorder are pervasive and resonant motifs. Things fall apart. The center can hold, however, for at the center is a belief that things are falling apart. In this book, I return repeatedly to the theme of loss because it is one I encountered time and again during my field research, expressed in many different ways, the various expressions reflecting off each other to shine with the clarity of a gemlike cultural truth. Society's decline is seen in the reflected light from a past golden age. A key characteristic of Fijian golden age discourse is the emphasis on power, rather than virtue, as what is lost. Buell Quain (1948: 203) wrote memorably of a Fijian informant, "[He enjoyed] proving to me that his forebears were virile men who ate their own children." Such a speaker would feel at home in Tavuki village, Kadavu Island, the locus of my research. In Tavuki the past is both valorized and demonized. The powerful and respected ancestors come back in dreams and curses, interrupting people's lives in the present; they provoke "awe and admiration," as Quain remarks of one dead chief in Vanualevu (203), but they also provoke anxiety. This anxiety can, ultimately, generate new kinds of hopefulness, new projects of recuperation for the land and its peoples in the future.

Introduction

Although it is often considered a religion of expanded horizons and improved futures, Christianity can create a profound sense of loss. In Kadavu Island, Fiji, where most people are Methodists, a sense of loss is prominent and pervasive, created and displayed through everyday talk and habitual practices. A commonly heard word is *leqa,* meaning "trouble" or "problem." Trouble, in Fijian understanding, comes from social disunity, which leads to the loss of power. This trouble comes in many shapes, but only one size. The ancestors were physically larger than people are today and worked together communally; each knew his or her proper place in the social hierarchy and followed customs respectfully. People in the present are smaller and infected by individualism; those who return to the village after spending time in the city bring disruptive new ideas, and as a result traditional customs are being neglected. The past golden age is a reflection of the present—but an inversion of it, shimmering in a cracked mirror. The present is fragmented by money, which undercuts the authority of traditional chiefs; by democracy, which divides the polity; and by the imitation of foreign cultures. This fragmentation leaves people at the mercy of non-Christian spirits, who still have the strength of the past and use it to curse people in the present. People who suffer from curses attempt to thwart them through prayer and other forms of Christian ritual.

The past is not a foreign country, but an intensely local one, a strong and sometimes dangerous one. In this book I argue that Kadavuans' visions of a dangerous past and a weakened present are the

5

result of competition between Methodist Church authorities and traditional chiefs. I analyze the interactions between Church and chiefs as *metaculture*—as Fijian reflections and commentary on Fijian social processes. The metacultural distinction between the *lotu* (Christianity) and the *vanua* (a complex domain encompassing chiefs, their people, land, and tradition) is a profoundly consequential one in Fiji. Metacultural expressions help frame debates over what life in Fiji is all about, or what it should be all about, who belongs "on stage" in public life, and what roles they are allowed to play in which contexts. Metacultural expressions of decline and loss are expressed regularly in church rituals and embodied nightly in kava-drinking sessions, where people's intellectual certainty that their world is getting weaker is reinforced by the beverage's sedative effects.

The sense of loss provokes intense anxieties, such as the perennial fear among indigenous Fijians that their lands will be taken over by foreigners. Anxieties about loss sometimes lead to efforts at recuperation, however. As I will show, support for recent political violence in Fiji can be seen as sympathy for attempts to recuperate *mana* (effectiveness), efforts to intervene in history and set Fiji on a new trajectory. Such projects of reclamation and reorientation can also be distinctly personal, projects in which individuals see their own lives running against the grain of history. Ultimately I argue that Christianity, specifically Methodism, has created this Fijian sense of loss and also raised hopes of recuperation.

Christianity, Power, and Loss

More than 99 percent of indigenous Fijians are Christian. In rural villages, Christianity is vibrant, visible, and active. The Methodist church is often the biggest, most expensive, and most well-constructed building, situated prominently on the village green, and a wooden drum is beaten loudly to announce the beginning of services. Enthusiasm for church projects waxes and wanes, depending partly on the charisma of the local minister, but for many people the Methodist Church is the pulmonary system of weekly life, a regular breathing pattern of scheduled worship and work. Christian calendrics are reflected in the names of the days of the week: Friday is Vakaraubuka (preparing firewood); Saturday is Vakarauwai (preparing water), because work is forbidden on Sunday, Sigatabu (literally, "taboo day"). Besides attending church, many people

support Methodism by raising funds for the church, assisting in garden-
ing, maintenance, and construction projects, and choosing to become
lay preachers, choir singers, and leaders of subgroups such as women's
or youth groups.

In towns and cities many Christian denominations have a conspicu-
ous presence: Methodism, Roman Catholicism, Anglicanism, Seventh-
day Adventism, as well as Assemblies of God and Latter-Day Saints.
Walking around the capital city, Suva, one is likely to see banners strung
across Victoria Parade advertising events such as Bible Week or posters
trumpeting the arrival of foreign evangelical ministers. International
evangelical superstars such as Benny Hinn and Reinhard Bonnke occasionally come to the islands and hold revivalist "crusades" that attract
tens of thousands of people. The beloved national rugby team publicly
displays its Christian identity: in the late 1990s, the team's jerseys had
the biblical reference "Phil 4:13" emblazoned on them, referring to
the verse in Paul's letter to the Philippians that declares, "I can do all
things through Christ which strengtheneth me." Eventually the team
began displaying corporate sponsorship rather than religious faith on
its jerseys, but the verse was not gone, only displaced: the team captain,
Waisale Serevi, began writing "Phil—4:13" on his wrist as he prepared
for games.[1]

Christianity's public presence has been reflected in official proclamations since the beginning of Fiji's colonial history. The Deed of Cession
of 1874, which made the islands subject to Queen Victoria, stated that
Fijian chiefs were "desirous of securing the promotion of civilisation
and Christianity" (quoted in Dean and Ritova 1988: 36). The 1997 version of the constitution declares in its preamble, "We, the people of the
Fiji Islands, seeking the blessing of God who has always watched over
these islands: Recalling the events in our history that have made us what
we are, especially . . . the conversion of the indigenous inhabitants of
these islands from heathenism to Christianity through the power of the
name of Jesus Christ . . ." (ICL 2000). The government insignia of Fiji
displays the phrase *Rerevaka na Kalou ka Doka na Tui* (Fear God and
Honor the Chiefs), from 1 Peter 2:17.

Indigenous discourse often binds religion and ethnicity together
in a tight package required for national citizenship: to be Fijian, the
claim goes, one must be indigenous and Christian. Many citizens are
neither, however. More than a third of the population is composed of
citizens of Indian descent, and these Indo-Fijians are predominantly
Hindus and Muslims; table 1 offers a demographic snapshot of the

major denominations. Overall, approximately 58 percent of Fiji's citizens are Christian, 34 percent are Hindu, and 7 percent are Muslim (Walsh 2006: 201). Although some indigenous leaders profess tolerance, many others insist on the conjunction of indigeneity, Christianity, and citizenship. Sitiveni Rabuka, the leader of two coups in 1987, claimed that his overthrow of the government was "a mission" from God and said, "If this land is run by Christians, or Fijians who are Christians, everything will be in place" (Dean and Ritova 1988: 11, 36; see also Malcomson 1990: 138). In his role as a lay preacher in the Methodist Church, Rabuka "loved to preach sermons on a text from the Old Testament exilic book of Lamentations (5:2): 'Our inheritance has been turned over to strangers, our homes to aliens' " (Heinz 1993: 433). He also said that he wanted Indo-Fijians to stay in the country after his coups, but added in the next breath, "It will be a big challenge for us [indigenous Fijians] to convert them to Christianity. . . . We either go that way, or they convert us and we all become heathens" (quoted in Dean and Ritova 1988: 121; see also Ryle 2005: 66–67). During the tumult of 1987, the Rotuman scholar Vilsoni Hereniko (2003: 78) observed such aggressive Christian nationalism with dismay: "I went to church, thinking it would provide a safe haven from the racist remarks I was hearing everywhere I turned. But I was shocked to hear the Fijian minister at the pulpit refer to the Indians as evil heathens who needed steering to the Light, and proclaim that until they converted, they deserved to be treated as second-class citizens. I couldn't help but be reminded that when the first British missionaries came to Fiji, this was the way they spoke of the Fijians" (see also Robertson and Sutherland 2001: 23).

Since the events of 1987, Fiji has seen a great deal of political turmoil, including two more government coups in 2000 and 2006; a Methodist "Church coup" following the 1987 military coups, in which ethnonationalist hard-liners kicked the serving president out of office; mass demonstrations for laws banning commerce on Sundays; the harassment of Indo-Fijians and the destruction of their property, resulting in massive emigration; and other chaotic events in which the division between indigenous and Christian and nonindigenous and non-Christian has been central.

Because of the Methodist Church's deep and continuing influence in many spheres of indigenous Fijian life, I went to my field site of Tavuki village, Kadavu Island, with the specific intention of studying Christianity. I chose Kadavu in consultation with Church and Fijian government

TABLE I. Religious demographics in Fiji, 1996

Denominations with at least 1 percent of the total national population

Denomination	Percentage of Indigenous Fijian Population Who Are Members	Percentage of Indo-Fijian Population Who Are Members	Percentage of Total Population in Fiji Who Are Members
Methodist	66.7	1.6	36.2
Sanatan Dharma (Hindu)	0.1	57.1	25.2
Roman Catholic	13.2	1.0	8.8
Sunni Muslim	0.0	9.5	4.2
Assemblies of God	6.3	1.4	4.0
Seventh-day Adventist	5.1	0.2	2.9
Arya Samaj (Hindu)	0.0	2.8	1.2

SOURCE: Adapted from Walsh 2006: 201.

officials because of its reputation for Christian conservatism; more than 93 percent of Kadavuans were members of the Methodist Church at the time (Government of Fiji 1995). Perhaps predictably, I sometimes felt myself pulled in the opposite direction from that of many other ethnographers: instead of noticing Christianity grudgingly, as many do, I had to acknowledge the contexts in which it is overshadowed. Specifically, I had to observe the ways in which the chiefly system is a locus of power and authority to which Methodism tends to be subordinate.

Observing the power of the chiefly system, I began to see, and then to analyze, the ways that interaction between Church and chiefs generates an understanding of the past as effective and dangerous compared to the present, which is considered ineffectual and threatened. The signs were everywhere. People spoke of the ancestors' strength and violence and worried about curses from those ancestors that afflict people in the present. A ritual called a chain prayer (*masu sema*) was occasionally performed to defuse curses, but the old spirits' malicious power never went away—it stayed like an infection, bound to flare up when the right conditions converged. The signs of ancestral strength were embedded in the soil: people could become ill by digging a taboo patch of earth. After bone and skull fragments were unexpectedly unearthed in Tavuki in January 1999, one man stated that the deceased must have been a big person; because the bones did not look particularly large, I wondered whether discourse about the ancestors' superior size had conditioned him to see the remains that way or whether he spoke that way to placate a possibly disturbed spirit. Either is possible—or both—because the claim that the ancestors had an inherent strength that people today lack is a canonical Fijian truth. People frequently substantiate it by referring to the Bible; the verse I heard used most frequently, in conversations, sermons, and other speech genres, was the beginning of Genesis 1:26: "And God said, Let us make man in our image, after our likeness." I came to understand that people often used this biblical passage to indicate humanity's loss of divine characteristics, because people are evidently not godly anymore. This was not just a moral critique but a lament about vulnerability. Everywhere I turned, it seemed, people were ready to criticize the present in terms of an idealized past. This is common cross-culturally, but I was continually struck by the fact that Fijian discourse was not nostalgia. It was lament—and lament that could motivate new kinds of religious and political action.

Fijians sometimes compare the ancient ancestors' lives to those of Old Testament Israelites and declare that Methodism is "traditional." Some people take this logic a step further and declare that parts of Fiji were already Christian before the first missionaries arrived (Kaplan 1990a, 1990b, 1995; Nacagilevu 1996; see also Jolly 1992), that "'the coming of the light' did not violate indigenous cultural practice but revealed the inherent Christianity of the Fijian people" (Toren 1988: 697), or even that Fijians' ancestors were "descendants of the lost tribe[s] of Israel" (Ratuva 2002: 21).[2] The arrival of missionaries is often recognized, however, as a rupture. It was the moment that Christian "light" came to the "darkness" of heathenism and its practices (such as cannibalism), which can now sometimes be joked about but whose vibrations still hum and buzz with an aura of lost power and lingering peril. As Geoffrey White (1991: 14) puts it, "Pacific perceptions of ancestors and their pre-Western ways may be fraught with ambivalence, encompassing both ridicule of primitivism and respect for a lost vitality and power." The ancestors from the dark past are dangerous because, as representatives of tradition, they can punish modern transgressions, and as non-Christian spirits they are potentially malicious. The Methodist Church positions itself as the force that can defeat these phantoms from the past, as a bulwark buffering the present era from the curses and sins of previous ages. In short, the Church is considered both traditional and a defense against tradition's darkness.

Buell Quain (1948), who worked in Vanualevu in the 1930s, diagnosed Christianity's role in generating the Fijian sense of decline and of loss. Observing how Christianity threatened local political orders, he wrote: "Wesleyan [Methodist] hatred of the devil-worshiping priests colored the entire British [colonial] attitude; without realizing the intimate interdependence of priest and chief, British law condemned forever the former and by so doing weakened the entire native political structure. Too late, Britain tried to reinstate the executive powers of the local chiefs; but the falsely royal 'chiefs' of church and colonial administration were well established, and the old authority continued to crumble" (71; see also Watters 1969: 218–219).

The dynamic described by Quain has become a kind of perpetual loss of power, a durable sense of powerlessness. Quain noted that Methodist missionaries disrupted local political relations and arrogated power to themselves by displacing power to Jehovah. Here, I want to develop Quain's insight about Christianity's role in creating a sense of loss by showing how descriptions and narratives of loss, once they begin to circulate, take on a logic and force of their own. The language of loss, I argue, plays a central role in generating anxieties about social decline and fragmentation. My interpretation of the Fijian sense of decline thus differs fundamentally from explanations offered by other anthropologists investigating decline, such as James Ferguson's 1999 description of Zambian frustrations with thwarted expectations of "modern" progress. In Ferguson's view, the idea that industrialization and urbanization would inevitably lead Zambia to material progress—an idea held firmly by scholars and the Zambian public alike—has been rudely disproved: the nation has suffered in the past three decades from a slump in copper prices and an increase in foreign debt, leaving the promises of modernity unfulfilled and snaring people in "a tangle of confusion, chaos, and fear" (19). In contrast to Ferguson, I emphasize religious language's force behind the creation of a sense of decline, disorder, diminution, and loss. People in Kadavu do not read from a teleological script about the benefits of material development, and they have not been left bereft by global economic shifts. In Fiji, to speak of loss is to speak in a Christian idiom.

Anthropological Analyses of Christianity

Until recently, many anthropologists have been disinclined to study and write about Christianity. This was especially striking in the case of researchers whose field sites were zones of intensive missionary activity. When Evans-Pritchard wrote *Nuer Religion* he wasn't referring to the

American Mission, and when Raymond Firth wrote *The Work of the Gods in Tikopia* he didn't mean Jehovah. Joel Robbins has recently identified several reasons for anthropologists' hesitancy to develop a coherent discipline of the study of Christianity. Because many anthropologists have backgrounds in societies suffused with Judeo-Christian influences, he writes, Christians living elsewhere can seem misleadingly familiar. Paradoxically, devout Christians seem intellectually incommensurable to anthropologists because of their different universalist epistemologies and stances on the limits and consequences of tolerance: "To claim, as anthropologists must, that Christians make sense in their own terms is at least to admit that it is possible to argue in a reasonable way that anthropologists do not make sense in their own" (2003: 192–193; see also Harding 1991; Robbins 2004, 2006). In short, many anthropologists have tended to think that Christians are both too easily understood and ultimately impossible to understand. Robbins recommends that scholars acknowledge the difficulties in developing an anthropology of Christianity, but he insists that the work should proceed.

A significant body of ethnographic literature on Christianity is now developing. Recent work has been particularly effective at illuminating topics of globalization, cultural change, and subjectivity (see especially Cannell 2006; Hefner 1993; Keane 2007; Robbins 2004). Three key facts have emerged in these studies: first, Christianity generates particular tensions that confound simple distinctions between local and global, traditional and modern, and individual and collective; second, it often fails to resolve the tensions it generates, and these tensions are, in fact, often irresolvable; third, such failures are not end points but drive people's ongoing efforts in ritual, doctrinal, theological, and other realms.

In regard to these three points, Webb Keane has offered an elegant argument concerning the relationship between Protestantism and modernity ("a term of self-description in a narrative of moral progress"), one focused on an ideology of signs' separation from objects in the world. He writes that within this ideology, subjects become "the source of [their] own authority," with God's agency becoming "an assumed background against which the person acts or seeks divine sources for the radical assertion of the individual's own agency" (2007: 201, 208, 208–209 n. 6). The ideology of signs' separation from the world is logically problematic, however, as semiosis necessarily has a material aspect. Protestant subjects are thus caught in an "irresolvable tension between abstraction and the inescapability of material and social mediations" (Keane 2006: 322), an endlessly looping effort of distinguishing inner truths from outer realities, insisting that religious practice be motivated by sincerity and worrying about the ways God is or is not manifest materially. Parts of Keane's argument have been taken up by scholars such as Matthew Engelke (2007: 246), who analyzes the case of a Zimbabwean Christian movement whose members "are committed to a project of immateriality." The "Friday apostolics" of Zimbabwe strive for a "live and direct" relationship with divinity, one unmediated by material tokens. Their antimaterialism is so extreme that they say reading the Bible is a sin: its physical nature as a book means that it obstructs spiritual inspiration, it degrades, and it can be burned or used as toilet paper. Yet even as they work to achieve an immaterial faith, their realizations of this faith are inextricably entangled in, emergent from, and dependent on a host of material tokens, from language's material aspects, to the ritual clothing they wear, to the special medicines they concoct. In short, the Friday apostolics can never entirely succeed in their project of immateriality, although they work energetically at it.

Two other recent ethnographies have shown the specific ways Christianity creates irresolvable tensions of evil and sin, Birgit Meyer's investigation of satanic obsessions in Ghana and Joel Robbins's analysis of the sense of sinfulness in highland Papua New Guinea. Meyer (1999) describes Pentecostals of the Ewe ethnolinguistic group who are fixated on Satan and his demons, continually invoking them and then expunging them in ritual action. She shows how daily concerns of kinship obligations, sickness, and thwarted hopes of material prosperity trouble the Ewe Pentecostals, who, rather than suffer their earthly trials meekly, want to fight back. They do so by treating Satan and his minions seriously as adversaries to be confronted rather than as outmoded superstitions to be ignored (as the older mainline Evangelical Presbyterian Church would have it). To understand how the Devil became such a galvanizing figure for Pentecostals, Meyer traces the histories of translation in which concepts of evil, sin, and demons were introduced to the local vernacular. One key term in Ewe, which means "breath," was used by German Pietist missionaries for the English term "spirit" and then extended with different adjectives to designate evil spirits, the Christian Holy Spirit, and "an individual's spirit" (145). The missionaries chose the term for breath specifically because it did not have any "heathen" ritual associations. The old meaning of "breath" and the new "suprasensory sense" of it as a spiritual force resonated with each other, and a "linguistic base was laid for a theory of spirit possession which integrated both non-Christian spiritual beings and the Spirit of the Christian [God] as comparable, though conflicting, entities, thereby opposing them on a single, spiritual battlefield" (146).

At the core of modern Ghanaian Pentecostal dilemmas, according to Meyer, lies a problematic of sameness versus difference inherited from the Pietist missionaries. As they drew on vernacular terms to articulate their novel vision of a Christian spiritual world, Pietists established a kind of equivalence within which different religious discourses could be engaged. But the missionaries were at pains to deny substantial sameness, asserting Christianity's rightness and truth in contrast to Ewe error and falsehood. Ewe religion was diabolized, meaning it was placed by Pietists within an overarching domain of Satanic practices. Ghosts and local deities were relabeled as demonic spirits, as they were in Fiji and many other places. According to Meyer, Pietists and Presbyterians saw conversion to Christianity as a sharp linear movement and a break from the past, after which those spirits did not matter anymore. Many Ewe, however, facing modern economic and social pressures as well as universal problems of sickness, seek "the opportunity to experience the satanic" (172), to express "hidden desires to return to the old, without actually doing so" (111)—indeed, to confront the forces of the past and then defeat them, repeatedly. In Ewe Pentecostalism, diabolization has become demonization, whereby old spirits clamor for a place in social life as "churches provide an elaborate discourse on particular demons and ritual practices related to them" (172). A key point to draw from Meyer's work is that Ewe Pentecostalism's vitality depends on the rich, vivid imagining of Satan and his demonic agents. The battle against the Devil is never won, and people are continually troubled by this, but they return to the ritual fight energized in their lives as Christians.

Whereas Ewe Pentecostals focus on demonic forces, the Urapmin of highland Papua New Guinea worry about sinfulness. They are obsessed with sin and their need to expunge it before Judgment Day, whose arrival they believe is imminent. Like Ewe Pentecostals, Urapmin become possessed by the Holy Spirit of the Christian Trinity. For the Ewe, the Holy Spirit functions mainly as "a negation of the satanic," and they are so focused on the satanic that Holy Spirit possession is "dull and meaningless" compared to possession by evil spirits (Meyer 1999: 211). The Urapmin, in contrast, become possessed violently by the Holy Spirit during "Spirit disko" rituals meant to ensure people's collective salvation. As Robbins (2004) shows, Urapmin are disturbed by the Christian doctrine of individual salvation, and in Spirit diskos they aim to achieve a good moral state as a community. Successful Spirit diskos are only temporary solutions, however, and anxieties about sinfulness always reemerge and thrive.

According to Robbins, when Urapmin adopted Christianity via the Australian Baptist Mission, they were responding to surprising new humiliations that reshaped their self-conceptions (see also Robbins and Wardlow 2005). Previously at the center of a regional religious network, Urapmin found themselves marginalized when their neighbors converted to Christianity, and they keenly felt the moral criticisms leveled at them by the new converts. Such humiliations led Urapmin to convert enthusiastically to Christianity even as the Baptists' core values devastatingly undermined previous cultural certainties. Whereas Urapmin valued willfulness (the force motivating people to act in ways that are often lawless but sometimes constructive; Robbins 2004: 185–186), Baptists damned all willfulness as inherently sinful. Moreover, as old taboos on consumption and social interaction were ended in the Christian era, Urapmin have been left with "the sense that their wills now lack control; they find themselves wanting everything and filled with envy, jealousy, and the ominous conviction that their community is full of potential thieves and adulterers" (221). Robbins describes the personal situations of various men and women who strive earnestly to avoid sin but remain anxiously convinced that they are mired in it and thus threatened with damnation. Christianity's "unrelentingly individualist" emphasis has created for Urapmin an irresolvable dilemma, a situation in which they "experience their own lives as ones of constant moral failure" (293, 249).

In this book I follow the lead of these scholars, describing a cultural scenario wherein Christianity creates irresolvable tensions while holding out the promise of recuperation.[3] For a crucial point in all of these cases is that—as deeply troubled as people are by loss, by the Devil, by sin, by signs' material embodiment—they nonetheless maintain a prospective orientation, a kind of hope that is defined not by its content but by its futurity (Miyazaki 2004). Although Christian tensions are often irresolvable, they are productive for this very reason; subjects do not give up on their projects, but strive ever more energetically to realize them. After all, for Ewe the Devil can be beaten, but he needs to be defeated continually; for Urapmin sin can be expunged from the community, but only temporarily. In Fiji the sense of loss generated by Christian conflicts with the chiefly system is pervasive and durable, but such loss also inspires hope of recuperation, of putting history on a new trajectory toward social and personal strength. In one way, I take a different approach from the authors discussed earlier: I argue that people's reflections on social processes must be analyzed in terms of metaculture, a topic to which I now turn.

Language, Culture, and Metaculture

Many anthropologists have come to appreciate the theoretical value and ethnographic precision of a language- and discourse-centered approach to culture.[4] Echoing Bakhtin's (1981: 293) famous dictum, "The word in language is half someone else's," one author writes:

> We do not live in private worlds, or speak private languages. In language resides our social being. Language is not only the technical means by which we can inquire whether reality is intelligible, but also the encompassing medium in which we investigate the relations between thought, action, and reality. . . . Conversely, it is within the medium of social life that language lives. Not only is language the primary means by which people are socialized, the chief way that they learn to participate in a society, it is also a primary means by which they participate in society. For these reasons, language is not only the most accessible social phenomenon but the most central social phenomenon. (Maskarinec 1995: 12)

Language is internal to our thoughts and external "in the world," a way of thinking abstractly as well as acting concretely, a way of summoning up and engaging with things that cannot be seen. In hearing, recording, transcribing, translating, and analyzing speech events, anthropologists can orchestrate sumptuously polyphonic ethnographies featuring distinct voices as well as common discursive themes.

Some of the most thought-provoking ethnographic research on Christianity has explicitly taken language use and language ideology as central concerns, showing how people's understanding of language's "proper" use and potential effects shapes their strategies and expectations in ritual performance. From ethnographies of Pentecostals who give exuberant testimonials, making and displaying their faith in terms of verbal power, to studies of contemplative Quakers who hesitate before speaking, anxious that the devil may lead them to mislead others, recent literature reveals an extensive range of Christian thought and practice about how language mediates humanity and divinity (e.g., Bauman 1983; Csordas 1997; Keane 1991, 1995, 1997a, 1997b, 1997c, 2002, 2006, 2007; Robbins 2001a, 2001b, 2004; Schieffelin 2000). Within the broad topic of language ideology, several distinct scholarly emphases have emerged, including Christian ideologies concerning the material dimensions of texts (Coleman 2000; Engelke 2007; Rutherford 2006) and ritual attempts to generate meaningfulness in Christianity (Engelke and Tomlinson 2006; Keller 2005).

I consider in-depth analysis of language to be integral to the argument in this book for two main reasons, both based on my ethnographic observations. First, speech often constitutes religious activity in Tavuki. Methodist services feature an array of verbal performances, including sermons, prayers, chiefly orations, hymns, and catechistic recitations, whereas forms of nonverbal practice involving bodily discipline have less consequence. In other words, although people engage in many significant nonverbal actions during services—for example, dressing formally, comporting their body respectfully, and giving money—it is verbal action that constitutes the most effective form of practice in Fijian Methodist ritual. Outside of church, language remains central to ritual effectiveness, as shown in the discussion of chain prayers in chapter 5.[5] Cross-culturally, language plays a foundational role in making spiritual presence palpable; spirits "come alive" when they make demands through shamans and mediums, appear in dreams that are turned into stories to tell others, and are whispered about in late night conversations. When people believe they are interacting with spirits by speaking to them or with them, linguistic characteristics such as ambiguity and allusion help generate a sense of danger and of uncertainty, and other characteristics such as reflexivity and formality may contribute to the sense that dangers are being controlled and risks overcome in ritual (see the works of Webb Keane, cited above).

The second reason I treat language as especially fruitful data is that speech, by serving as a primary means of representation, can become a focus of local debate. Some questions I heard posed in Tavuki about doctrine and practice were specifically questions of language use, for example, whether the Christian God has or needs a name, and whether the formulaic announcements made at kava sessions can summon demonic spirits. These are religious questions that depend on a particular understanding of how language works and how human agency is expressed and effected verbally. In addition, conflicts between Church and chiefs were sometimes contests over language. For example, one argument concerned whether it was appropriate to call on villagers to make their church contributions according to subclan name (the chiefly assertion) or according to village name (the Church assertion; see chapter 1).

Close analysis of language use and language ideologies can lead scholars to investigate broad questions about how culture circulates: What motivates the transmission of culture generally? What propels different kinds of social learning—intellectual, practical, aesthetic, and so forth? Although these questions sound almost crudely mechanical, they can be investigated with considerable nuance. As Greg Urban (2001; see also Urban 1991, 1996) argues, culture can be conceptualized as motion, as a force moving through the world, transmitted between people and manifest in what I call cultural products. According to Urban, culture shapes social space, which, correspondingly, channels cultural motion, but not all cultural products move in the same way.

Even though culture is not reducible to physical objects nor subject to the laws of physics, it shares certain properties with physical objects in motion through space and time. For example, inertia is one force generated by and acting on culture. Urban (2001: 15) characterizes as "inertial culture" the kinds of social learning that are simply imitative: "Something tends to be copied just because it is there already. This is most apparent in the case of cultural and, especially, language learning by young children, for whom the models that are present are what tend to be reproduced. Why does a child learn the language it does? The answer is that it is the language spoken by those around it. This is inertial culture. The child does not set out to create something new." In this ideal-typical example, culture is transmitted—a child learns a language—but nothing novel is created (cf. Makihara 2005). Under ideologies of "tradition," as anthropologists know well, great effort is expended in maintaining apparent inertia. People strive to make sure that transmission does not deform the cultural products, and so myths, rituals, and styles are (supposedly) kept constant from generation to generation.

Urban (2001: 15) opposes inertial culture to "accelerative culture," which is "culture on the side of futurity, looking forward rather than backward, characterized by newness and novelty, rather than oldness and familiarity." In other words, accelerative culture is culture of a new kind, novel social learning, breaking with tradition. Urban argues that to circulate successfully, such new culture must not only conform to some extent with perceived realities in the natural world, but must also conform to some extent with prior cultural expectations. So, for example, missionaries who translated the Bible into Fijian rendered "strong drink" as *yaqona,* meaning "kava," which is a Fijian beverage. No cultural product can be accepted if it is entirely novel; there must be a moment of recognition in which people can interpret newness via oldness. In ideologies of "modernity," however, newness itself often becomes a criterion of success or desirability, and pointing out that something "has been done before" can become an insult—in anthropological theory as well as popular arts. Accelerative culture is necessarily transformative: when Christianity was introduced to indigenous Fijians in the nineteenth century it profoundly reshaped local social processes, although it is now often recast by Fijians as something "traditional."

If culture can accelerate, it must be able to decelerate as well; recall that this is an analogy about the ways that social learning takes place, not an assertion that culture follows Newtonian laws. Urban writes that some forms of culture decelerate because of competition. For example, certain pre-Christian Fijian religious practices (including those ethnographic starlets, cannibalism and widow strangling) died out because missionaries banned them and introduced new ritual forms. Now the old practices exist discursively as echoes of the dangerous, powerful past: "Fijians have long talked privately and publicly of cannibalism as a cultural practice, for instance in my own conversations with them on the subject (in Fijian)" (Hooper 2003: 20). Some culture decelerates, however, simply because of entropy. To put it another way, if culture moves, then entropic forces—decay, disorder—come into effect. Seen in this light, conscious attempts to preserve tradition are recognized as active, creative efforts to correlate past and present in an iconic relationship where each side resembles the other.

Metaculture, according to Urban (2001: 281 n. 4), is "culture that is about culture," operating "as a distinct . . . layer of circulation articulating in various ways with the cultural plane." It is a cultural product, but one that reflects on, or comments on, aspects of culture, and as such it is necessarily comparative. Comparisons can be made along axes— themselves culturally shaped and calibrated—such as oldness and newness, effectiveness and ineffectiveness, and success and failure. In his monograph, the main metacultural categories that Urban analyzes are "tradition" and "modernity," the former defined by judgments of oldness and equivalence and the latter by judgments of newness and uniqueness (43). But metaculture is not a static reflection, not just an act of categorization after the fact of expression; it is creative and consequential, functioning as an accelerative force propelling other cultural products into social circulation.

Metacultural statements are easiest to recognize when the object upon which they reflect is the social group, the very thing often reified in popular terms as "a culture," such as "Fijians respect their village traditions" or "Australians give everybody a fair go." But metaculture does not need to encompass social wholes, imagined or otherwise; it simply needs to reflect on culture and affect its circulation. As an example of metaculture's nuances, consider the statements commonly heard in Fijian villages about Fijians being traditionally Christian, such as this one made in a speech given by a Fijian Affairs government representative in Naqalotu village, Yawe district, Kadavu, in June 1999: "We also see that the times are changing, life is changing, oh, the ways people look up and recognize chiefs' status have changed [lit., 'our recognizing the truth of the noble dwelling is also changing']. . . . The landowners' government [Fijian Affairs] believes the time our honorable chiefs accepted Christianity which had arrived in our land, they thus accepted that Christianity is a part of Fijian life today, and we also believe the word of creation in His beginning to create the world when the creation was finished, the Holy Trinity said something: 'We are making man in our image, after our likeness' [Genesis 1:26]."[6]

The speaker's claim that "Christianity is a part of Fijian life today" is an explicitly metacultural one, and it resonates with his statement about "the time our honorable chiefs accepted Christianity." In other words, Christianity is traditional—sanctioned by chiefs' acceptance more than 150 years ago—and, as a traditional part of Fijian life, it is now something potentially threatened and necessarily safeguarded. (For this speaker, the primary threat to traditional Fijian Christianity was not the Hinduism or Islam practiced by Indo-Fijians, but the newer evangelical forms of Christianity embraced by some indigenous Fijians. These sects forbid kava drinking, thereby refusing to recognize the authority of chiefs, whose position is socially inscribed in kava circles.) His statement "We also see that the times are changing" is not a Dylanesque celebration of newness but a resolutely Fijian warning about weakness and chaos. The event at which he was speaking was a government-organized workshop echoing with metacultural statements about problems in Fiji and how tradition should be honored appropriately.

Christianity is cultural; it does not stand outside of social processes in any meaningful anthropological sense. But I argue that, culturally speaking, Christianity is especially effective at generating metacultural reflections expressed as dissatisfaction with reified "culture." It prompts people to reflect on the social processes in which they are enmeshed and to see the mesh as a net or trap rather than a liberating network. This broad claim about Christian metaculture and the irresolvable tensions it generates needs to be substantiated ethnographically, and that is my aim in this book. The version of Christianity I am analyzing is quite particular: a form of Wesleyan Methodism practiced in a chiefly district of a rural island in southern Fiji in the late twentieth and early twenty-first century. If my argument is fruitful, however, it will be precisely because the particular situation of Methodists in Kadavu helps illuminate Christian metacultural dynamics in a way that resonates productively with other cases in different contexts.

THE METACULTURAL FORCE OF *MANA, LOTU,* AND *VANUA*

Three Fijian terms play an especially prominent and consequential role in generating people's sense of loss: *mana, lotu,* and *vanua.* They are key indexes used in the engagement between Church and chiefs. Their interrelationships reveal the constellation of social power in Fiji, identify the things that Fijians are most anxious to hold onto and strengthen, and trace trajectories of perceived decline.

Of the three terms, *mana,* which is found in cognate forms throughout Oceanic languages, is the best known in the scholarly literature. At the end of the nineteenth century, R. H. Codrington (1957: 118–119) wrote that *mana* "is what works to effect everything which is beyond the ordinary power of men, outside the common processes of nature." Building on Codrington's work, Marcel Mauss described *mana* as one form of a universal category of magical power, comparable to the Iroquois *orenda* and the Algonquin *manitou.* "We could extend . . . the meaning of this word," he wrote, "and maintain that *mana* is power, *par excellence,* the genuine effectiveness of things which corroborates their practical actions without annihilating them" (1972: 111). Lévi-Strauss (1987), Evans-Pritchard (1965), and Keesing (1984, 1985) all criticized scholars' tendencies to smuggle their own metaphysical understandings into their definitions of *mana,* and a critical retheorization of the term is under way (Tomlinson 2006b).

Historically, the standard usage of *mana* in Fijian has been as a verb meaning "to work successfully," that is, to be effective. An unpublished monolingual Fijian dictionary defines *mana* as "yaco dina na kena inaki," meaning "achieving its intended purpose" (Qereti n.d.). It is also used as an adjective meaning "effective." When writing of Fijian *mana* in English, it would be ideal to keep it as a verb or adjective, but this is often grammatically awkward. And, indeed, contemporary Fijian authors use *mana* as a noun, giving it the Polynesian sense of abstract power made substantial (which Keesing accused anthropologists of doing indiscriminately). For example, the anthropologist turned politician

Asesela Ravuvu (1983: 91) defines *mana* as "the power to effect," and Ilaitia Tuwere (2002: 136), a theologian and past president of the Fijian Methodist Church, writes, "*Mana* is power or influence, not physical and in a way supernatural, but it shows itself in physical force or excellence which a person possesses." Writing in Fijian, Semi Seruvakula (2000: 120) claims that an earlier generation "believed that the elders were endowed with 'mana,' or the ability to make things happen by saying them."

Talking about *mana* is metacultural commentary on the effectiveness of action. It is a term strongly associated with chiefs because in the old days, supposedly, their speech was automatically effective. However, the decoupling of *mana* and chiefliness features prominently in the fall-from-a-golden-age theme. Tuwere (2002: 138) writes, "I often hear young men in the village saying, *Ke ra vinaka walega na noda i liuliu* (if only our leaders were good), referring to traditional leaders in general and imply-ing that *mana* is slipping away from its source" (see also Toren 1990: 102; Toren 2004). Here, then, is a great anthropological irony of mod-ern Fiji: now that scholars can define the term more precisely than be-fore, what we see is that it is characterized by absence and loss. *Mana* is what's disappearing, or already gone.

The second term is *lotu*. Methodist missionaries introduced the word from Tongan, where it originally referred to a pre-Christian form of prayer (see Martin 1979: 189). In the South Pacific, missions often ad-vanced through networks of local teachers, and Tongans in eastern Fiji shaped early mission development there; the term *lotu* is one token of this early influence, and once it was adopted in Fiji, Fijian missionaries brought it to other parts of Oceania (Garrett 1982: 233). As a noun standing alone, *lotu* can usually be translated as "Christianity." In some contexts, the most accurate translation is "religion," as when Seruvakula (2000: 14) claims, "If we gently disentangle the beliefs of today's lotu and the ancestors' lotu, we will see that the difference is not so great." He is referring to Christianity when he writes of "today's lotu," but he also uses the term for the ancestors' non-Christian practices. As a proper noun, Lotu is part of the official name of the national Methodist Church organization, the Methodist Church in Fiji and Rotuma (Lotu Wesele e Viti kei Rotuma; Viti is the indigenous name for Fiji, and *We-sele* is the Fijian spelling of John Wesley's surname). Finally, as a verb *lotu* can be translated in different contexts as "worship," "convert," or sim-ply "attend a church service."

The third term, *vanua*, is often used in close conjunction with *lotu*, but *vanua* has a wider range of meaning. If one had to translate it with a single word, the best choices would be either "land," "place," or "people." Regarding location, *vanua* can indicate a wide range of places, and like the English word "place" it can mean something as small as a spot on one's body or something as large as a nation. Sometimes *vanua* means the physical landscape generally; sometimes it means dry land, as opposed to water. As a social designation, the *vanua* are commoners, the "people of the land," as opposed to chiefs. The issue is complicated, however, by the fact that chiefs represent the *vanua:* "The chief . . . is the focal point, the central organizing figure who stands for the whole of the people" (Kaplan 1995: 27). Thus *vanua* can also be translated as "chiefdom." Chiefs' role in representing the *vanua* is highlighted when the *vanua* is opposed to other entities such as the *lotu* or Indo-Fijians. Thus the frequently made distinction between *lotu* and *vanua* should be translated "Church and chiefs," with the understanding that the chiefs in turn represent commoners and "tradition."

Vanua often appears in the adjectival or adverbial form *vakavanua*, which can be translated as "customary" (Nayacakalou 1975: 66), "in the nature of the land people and customs" (Ravuvu 1983: 122), or simply "traditional." *Tradition* is a contentious word in anthropological theory, but its colloquial English sense conveys the meanings of *vakavanua* well; it connotes older things, local things, and therefore carries an emotional charge (Tomlinson 2002; Williksen-Bakker 1990; Young 2001). Chiefs are guardians of tradition, which includes Christianity in some respects and excludes it in others. Of all these terms, *vanua* is the one subject most often to explicit metacultural representation. The self-consciously traditional order of rural Fijian life is the focus of radio broadcasts, government workshops, and publications, including newspaper columns, websites, and books such as Semi Seruvakula's *Bula Vakavanua* (Traditional Life, 2000) and Ilaitia Tuwere's theological work *Vanua* (2002).

One additional term needs to be mentioned: *matanitu,* the term used for national government, which was originally applied to the large and powerful "confederations" that emerged in Fiji in the late eighteenth century (Routledge 1985; Thomas 1986). In Fiji, the trio of *lotu, vanua,* and *matanitu* is often invoked rhetorically and proclaimed to be the basis of Fijian culture. In other words, they constitute a metacultural formula through which Fijians describe, evaluate, and engage with a reified Fijian culture that has become hallowed as traditional. For example, Paula Niukula (1994: 14–15), who served as president and general secretary of Fiji's Methodist Church, wrote, "When our grandfathers accepted the Church and the Colonial Government, that which bound the people together was divided into three: the Community [*vanua*], the Church [*lotu*] and the Government [*matanitu*]. They became the bases of Fijian life. They are the three pillars of Fijian society." In comparison, a Tavuki man who was explaining to me the interrelationships of Church, community, and government drew a picture of his own home-spun version: the Church as boat pilot, the community as the boat itself, and government as the outboard motor. The missionary-anthropologist Alan Tippett (1955: 74–75) similarly wrote:

We may fairly say that the Fijian out-look on public affairs today may be found in a phrase heard time after time in native prayers and public speeches— *vakavanua, vakamatanitu ka vakalotu talega,* This may be rendered—"in the way of the land, in the way of the government and in the way of the Church." The phrase sums up the Fijian way of life.

Let us admit that it is modern and artificial. It is like a three-stranded rope, but the Fijian people stand in the strength of that rope. (Emphasis added; see also Tippett 1976b)

Although *lotu-vanua-matanitu* is a standard formula, the strong elements in it are *lotu* and *vanua*. *Matanitu* is invoked with less frequency and passion than the other two terms, a weak partner both conceptually and practically. Also, it is not always the third term attached to *lotu* and *vanua*. During fieldwork, other words I heard used in the third position behind *lotu* and *vanua* were "service" (*viqaravi*), "responsibility" (*itavi*), "study" (*vuli*), and "family" (*matavuvale*). Evidently, the rhetorically appealing triadic structure demands that *lotu* and *vanua* have a third element, a triangulation; the third element is the variable one, and *lotu* and *vanua* remain the core metacultural pair, sometimes complementary, sometimes oppositional.

In this book, sometimes I translate *mana, lotu,* and *vanua* by using their most relevant contextual meanings, but sometimes I leave them untranslated. Following Piers Vitebsky (1993: 9), I would rather "set the word free in order to see how it behaves," letting the nuances breathe and grow in these pages. The terms are used very often in Fijian public discourse, spoken again and again by chiefs and commoners, preachers and prayer givers, men and women, on formal and informal occasions. Their very frequency suggests their salience to Fijian public life, so I would rather keep them prominent in this ethnography as well and I also do not italicize them hereafter.

Commentary on the lotu-vanua interaction sometimes highlights their rivalry. For example, the same man who drew the picture of lotu, vanua, and matanitu as pilot, boat, and motor also told me, "The vanua should be Christianized; [but] today, the lotu is being influenced by the vanua" (*E dodonu me vakalotutaki na vanua; nikua, sa vakavanuataki na lotu*). Similarly, Ilaitia Tuwere (2002: 160) describes "a form of captivity of the church under the vanua" (see also 101, 104), noting, "One often hears in church the admonition under the guise of a statement . . . [that] land, church and state each has its own path . . . meaning, they must not be mixed together"; in an endnote he adds, "I began hearing this as a child, particularly during church services on special occasions. The distinction to be clarified was understandable but it did not always filter down into practice. Chiefs were often involved in church politics and church ministers were not totally innocent of village and even national politics" (70–71, 75 n. 35; see also Halapua 2003; Ryle 2001, 2005). The relationship between lotu and vanua, like that between many long-married couples, is complementary and competitive, supportive and antagonistic, and always tightly joined. As I will show, Methodism in Fiji motivates attempts to define the terms' categorical independence—the work of "purification," in Latour's critical discussion of "modern" practice (1993). Yet the close ties between lotu and vanua are celebrated especially when they support the authority of chiefs. In other words, Methodism is valued as traditional to the extent that it supports chiefly authority.

Lotu, vanua, and matanitu are routinely identified as the bases of Fijian culture, but their metacultural distinction is an ongoing project for Methodists. Projects of boundary drawing are never fully successful, and they provoke anxieties that are manifest in and reinforced by talk about the fall from a golden age of power. Not quite the opiate of the masses, Fijian Methodism is more like the caffeine of the masses, energizing people while intensifying their anxieties. Stories of decline and loss are not end points in a historical process; they circulate in their own right as metacultural commentaries, framing analyses of unfolding events and provoking new political actions. In carving out spaces of its own authority and responsibility in Fijian life over the past century and a half, the Methodist Church has been engaged in a superficially harmonious but ultimately rivalrous relationship with chiefly systems. This conflict has been engaged temporally in one key way: the past has been turned into a realm of "demonic" spirits whose non-Christian ways are rejected but whose admirable power remains.

The lotu is an emblem of tradition that gains its authority by demonizing certain aspects of tradition. The vanua is more unambiguously associated with the past. The missionary A. C. Cato (1947: 156), writing about Kadavu in the mid-twentieth century, noted, "I listened to stories expressing ancient beliefs as recounted by a Methodist Circuit Steward. When I asked him whether he believed these things or the Christian New Testament, he unhesitatingly replied that he believed both. I asked him which he would believe if they were in conflict. Slowly, and with some reluctance (perhaps because of his position in the church) he replied that the ancient beliefs were very important to Fijian people, that it was from them they derived the truest consolation and they therefore would believe the old." Cato's phrase "truest consolation" is striking. It indicates that the Fijian past, despite its host of dangerous spiritual agents that haunt the present, is still a source of positive emotional feelings. It also suggests that there is something discomfiting about the present—otherwise, why would one need consolation?

In the present, people defend themselves from punitive and malicious ancestral spirits. In the future, the vanua is threatened by supposed Indo-Fijian greed and all the corrosive forces of the modern West: money, business, education without wisdom, alcohol—the list spirals down into a murky space of perpetually anticipated threat. If the land is ultimately lost to outsiders, Fijians reason, their divine inheritance—God's gift—will be finished, gone, dead. How, then, does one save the vanua? What role does the lotu play in defeating ancestral malignance and creating a future paradise? Where, finally, does mana now become manifest?

Plan

This introduction and the first chapter constitute part 1, "Situation." In chapter 1 I introduce Kadavu, situating it culturally and describing the history of Methodist missionary efforts and the present-day structure of the Church.

In part 2, "Lamentation," I analyze the theme of the fall from a golden age. Chapter 2 introduces this subject and gives prominent examples of its expression, including discourse about weakened bodies, loss of chiefs' mana, and the fragmentation and disorganization of social order. Chapters 3, 4, and 5 describe Fijian ritual practice in light of the golden age theme. In chapter 3 I analyze preaching as a metacultural performance in which speakers circulate discourse of decline, loss, and fragmentation. Examining kava drinking in chapter 4, I consider how drinking sessions foster the circulation of narratives of decline and loss and turn them into palpable, embodied experience. That is, in drinking kava, and in talking about drinking kava, people in Tavuki come to know and feel a history of decline. Chapter 5 turns to the vanua and a consideration of the ways soil is made sacred. It concludes with a detailed analysis of the ways spiritual power is managed by Methodist authorities in chain prayers.

Part 3, "Recuperation," faces the future, asking how histories of decline and loss are challenged and how trajectories are altered. Chapter 6 is an examination of Fiji's coups and the Methodist Church's role in political violence. My goal is to understand the context in which riotous and destructive acts can seem to many local observers to be the positive acts of moral Christians. In chapter 7 I present the autobiography of a man who describes his life in terms of St. Paul's famous "road to Damascus" experience. It is a narrative of finding a new voice and agency within Fijian Methodism. These concluding chapters unite the topics of Christianity, power, and loss by focusing on responses to decline and hopes for the future.

CHAPTER I

Situating Kadavu

Church, Chiefs, and the Creation of a Sense of Loss

Kadavu is Fiji's fourth largest island, at 408 square kilometers (Nunn 1999: 36). Seen from offshore, it is a vivid tableau of green forest, gardens, grassland, palms, and planted pine. Although there are no major rivers, many streams and creeks flow down from the hilly interior. Derrick (1957: 267) compared the shape of the island to "the body of a wasp, whose head, thorax, and abdomen are linked by narrow waists," with much of the coast notched by deep-cut bays of iridescent blues and greens. A standard geographic distinction that Kadavuans make is north shore (*baba tokalau*) versus south shore (*baba ceva*).

The island is a six-hour ferry ride from Suva, Fiji's capital city, or a short airplane flight from Suva or Nadi. Its main jetty and only airport stand near each other in the town of Vunisea and the neighboring village of Namalata. In western Kadavu, a northern road reaches Tavuki village and a southern one reaches Nabukelevuira; one can drive from Vunisea to Tavuki in around twenty minutes, about the same length of time as a quick boat trip. In 1998–1999 there were only twenty-six registered road vehicles on the island, and small boats with outboard motors are the standard form of long-distance transportation within Kadavu.

In Tavuki Bay, as in much of Fiji, people distinguish between the area's original inhabitants and later arrivals, also indigenous Fijians, who became the chiefs.[1] The original inhabitants are the vanua proper, who are expected to support their chiefs; the chiefs, in turn, are expected to work for the welfare of the vanua. Many people in Tavuki agree that the Nukunawa clan was the first to arrive. They are said to have come

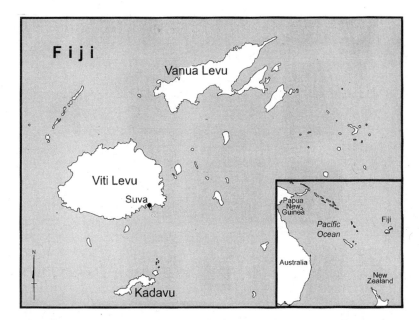

MAP I. Fiji

from Verata, on Vitilevu, and passed through other lands on their way to Kadavu.[2] After Nukunawa settled the land as its original inhabitants, another clan, Nacolase, arrived and gained political supremacy.

The story of how Nacolase became chiefs is an elegant expression of Fijian visions of the strong, noble past. The plot hinges on the *vasu* kin relationship, by which a nephew has the right "to take certain liberties against the whole of the mother's [patri]lineage group" (Nayacakalou 1957: 47). The hero of the story is the Nephew-to-Naceva, a man of great physical prowess who called on his mother's relatives from the Naceva region of Kadavu.[3] Here is the version that A. M. Hocart (n.d.: chapter 9) recorded a century ago:

When [the Nephew-to-Naceva] grew up Tavuki was at war with Nabukelevu and Yawe. The Nephew-to-Naceva went to bring over the Naceva people without informing his own people. He came to an ascent (Kadavu is all steep hills) and said, "If I run up to the top without a halt I shall certainly be Lord of Tavuki." He ran up to the top without a halt and came down on the other side, "If I can get to Naceva along this reef before the tide comes in I shall certainly be Lord of Tavuki." He reached Naceva and sat on the threshold. The Lord of Naceva asked him who he was, and he explained. "You are my grandson," said the Lord of Naceva, "let us embrace." They embraced and the Nephew-to-Naceva asked them

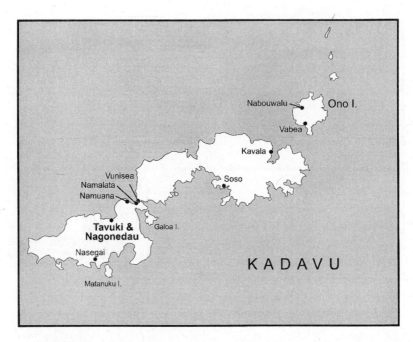

MAP 2. Kadavu

to come and help in the war against Nabukelevu and Yawe and added, "If after the war they want to prepare gifts for you tell them to make me Lord of Tavuki, and that you will go home." He went back to Tavuki but told no one. On the appointed day the men of Naceva came. The people of Tavuki were angry with the Nephew-to-Naceva. "Why did you not tell us? They have come here and are hungry and there is no food for them. If you had told us we might have made a feast to await them with." . . . The Lord of Tavuki ordered sugar cane and plenty of food. Then they went out to battle and defeated the enemy. When the army returned the people of Tavuki told the men of Naceva, "Wait till we have prepared a small thing for you." The men of Naceva answered, "All we desire [is that] you should make our nephew Lord of Tavuki. . . ." So the Nephew-to-Naceva was made Lord of Tavuki and from him are descended the present chiefs.

By enlisting the aid of his mother's patriline, the Nephew-to-Naceva was able to ensure Tavuki's victory over Yawe and Nabukelevu, making Tavuki the leading power on the island. He also made sure that by putting Tavuki in Naceva's debt, the latter could insist that Tavuki make him their leader.

I was told that this hero was the first, and only, person to be installed formally as the Tui Tavuki, the paramount chief. However, the anthropologist Rusiate Nayacakalou (1975: 40) was told, "The last *Tui* Tavuki to be formally installed according to custom was Ratu Naulivesi," the great-great-grandfather of the man who took Nayacakalou on his tour of Kadavu in 1960. In either case, no Tui Tavuki has been installed for many decades. In years of inquiries, I have never received a definitive answer as to why this is the case, although the general theme that has emerged is one of disagreement over who the chief would be and who would have the right to choose him.[4] This ongoing situation is politically consequential, because chiefs depend on installation by the vanua—specifically through the subclan of chiefly installers (*sauturaga*)—for formal recognition of their legitimacy. Without a base of support, chiefs cannot claim the right to rule. Rather than attempt a definitive answer of exactly how many Tui Tavukis were installed, or who was the last to be installed, I simply wish to point out what most people would agree on: that the last installation was a long time ago, and installation is a ritual performance in which chiefs become effective.[5] Despite this fact, a senior man is generally recognized as the Tui Tavuki. During the entire period of my research it was a man of the Naocovonu subclan, Ratu I. W. Narokete. As Nayacakalou observed, men now filling the role of Tui Tavuki are in the tricky position of serving as paramount chief but not emphasizing their authority too much; he described the case of one man who "normally acted in the capacity of *Tui* Tavuki, [but] never pressed the point too far, for if he did, the other members of the clan were entitled to refuse to recognize his authority" (63).

Tavuki village has a population of approximately 125 people.[6] Besides being the seat of the Tui Tavuki, it is also the village of residence for the superintendent minister of the Methodist Church in Kadavu. In addition, it is the location of the Kadavu Provincial Office and its leading official, the Roko Tui Kadavu. The provincial office is run by employees of Fijian Affairs, a branch of government for indigenous Fijians that stands alongside the multiracial, democratic national government. Thus Tavuki is home to the leaders of the chiefly system (vanua), the Methodist Church (lotu), and influential government (matanitu) authorities. The town of Vunisea has the hospital, police station, and main post office, but Tavuki has the prestige and traditional power. Nayacakalou (1975: 62) wrote, "These three high-powered orders of authority co-existed in the same village without apparent conflict, partly because their jurisdictions were fairly distinct, and partly because the village was run mostly on the basis of traditional authority."

Nayacakalou (1975: 61–62) wrote evocatively of Tavuki's distinctive-ness when he visited it in 1960:

Tavuki bore the true marks of a chiefly village. It was the seat of the high chiefs of Nacolase, the traditional leaders of the confederation of twenty-two villages which comprised Tavuki [as a vanua]. The huge native-style houses (and two with iron roofs) reflected, by their size, the height of their earth platforms, and their gables, the rank of their occupants in the traditional hierarchy. These chiefly houses were arranged more or less neatly around the central village green on which ceremonies took place. The first impression I had was of a disturbing si-lence, but it was a reflection of the awe and respect with which the chiefs were held, not only by lower-ranking men but also by themselves in their relations with one another. There seemed to be a standing rule that children should not cry and cocks should not crow. The babbling of women beside houses working under the shade of trees, the laughter of young men preparing to go to the bush or to the sea, which often characterize village life in Fiji, were not at all common in Tavuki. Here the chiefs' houses dominated the village scene, and lesser men were bound by rules of respect towards chiefs to maintain silence in their presence. It was, in-deed, a strongly tradition-oriented village. (See also Spate 1959: 112)

Tavuki is still an impressive and well-maintained village, with one of the finest churches in Kadavu. The church is located in a section of the village that includes the minister's and catechist's houses and the church social hall. Tavuki also has an attractive town hall, Ratu Nacagilevu House, where large meetings are held. Large old earthen house foun-dations remain, although the "native-style houses" described by Naya-cakalou have been replaced by more durable structures of corrugated iron, lumber, and concrete. Water is piped into the village from the hills, although many houses do not have private taps. Electricity is available for a few hours each night from the village generator or private genera-tors. When power is turned off, people drinking kava late into the night will light kerosene or benzene lanterns.

Tavuki village sits on the shore of Tavuki Bay, in the middle of six other villages. In Fijian terms, the villages of Solodamu, Natumua, and Waisomo sit "above" Tavuki. The villages "below" them are Tavuki, Baidamudamu, and, at the far edge of the bay, Nukunuku. Nagonedau village stands adjacent to Tavuki, just "above" it along the shore. In the mid-1990s the total population of the seven villages in the bay was ap-proximately seven hundred, and almost 82 percent were members of the Methodist Church (Government of Fiji 1995; Vale ni Volavola ni Yasana ko Kadavu 1995). The total population of Kadavu was approximately ninety-five hundred, nearly all of whom were indigenous Fijians (Fiji

FIGURE 1. The choir enters the Tavuki Methodist church before a Sunday service.

Islands Bureau of Statistics 1998: 30–31) and over 93 percent of whom were members of the Methodist Church (Government of Fiji 1995). It is a rural island, ranking eleventh out of Fiji's fifteen provinces in population density, at twenty people per square kilometer (Rakaseta 1999: 6).

Many of Tavuki's inhabitants are subsistence farmers who grow taro, cassava, yams, other root crops, and kava; some earn money by selling surplus produce, especially kava. Women weave mats, baskets, and fans and gather fish in the lagoon; in Baidamudamu village, they gather delectable freshwater prawns. Some men go spearfishing at

FIGURE 2. Inside the Tavuki church.

night and take boats out to pursue bigger fish in deeper waters. Kadavu is well known internationally as a dive site because of the Astrolabe Reef, and the eastern half of the island has numerous small scuba-diving resorts, but the impact of these resorts is negligible in Tavuki and tourists are very rarely seen in the village. Many Tavukians spend time on Vitilevu for education or work, but, like many Fijians, at Christmastime they return to their true homes "on the foundation" (*dela ni yavu*), streaming back to the village for weeks of celebration.

Kadavuans have a two-section Dravidian kinship system, as described for Fiji by Groves (1963: 278; see also Cook 1975; Nayacakalou 1955, 1957). Descent is patrilineal; postmarital residence is often patrilocal; and authority is generally patriarchal. Parallel cousins are treated as siblings, whereas cross-cousins are one's joking companions and, especially in earlier days, were one's ideal marriage partners. In practical terms, one of the most significant kin groups is one's *mataqali*, an extended family defined by Nayacakalou (1975: 165) as "a primary division of a village; a sub-clan" (see also Arno 1993: 9 n. 9). It is also "the fundamental landowning group," and each *mataqali* is associated with a traditional social role, such as chief, priest, or warrior (Nayacakalou 1957: 50–51; cf. Tuwere 2002: 65). *Mataqali* membership is officially supposed to be subsumed within *yavusa* membership. Logically, this would seem to make a *yavusa* a clan, but Fijian anthropologists are reluctant to

FIGURE 3. Sereti Liu weaves a mat.

apply the word too literally: Nayacakalou (1975: 166) defines *yavusa* as "the widest patrilineal kinship unit (real or imputed)," and Asesela Ravuvu (1983: 123) has called it "a social unit of agnatically related members [larger] than the *mataqali* and the members of which claim descendants from a common founding male ancestor."[7] For the purposes of this book, I gloss *yavusa* as "clan" and *mataqali* as "subclan" because, I argue, an analytical focus on lotu, vanua, and mana—the core terms that I prefer not to translate—will illuminate local social dynamics more effectively than a focus on structural debates.

Kadavu is well known in Fiji for its independent chiefdoms.[8] Although the Tui Tavuki drinks the first cup of kava when Kadavuan chiefs gather, displaying his paramount status, a well-known saying describes the island's politics as "each rooster its own cry" (*manu dui tagi,* meaning the place is balkanized; see Rokowaqa 1926: 59; cf. Kuhlken 1994: 295). Within Fiji's three major indigenous confederacies, Kadavu is affiliated with Burebasaga, whose leading power is Rewa; the others are Kubuna, led by Bau, and Tovata, led by Lau and Cakaudrove.

Walking in the Mouths of Sharks: Mission History

In October 1839 the Wesleyan missionary Thomas Jaggar wrote in his journal that a teacher at the Rewa mission had described his situation as "walking in the mouths of sharks."[9] The historian Andrew Thornley (2000: 157), who relates this comment, adds, "This apt remark might fittingly be applied to the Wesleyan cause in most parts of Fiji from 1839 to 1842," an early and unstable period for the Methodists. The first British missionaries arrived in Lakeba, eastern Fiji, in 1835.[10] From then the European effort, directed by the London-based Wesleyan Methodist Missionary Society, would have a seismic effect throughout Fiji, although its beginnings were inauspicious and the early mission workers struggled against warfare, cannibalism, disease, and exhaustion.

To the missionaries, indigenous religion seemed a polyglot affair wherein deified ancestors, gods of war, and fantastical human-animal spirits mixed easily. Some spirits or gods were local figures; others were known in most of Fiji. Methodists offered predictable judgments on Fijian gods—"monster expressions of moral corruption," for example (Williams 1982: 217)—but there were some elements in Fijian religious life that the Christians appreciated. For one thing, "the idea of Deity [was] familiar"; Thomas Williams even suggested that Degei, the snake god known throughout the islands, might "be an impersonation of the abstract idea of eternal existence" (215, 217). For another, Fijians generally did not create iconic figures of gods, although they did perceive spiritual forces within natural vessels. The most practical difficulty facing the missionaries was thus not to build up a belief in deity or to knock down wooden representations of it, but to challenge the authority of hereditary priests (*bete*) who served particular gods on behalf of chiefs.

From the beginning of the missionary encounter, lotu and vanua used each other in ways that both supported and challenged the other's claims. Missionaries and chiefs were locked in a dynamic of mutual dependence and aggression, each side needing and distrusting the other. Methodists sought chiefs' support for strategic reasons. Once a chief converted, it was assumed that his subjects would follow. Missionaries also turned to chiefs for practical needs of land and gardens and necessary considerations of safety. Chiefs appreciated the material resources and prestige they gained by hosting white foreigners, as they had already benefited by appropriating the services of castaways and beachcombers.

Despite their fundamental dependence on chiefs, missionaries threatened chiefs' authority in four main ways. First, in the years before Wesleyan efforts had become effective and stable, Christianity was spread in Fiji largely through the efforts of Tongans, who also aimed at military conquest (see Derrick 1946; Scarr 1984; Thornley 2000, 2002). Second, missionaries inevitably challenged chiefly mana by proposing the existence of a supremely effective deity for whom they alone spoke. The supreme deity was said to dislike cherished practices such as chiefly polygamy, so accepting Jehovah meant that chiefs would be stripped of important components of their temporal power. Third, although Methodists often focused their efforts on converting chiefs so that commoners would follow, commoners sometimes took the initiative in converting. Fourth, despite their self-image as benevolent men working only for godly purposes, missionaries were occasionally guilty of abusing their authority in non-Church affairs. In fact, in the opinion of some indigenous Fijians, missionaries were just as ambitious and avaricious as other settlers were, and accepting Christianity might lead to the ultimate loss of land as well as custom. For example, in September 1838 the Rewa village of Sigatoka was burned down as a protest "against [Chief] Rokotui Dreketi's leadership, including his patronage of the missionary [William Cross]. . . . Shortly after the burning, there were talks between Rokotui Dreketi and his elders on the question of whether to accept Christianity" (Thornley 2000: 69). The ensuing debate revealed the threat that missionaries posed and that chiefs recognized the dangers but also felt they could not fight the Christians: "Some advised the high chief against it, saying that the coming of [William] Cross was the beginning of a flow of outsiders. Soon, they said, many more would come 'to dwell and they will all join together, build themselves a city, take our land from us and rule over us.' Rokotui Dreketi responded with a more pragmatic outlook: 'Christianity has taken hold of the land and we cannot send it away or stop its progress.' " (Thornley 2000: 69; see also Thornley 2002: 77; cf. Keesing-Styles and Keesing-Styles 1988: 88).

The early period of missionary work in Fiji created a situation in which Church authority both depends on and opposes chiefly authority; Christianity in Fiji has created a contest in which lotu and vanua struggle to define their proper places in Fijian society with reference to each other. I will discuss this dynamic at length in succeeding chapters. To set the stage for these later discussions, here I examine four themes that emerge from the early mission encounters. These themes illuminate the origins of lotu-vanua rivalry and suggest ways of thinking productively about its metacultural elaboration. They are (1) difficulties of translation, (2) sin and diminution, (3) disease and paternalism, and (4) the persistence of ancestral spiritual agency.

TRANSLATION

Methodist missionaries vigorously translated and published biblical texts and other materials in order to convert Fijians and organize them into religious communities. As table 2 shows, a great deal of effort was expended in translating, and retranslating, certain parts of the Bible, most notably the New Testament (especially Matthew) and Genesis. A great deal of secondary literature was also produced in Fijian during the early years of the Church, including catechisms, hymnals, sermon outlines, paraphrases of Bible stories, biographies of biblical figures, and textbooks for biblical instruction (Clammer 1976: 24; Thornley 2002: 222; Tippett 1974a: 403–408). A particularly influential early text was *Pilgrim's Progress*, John Bunyan's seventeenth-century allegory of a man named Christian who journeys from the City of Destruction to the Celestial City (Nettleton 1866a; Tippett 1958a: 141). In 1861, the missionaries Royce and Baird wrote, "The scriptures have now a wide circulation on Kadavu, and are frequently sought by numbers. . . . We have received more than three tons of oil during the past year as proceeds for the sail [sic] of books."[11] John Clammer (1976: 25) estimates that "by 1870 the total number of volumes produced [by the Wesleyans] for distribution in Fiji must have [been] 200,000, at a conservative estimate."

The publication of new texts intrigued many Fijians and attracted them to the Church, but not all texts were appreciated for their intelligibility. When John Hunt introduced a revised catechism in 1843, cleaning up an inaccurate earlier version, some members of the Viwa congregation complained that it was now too easy to understand (Thornley 2000: 232; Tomlinson 2006a). Bible translations are not models of clear prose, either, although missionaries spent decades revising and refining their work. In 1843 the Wesleyans chose the dialect of Bau Island in which to produce the scriptures, but they were not fluent in Bauan

TABLE 2. Methodist missionaries' early translation and
publication efforts in Fiji

Date	Event
1835	British and Foreign Bible Society gives one hundred reams of paper to the Mission in Tonga, where Fijian material will be printed.
1836	David Cargill's translation of parts of Matthew in the Lakeban dialect are printed in Tonga.
1838	Printing press arrives in Lakeba.
1839	Mark is printed at Lakeba, in the Lakeban dialect.
1841	William Cross's translation of parts of Genesis in the Bauan dialect is printed at Rewa; parts of Matthew, perhaps a new translation by Cross, are printed there in the Rewa dialect.
1843	The missionaries' language committee decides to choose a single dialect for future translations and selects Bauan.
1844	Two thousand copies of John Hunt's sermons and lectures, hymn books in Bauan and Rewan, and a liturgy in Lakeban are printed at Rewa.
1846	John Hunt's translations of Matthew and Acts are printed in Bauan at Viwa; three thousand copies are bound for distribution, but one thousand are held for future binding in a complete New Testament.
1847	One thousand copies of the entire New Testament are printed in Bauan at Viwa, translated by John Hunt with assistance from a Fijian man named Noa Koroinavugona, except for the Gospel of John, which is translated by John Watsford.
1853	Five thousand copies of the "London edition" of Hunt's New Testament are printed, as well as three thousand copies of Watsford's own revision of Hunt's New Testament, which is printed in Viwa; three thousand copies each of Matthew, Romans, and Philippians are individually printed and bound.
1854	Five thousand copies of Hunt's and David Hazlewood's translations of Genesis, Exodus, and Psalms are printed.
1856	The complete Bible is apparently available in Bauan for the first time.
1858	James Calvert's revision of the New Testament is printed.
1864	The complete Bible is printed in London by the British and Foreign Bible Society.
1884	The complete Bible is printed with Calvert's and Richard Lyth's revisions of the Old Testament and Calvert's New Testament.
1885	A new edition of the New Testament, revised by Calvert, is printed.
1890	Another new edition of the New Testament, revised by Calvert, is printed.
1899	A new version of the New Testament, revised by Frederick Langham, is printed in London by the British and Foreign Bible Society.
1902	Langham's complete, revised Bible is printed in London by the British and Foreign Bible Society.

SOURCE: Adapted from Tippett 1947: 67–69; Thornley 2000: 261; Thornley 2002: 192; see also Clammer 1976.

themselves. In the mid-1850s James Calvert decided to revise Hunt's translation of the New Testament, seeking a more strictly literal version. "This revised edition was published in 1858," Thornley (2002: 193) writes, "and greeted with dismay by the senior missionaries." Calvert had worked with an editor at the British and Foreign Bible Society, and together they managed to produce a text that "clearly carried the imprint of a missionary unskilled in translation and an advisor [editor] ignorant of the language. [The missionary] William Moore was blunt about Calvert's efforts: 'We have much that is not Fijian, not the sense of the Holy Spirit, but Fijian [as spoken by white men] . . . and making what was clear into mud' " (193). The Bible translation used most widely in Fiji today was completed in 1902 by Frederick Langham. This version still contains awkward grammar and Eastern dialectal forms.[12]

In their translations, missionaries staked claims to their own authority in their translation of *God* and their use of new terms and concepts. Lamin Sanneh (2003) has argued that local Christianity flourishes when the word used for God comes from the local vernacular. The Wesleyans in Fiji followed this approach, using the common noun *kalou*, which was "a blanket term for the general class of spirit beings" (Clammer 1976: 36; cf. Hocart 1912b). Quite simply and ingeniously, however, they added the definite article *na* in front of *kalou*, referring to the Christian God as "*the* Spirit." This shift toward prototypicality meant that missionaries were the exclusive agents of the most powerful deity. It also meant that the old *kalou* were still alive. These old spirits were displaced into the newly created categories of *tevoro* and *timoni* (Kadavuan *jimoni*), meaning "devils" and "demons," with results that I describe in later chapters.

The Wesleyans introduced loanwords such as *kameli* (camel), *ose* (horse), *lami* (lamb), *laioni* (lion), *olive* (olive), and *oki* (oak), as well as characters, identities, and places from the Bible, including *Jiu* (Jews), *Parataisi* (Paradise), and *Etesi* (Hades). Invisible beings inhabited new terms, including *Jiova* (Jehovah), *agilose* (angels), and *Setani* (Satan). But perhaps the most profoundly transformative terms were ones like *papitaiso* (baptize), *sakaramede* (sacraments), and the frequently heard *emeni* (amen), words that define ritual practice.[13] By introducing these terms, missionaries were carving out a sphere of authority for themselves, positioning themselves as mediators of new significance.

Methodists believed that once people had converted, their familiarity with holy texts would guard them from other missionaries looking to poach their followers. In the mid-1860s, when two French Catholic priests arrived at Ono Island off northeastern Kadavu, Joseph Nettleton

(1866a: 541) assured readers of the *Wesleyan Missionary Notices*, "Popery can only gain ground where there are political disturbances. Where the people are at peace and can read the Sacred Scriptures, popery cannot make headway" (see also Thornley 2002: 192). He was a bit too confident, however, for Ono remains the stronghold of Catholicism in Kadavu to this day.[14]

SIN AND DIMINUTION

Methodist missionaries introduced the notion of sin to Fiji. In doing so they gained a potent weapon for their arsenal: a means by which to claim they had more mana than chiefs did.

The translation of *sin* provoked some contention. *Ca* is the Fijian word meaning "bad" (Dixon 1988: 358). In his New Testament of 1848, John Hunt used the phrase *ai valavala ca* for "sin" because "valavala" denotes "an act habitually carried out" (Capell 1991: 254; *ai* is an article plus nominal prefix). This phrase, which might be translated "bad habits," was considered "an unsatisfactory substitute [by] many missionaries," too weak to convey the sense of human depravity (Thornley 1979: 105). "When the worst you can tell a man about the most heinous offence he can commit is that it is *ai valavala ca* — the difficulty of bringing him to see the repulsiveness of it can be appreciated," wrote William Aitken Heighway in 1913 (quoted in Thornley 1979: 105; see also Clammer 1976: 39).

Nonetheless, the effort to teach Fijians about sin and encourage them to feel it in their marrow proceeded through the decades. A. J. Webb (1870: 213) reported on his efforts to convince "a queer-looking old man" in Nakasaleka district, Kadavu, that he was a sinner:

On being asked what is the natural state of our hearts toward God, he replied "Oh! very good."

"But just think! what was the state of your own soul before you came to God and sought life through the Lotu?"

"Good, very good."

"What then was your conduct and the state of your heart before the 'Lotu' came, and while you were yet a heathen?"

"Well, not bad, very fair."

"Well, you are the first heathen that I ever heard of as being in such a remarkable state. Do you mean to say that you were good when you were a cannibal, and everything else that was dark and wrong?"

"I did *some* bad things."

"Yes, I rather think so! Tell me, then, what was the natural state of your heart before you came to Jesus to be saved from your sins?"

"Vinaka, Vinaka ga" [Fine, just fine].

And this was all that I could get from him on the great subject of Original Sin. The old man would have delighted a Socinian, as being an advocate for man's natural goodness and moral nobility, and a living proof that a savage and a heathen may be a singularly innocent and happy creature. But we were obliged to defer baptising him until he had been instructed more fully in the leading truths of the Gospel. (Emphasis in original; cf. Rafael 1988: 100; Robbins 2004, 2005)

This example highlights an aspect of the relationship between recognizing sin and deferring to authority. Teaching Christian converts that humankind was inherently depraved and essentially sinful was only half of the process; the other half was getting converts to say this themselves and for them to acknowledge the right of men such as Rev. Webb to be authorities on whether they had learned the lesson well enough to participate in central rites of passage such as baptism.

In a move paralleling their introduction of sinfulness, missionaries helped introduce a sense of smallness and insignificance to Fijians. In a grave irony, it was not primarily the missionaries' lessons about heaven that taught people to feel diminished, but their lessons about earth. "We are . . . very much in want of maps," the Rev. Joseph Nettleton wrote in 1865 to the *Wesleyan Missionary Notices*. "The students are much interested in geography. . . . If any one could send us a map of the World, of Asia, Europe, Africa, America, and of Polynesia, it would do their generous hearts good to receive the warm thanks of these young men." But then he continued: "A Fijian has strange notions about the world, especially about its magnitude. . . . The world to the Fijian is composed of small Islands and all is sea besides. The Globe confuses all his notions of creation, and enlarges his view wonderfully. But he cannot see how Fiji can be so little comparatively, as it is represented on the Globe" (1866b: 542). Similarly, in 1858 the missionary Thomas Williams (1982: 120–121) wrote, "The Fijian is very proud of his country. Geographical truths are unwelcome alike to his ears and his eyes. He looks with pleasure on a globe, as a representation of the world, until directed to contrast Fiji with Asia or America, when his joy ceases, and he acknowledges, with a forced smile, 'Our land is not larger than the dung of a fly'; but, on rejoining his comrades, he pronounces the globe a 'lying ball.' "

In August 1999 I was sitting with a middle-aged man—a man who had traveled more than most of his fellow islanders; he had even been to Japan—when he used the phrase *da ni lago* to describe Fiji. *Da ni lago* means "dung of a fly," and I was astonished to hear him using the phrase

I remembered reading in Williams's book. But perhaps I should not have been surprised at how effectively that phrase had wended its way through history, for sentiments of Fiji's small stature in the world were evident during my fieldwork. People sometimes said that places like America were big and Fiji was small. A phrase I occasionally heard in Tavuki, *vuravura levu,* literally means "big world" and indexically points to someplace else, that is, not here, not Kadavu.[15] A sense of smallness is thus a product of Fiji's engagement with white foreigners, not of their engagement with other Pacific Islanders. Missionaries' globes and maps helped introduce a discourse of smallness to Fiji, with significant consequences: a sense of weakness, diminution, threat, and loss. Gone was the expansive Oceanic universe in which Fiji, Tonga, and Samoa were large, mighty places in a living sea (cf. Hau'ofa 1993; Kempf 1999).

DISEASE AND PATERNALISM

Measles and whooping cough decimated Kadavu and much of Fiji in the second half of the nineteenth century. In 1868 William Moore reported about whooping cough at Tavuki, "I may say here that the land is being depopulated fast with this epidemic" (85). In 1875 John Robson counted 1,811 deaths from measles in Kadavu out of a population of approximately 10,000—a staggering amount.[16] Alfred J. Collocott's 1884 report from Kadavu mentions that "scores" of children died that year of whooping cough. Then influenza took a heavy toll in 1918–1919, in Fiji as it did worldwide (Lal 1992: 18, 57–59; see also Colony of Fiji 1896; France 1969: 152, 163).

These terrible epidemics led to salutary campaigns for better hygiene, but those campaigns reinforced missionaries' ethnocentric notions that Fijian society needed to be "civilized" generally. The earliest missionaries had been appalled by cannibalism, widow strangling, and other such practices, but it was not until the later Victorian age that the evangelists' tone of moral superiority became cartoonishly uncompromising. For example, consider the wife of William Aitken Heighway, who served in Kadavu from 1897 to 1901. Mrs. Heighway, seeing an old woman's house that did not meet her domestic standards, ordered the woman's belongings taken out and the mosquito net burned. "Then [I] told a lad to push the hovel over. This I did to prevent the old dame re-occupying it when I had departed" (Heighway family 1932: 95–96). Not content with merely destroying old women's homes, she also sent a report to the colonial government insisting that Fijian houses should henceforth be built with partitions: "I long to see more privacy secured for the sleeping part of the house and for women, and think it would be very helpful in inculcating a sense of modesty, and also a sense of the value of that virtue which is well known to us all" (96; see also Firth 1997; Jolly 1998; Thomas 1990).

Mrs. Heighway's program of harassment reflected the Methodist Church's turn to paternalism in the later nineteenth century. After the pioneers had established Christianity in Fiji, along came "a new kind of missionary—more Victorian in style and message than his predecessors, much more paternal, more disposed to rule over his 'children' as a stern 'father' " (Tippett 1985: 22). Surveying the history of the Church in Fiji, Alan Tippett lamented this period but also pointed out that the increasingly rigid and authoritarian Methodists were responding to social upheavals—not only the devastation of disease, but also a flood of land-hungry settlers and the introduction of alcohol. Defensively, Church leaders "met extreme vice with extreme puritanism" (Tippett 1961: 219). As their standards grew more stringent, they naturally grew more disappointed at their own results and more inclined to see the negative side of things. In 1912 C. O. Lelean complained about the contemporary state of Fijian Methodism by listing "dull sermons, poor singing, long prayers, too much public and too little private devotion, late [kava] drinking, stereotyped forms, shortage of hymn books, a lost fear of God, and an absence of power" (quoted in Garrett 1992: 176).

Victorian missionaries' complaints about sin, vice, and backsliding buttressed their efforts to maintain authority over Fijian ministers. The first Fijian ordained ministers, although given many of the same responsibilities as European and Australian missionaries, could not attend the annual district meeting until 1863, when they were made to meet on their own separately; they were given the subordinate title "native assistant missionaries" until 1869; and "in 1870, a missionary was paid £160 a year while Fijian ministers received £5" (Thornley 2005: 135–137). Dissatisfied with their subordinate status, indigenous Fijian ministers proposed in 1875 that they be allowed to attend the district meeting as equals of the missionaries, to have their supervisory responsibilities increased, and to receive economic assistance (145). The missionaries, in response, asked the Fijian ministers to vote on a new proposal that they be allowed to attend the meeting on a representative basis, whereby one Fijian minister would attend for each ten circuits of the church. Apparently because of coercion and misunderstanding, twelve of twenty-one indigenous Fijian ministers voted for the change; one voted against the representation plan, and the rest abstained (143–145). In 1878 the

Australasian Methodist Church's General Conference approved the representational system for Fijian ministers,[17] and, with the autocratic Frederick Langham running the Fiji District until nearly the end of the century, their subordinate status became entrenched: "The new generation of missionaries, greatly influenced by Langham . . . had the same lack of faith in the abilities of Fijian ministers as had their predecessors. On numerous occasions throughout the later part of the 19th century and into the next, pronouncements were made lamenting the unsuitability of Fijian ministers for senior positions of authority. . . . Missionaries largely trained in Australia maintained effective control of Fijian Methodism until after World War II" (149–150).

In reaction to this haughty approach and its demoralizing consequences, Tippett was part of the progressive post–World War II effort to "indigenize" the Fijian Methodist Church, to weaken Eurocentric paternalism and, ultimately, to have Fijians run the organization. Accordingly, a new constitution was written: "[It] committed us all to terminating the overseas mission in twenty years in favour of an independent Church" (Tippett 1985: 23). In 1964 the Fijian Methodist Church became independent.

SPIRITS OLD AND NEW

From the beginning, Fijians blended John Wesley's religion with local concepts and practices to produce new kinds of Methodism. They reshaped the lotu in terms of the vanua, bringing understandings of place, spirit, and spiritual effectiveness into an imported organizational framework. Ancestral phantoms never died in people's thoughts, flickering in ritual life just beyond the gaze of many missionaries.

When they did notice the vanua's imprint on the lotu, missionaries were surprised and offended. Jesse Carey (1867–1874: 119) wrote in 1868, "Even among the coast tribes, almost all of whom now 'profess and call themselves Christians,' there is unquestionably a *hankering* after the old ways." In another letter written less than a year later, he put the matter more forcefully: "When I first thought of coming to Fiji, it was with the hope that I might help with my brethren in works more abundant in *sapping the old foundations,* rather than by attempting to build *Christianity* upon them, which I am afraid we have in some degree—perhaps even to a dangerous one—been doing" (278; emphases in original).

In 1944 Alan Tippett was sent to Kadavu because the missionary there at the time, A. C. Cato, was alarmed by an "outbreak of sorcery"

(Dundon 2000: 49). In Kadavu, Cato (1947: 156) wrote, "Methodist Church members . . . serve the ancestral spirits but attend the Sunday services of their denomination." This is indeed what Tippett found, observing a wealth of non-Wesleyan practices carried out by Methodists, including malevolent spell casting, invulnerability rituals, and séances in which people used mirrors to contact the recently dead and ask about the causes of their deaths. In a 1945 report on mission education, he complained that Kadavuan Christianity was relatively "primitive" and claimed, "Ancestor worship, totemism and sorcery still exist in most villages. In many cases accepting Christianity has never meant to these people rejecting the earlier forms of belief." Later he would phrase his observation neutrally: "Possibly the idea that the ghosts of the recently dead impose themselves on the fortunes of the living has been the most tenacious idea coming down from old Fiji" (Tippett 1971: 363; see also Williams 1982: 239–248).

Thus, after an apparently decisive conversion by Kadavuans to Methodism in the late 1850s and 1860s, almost a century later islanders were still reshaping their religious practices in novel directions. Some new influences came from other Christian denominations. For example, Tippett (1974a: 426) speculated on the influence of Jehovah's Witnesses' publications in spurring a mid-twentieth-century charismatic movement in the village of Nacomoto. The greatest influence in reshaping the lotu, however, was the vanua. Chiefs and commoners remade Fijian Methodism as a new institution that appealed to people more than severe British Victorianism did. The hybrid of lotu and vanua was lush and lively, but its vitality grew from a complicated dynamic: Christian leaders both depended on chiefs and challenged their authority at the same time. This dynamic generates the sense of decline and loss that is the subject of the rest of this book. To begin analyzing how this process works in the present, I now turn to examine lotu and vanua in the 1990s and 2000s.

Competition between Church and Chiefs: Kadavu in the 1990s and 2000s

The Wesleyan stamp on Fijian Methodism is profound in at least two ways. First, the organizational structure is not much altered from John Wesley's "hierarchy closely knit and wonderfully efficient" (Edwards 1955: 178; see also Tippett 1976a). The British system remains intact in

Fiji: ministers are responsible for local congregations, but lay preaching is encouraged; superintendents oversee the ministers, and a president stands at the institution's apex; quarterly meetings are held for local circuits, annual synods for districts, and annual conferences for the national organization. Second, Wesley's conservative political stance has endured. Wesley admired the admonition in 1 Peter 2:17 "Fear God. Honour the king," including it in some of his correspondence to political figures, and this dual imperative is emblazoned on Fiji's national coat of arms. British Methodism "was at once the most conservative in the political opinions of its members, and the most hierarchical in its internal organization, of all the Protestant sects" (Halèvy 1971: 76; see also Thompson 1963: 398). This hierarchical conservatism is a defining feature of Fijian Methodism today.

The Fijian Church bears its Wesleyan heritage in other ways as well. For example, Wesleyanism was not noted for giving women many opportunities to preach (Hobsbawm 1964: 26; McLeod 1996: 160), and Fijian Methodism, like Fijian society generally, limits women's public and institutional roles. For example, few women become ministers, those who do are appointed only to special circuits such as schools, and women never become superintendent ministers.[18] Economically, Wesleyans moderated the Protestant ethic by encouraging not just production but also consumption. As Maldwyn Edwards (1955: 183) put it, John Wesley "strongly urged not only that Methodists should gain and save money, but that then they should spend it"; in Fiji, this ethic is displayed in communal contributions to the Church, as I describe below. Discursively, Wesleyan Methodist missionaries energetically constructed demonic cultural "Others," introducing Christian reading publics to a host of wicked characters, such as Fijian cannibals, Chinese foot binders, and Indian widow burners (Birtwhistle 1983: 71). Inheriting this legacy, the Fijian Methodist Church now sets up a new kind of Other: Indo-Fijians who mostly remain Hindu or Muslim despite missionary efforts to bring them into the Christian fold. Some of the British missionaries' distrust of Roman Catholicism lingers too. For example, one Methodist official in Kadavu asked me if it were possible that the pope was the Antichrist. In these various ways, Fijian Methodism is notably Wesleyan.

Kadavu constitutes its own division of the Methodist Church along with Ono and several small islands nearby. At present, the number of divisions in the national organization is forty-seven. That number has grown in recent years, but this has resulted from divisions being splintered rather

TABLE 3. Church denominations in Tavuki Bay villages, 1995

Village	Methodists	Seventh-day Adventists	Assemblies of God	Roman Catholics	Muslims	Others*
Tavuki	161	5	0	0	0	0
Nagonedau	46	0	0	1	0	0
Baidamudamu	53	0	0	0	0	0
Nukunuku	56	29	0	0	0	0
Waisomo	84	20	0	0	1	2
Natumua	80	0	15	0	0	37
Solodamu	105	3	5	0	0	12

*This category is almost entirely composed of smaller Christian denominations.
SOURCE: Vale ni Volavola ni Yasana ko Kadavu 1995.

than from demographic expansion. In fact, Methodism's numbers have declined nationally from being the denomination of 74.2 percent of indigenous Fijians in 1986 to 66.6 percent in 1996 (Ernst 1994: 206; Ratuva 2002: 19). As Fiji's population increases, Methodism's numbers are being outpaced by the gains of other denominations, most notably Assemblies of God and Seventh-day Adventism (Ernst 1994: 203). In 1995 statistics showed that Methodism was still dominant in Kadavu, where more than 93 percent of the island's population were members of the Methodist Church. Of the 715 villagers living in Tavuki Bay, 585 were Methodist, approximately 82 percent. Methodist church buildings stand in each village of the bay—counting Tavuki and neighboring Nagonedau as one large conjoined village—except for Nukunuku, where the building would more appropriately be called a chapel. Solodamu was building a new Methodist church during my periods of fieldwork, and Baidamudamu opened a new church in April 1999. But several villages in Tavuki Bay had sizable non-Methodist groups, and Seventh-day Adventists had their own church in Nukunuku; in Natumua village, the Methodists let other denominations meet in their church building. Even within Tavuki village, not everyone was under the sway of Methodism. A few villagers had experimented with or joined other religious sects, sometimes going to the town of Vunisea to do so. Such individuals were not barred from attending Methodist services in Tavuki. However, one of Tavuki village's twenty village laws states, "It is forbidden for another lotu to come into the village" (*Sa tabu ni dua tale na mata lotu me curu mai e loma ni koro*); thus, missionaries are legally forbidden from proselytizing locally.

A superintendent minister (*talatala qase*) leads each division of the Methodist Church. Chosen and appointed at the annual Methodist Church conference, superintendents serve five-year terms, then rotate to new divisions when their terms are finished. This policy of mandatory mobility applies to all ministers, not only superintendents, and was designed by the British so that Church leaders would "not . . . be subjected too strictly to the influence of those whose spiritual guidance has been delegated to them" (Halèvy 1971: 51). The policy serves to keep ministers as permanent guests of their congregations—perpetually subordinate to, and dependent on, local chiefs. In other words, the rotational system keeps the lotu perpetually dependent on the vanua, since the lotu is usually represented by an outsider. In 1999, of the twelve Methodist ministers serving in Kadavu only one was originally from Kadavu; in 2003 the number had risen to four, but I believe this increase was not indicative of any trend. Church officials may become affiliated with a particular subclan in the villages where they are stationed. In Tavuki superintendent ministers customarily become affiliated with the Nadurusolo subclan and catechists become affiliated with Naocovonu.

Rev. Isikeli Serewai was Kadavu's superintendent minister from 1995 through the end of 1999. Born on August 20, 1952, Rev. Serewai was a native of Ra province in northern Vitilevu, meaning he enjoyed a *tauvu* relationship with Kadavuans. The *tauvu* relationship is a connection based on ancestral kinship links; interactions between *tauvu* are expected to be mutually beneficial, relaxed, and jocular. It was an ideal position for Rev. Serewai to be in, because he was jovial, funny, and generous but publicly respectful of chiefly authority. His personal good humor and friendliness, his willingness to walk about the village chatting and joking, his enthusiasm for drinking kava, and his respect for Tavuki's chiefs all combined to make him immensely popular. He was compared favorably with his predecessor and successor, and Church life was noticeably more energetic during my first two field visits (1996, 1998–1999) than it was in 2003, after Rev. Serewai had departed. When he was in charge of the Church, people wanted to work for it. He also established his own local kinship links: one of the reverend's classificatory daughters married a Tavuki villager, and a man from Baidamudamu village named his son Isikeli Serewai in honor of the minister.

One night at a casual kava-drinking session, I asked two Tavuki men (one middle-aged, one quite elderly) who had been the best superintendent minister in Kadavu. They both named Rev. Serewai and another man, Esaroma Muasobu. Although the mention of Rev. Serewai

FIGURE 4. Rev. Isikeli Serewai.

may have been partly diplomatic—I was living in his house at the time, after all—the elderly man said something else. He explained that Mua-sobu and Serewai were both from places *tauvu* to Kadavu, and that this meant they worked well in "traditional" matters (*vakavanua*), unlike ministers who came to Tavuki and paid attention only to Church matters. In other words, the old man was claiming that a Church leader should not focus on the lotu alone; a minister should pay attention to the vanua as well, and to all the practices that are the lifeblood of a chiefdom. Rev. Serewai was particularly good at this. He was good friends with the Roko Tui Kadavu, and even accompanied him on a trip to Australia, the United States, and Canada to solicit contributions for Kadavu's ceremonial honor of opening the annual Methodist Conference in 2000.

I asked Rev. Serewai how he knew as a young man that it was right for him to work for the Church. He answered that when he was a schoolchild he used to get bad headaches, but that when he was a teenager studying to become a catechist his head did not hurt. In 1970, still a young man, he entered the Methodist training institution at Davuilevu to begin studying for the ministry. He finished in three years and received his first ministerial appointment, to Nadrau in the division of Ba, in 1974. After Nadrau his appointments ranged widely over Fiji's largest islands, Vitilevu and Vanualevu: to Wainibuka (Bau division), Nawaka (Vuda), Seaqaqa (Macuata), and then Buretu (Bau). In January 1995, at age forty-two, he became a superintendent minister for the first time when he came to Tavuki.

He did a great deal of organizational work. For example, he often attended quarterly meetings held in the different circuits around Kadavu. He drew up the Tavuki circuit's "preaching plan," the document assigning particular preachers to services in different villages. He frequently delivered sermons, sometimes appointing himself as the preacher for a particular Sunday service and sometimes being asked to fill the role by a member of the group responsible for organizing the day's service (see below). When he was not giving a sermon, Rev. Serewai was often asked to provide the closing prayer at the end of the service. He responded to occasional religious crises, as I describe in chapter 5. In addition, Rev. Serewai performed ceremonial duties at non-Church events, such as giving public prayers. Finally, through many informal day-to-day practices, Rev. Serewai acted in ways that displayed his religious authority, for example, giving advice on preaching and serving as the voice of the lotu at kava-drinking sessions.

Serving under the superintendent are his ministers, either first-time appointments ("training ministers," *talatala vakatovolei*) or full ministers (*talatala yaco*). They have the authority to conduct weddings, funerals, baptisms, and communion. Eleven ministers are stationed in Kadavu under the superintendent: eight are in charge of circuits (*tabacakacaka*); two work at the Methodist high school and catechist training center at Rijimodi; one serves in the town of Vunisea.

Below the ministers are the catechists. Catechists, called *vakatawa* in Fijian, might be described as the minister's righthand men.[19] Like ministers, catechists undergo three years of training. They can conduct funerals but not weddings, nor do they baptize or give communion. If they are serving actively, catechists receive a salary. A circuit may have more than one catechist, and if so, his bailiwick is called a "small circuit" (*tabacakacaka lailai*). Three catechists serve the full circuit of Tavuki, which includes ten villages, the town of Vunisea, the school at Rijimodi, and the settlement of Busa; one of them serves the Tavuki Bay area specifically.

In the late 1990s Rev. Serewai's catechist in Tavuki Bay was Tomasi Laveasiga. Born on April 9, 1960, and hailing from Muani on Kadavu's south coast, he studied at Rijimodi from 1978 to 1980 to become a catechist. Before coming to Tavuki in January 1996, Laveasiga had been assigned to three other villages in Kadavu. He worked energetically, often traveling to other villages to conduct services and occasionally serving as a replacement for preachers or prayer service leaders who neglected their duties. On one Sunday in July 1999, for example, he substituted for the morning prayer service leader in Tavuki who was unable to fulfill her assignment; then he went to Rijimodi, down the coast from Tavuki, to preach the noon service there; and finally he returned to Tavuki to preach at the afternoon service. His sermons were always solid and straightforward, probably closest among local preachers' efforts to the early Wesleyan ideal of plain speaking. Besides his heavy workload on behalf of the Church, Laveasiga was an impressively powerful manual laborer. He cleared gardens, chopped firewood, and gathered coconuts with seemingly inexhaustible vigor.

Besides the catechists, circuits have treasurers, secretaries, and leaders of various social groups, such as the women's group and the youth fellowship. Each village ideally has one pastor (*qase*) or teacher (*vakavuvuli*); the roles are interchangeable. Tavuki village, however, neither has nor needs a pastor because both the superintendent minister and the circuit catechist already reside in the village. Pastors and teachers, who need no formal training, are like lower-level catechists; they are executives' executives, local men in charge, carrying out much of the labor the Church requires. Each village also has several lay preachers (*dauvunau*) and prayer service leaders (*daujili lotu masumasu*).[20] These positions are typically gendered, with preachers being male and prayer service leaders being female; I discuss these roles further below.

A key position is the steward (*tuirara*), who represents the Methodist Church to the chiefs and vice versa. When people explained to me the responsibilities of a steward, they sometimes described the position as a "mouth" between lotu and vanua, speaking from one side to the other. Individual villages may have their own steward, and the head steward in charge of a circuit is called the *tuirara levu*. In Tavuki, the position of head steward was one marked by conflict during my early period of fieldwork. The first man holding the position was the descendant of one of Tavuki's greatest chiefs, so I will call him "the high chief" even though he was not the Tui Tavuki. (In fact, it would be odd for a Tui Tavuki to serve as a steward, because the steward is a go-between, not a paramount leader.)

In November 1998 I learned that the high chief had been replaced as head steward. The switch had happened a week or two earlier, while I was in Suva. When I asked why, I was given several reasons, most focusing on the high chief's lack of attention to his responsibilities. I learned that men of the neighboring village, Nagonedau, had brought kava to a Tavuki village men's meeting one morning and formally requested that the chiefs of Tavuki appoint a new head steward. Their request, called a *kerekere,* is well known in the ethnography of Fiji as the sort of entreaty that cannot respectfully be denied (Nayacakalou 1978; Sahlins 1962, 1993; Thomas 1992). But this request was especially remarkable: the high chief was, after all, a high chief, and the men's meetings were held in the house of one of his subclan members. Moreover, Nagonedau is not a village of chiefs, but the village of *sauturaga,* the installers of chiefs. In the somewhat awkward position of kingmakers who refuse to make kings, the Nagonedau villagers nonetheless had enough influence to successfully request a new head steward.

But why was the vanua orchestrating the affairs of the lotu? At the time, Anaseini Serewai, the wife of Rev. Serewai, explained to me that in Tavuki the vanua, not the lotu, chooses the head steward. In other words, the pivotal position of go-between—the person who will represent the Church to the chiefs and the chiefs to the Church—is chosen by the people and the chiefs, not by the Church. According to Rev. Serewai, this power of the vanua over the lotu was unique to Tavuki; in the other places he had worked as a minister, Church authorities chose the *tuirara levu.* This fact illuminates the vanua's strength in Tavuki, a topic to which I return below.

The new head steward in late 1998 was Ratu Meli Qaravanua ("Ratu Qara"). He was born on December 19, 1953, and was a member of the subclan Touluga, which made his appointment as head steward in Tavuki somewhat surprising. Toulugans are descended from Qaraniqio, a warrior from Rewa who was a fierce enemy of early Christian converts in Kadavu. Not only did Ratu Qara stand in the daunting shadow of his ancestor, but, until his appointment as head steward, he had not served in any Church role. In some ways he was an ideal candidate, however. He was intelligent, hardworking, and committed to doing a good job of representing the lotu to the vanua and vice versa. When I asked him how he felt when the chiefs asked him to take the position, he said he was "happy" (*marau*). I asked him if it were possible to refuse the chiefs' summons, and his answer surprised me: not only was it possible, but other men—I am not sure how many—had been approached before him and had declined to take the position.

For several months he worked without any notable disruption. Then, on June 13, 1999, he helped make a decision that would cause strain between lotu and vanua. Church leaders, including Rev. Serewai, decided that at the next Sunday afternoon's service people would be called on to give financial contributions by village rather than by subclan affiliation, the usual practice. In other words, the ceremonial names of each village (*icavuji*) would be announced and people would contribute accordingly. As it turned out, the plan did not go into effect until the afternoon service of the third Sunday in July. It sounded like a minor change to me, but, as it turned out, its effects metastasized.

The controversy unfolded at the kava session that took place in the church social hall after the service at which the change was initiated. Normally, these sessions after big church services are pleasant affairs where chiefs discuss matters of importance, people chat and enjoy camaraderie, and kava flows in like a tidal river. This time, however, events took an unusual turn when the Tui Tavuki asked why the call to the collection plate had not followed the usual pattern. I was not present at the beginning of the debacle because I was helping to pound kava outside. By the time I entered the church social hall, the paramount chief and the head steward were arguing and the atmosphere was painfully tense. The head steward even interrupted the Tui Tavuki during their dispute, which was a shocking act—people almost always listen to chiefly speech without interruption.

Ratu Qara was asserting that these financial contributions were purely an affair of the lotu. It was a Church collection, he said, so the Church decided how it would be conducted. In short, this was one arena in which the lotu did not need to defer to the vanua, in his opinion. A third party had to step in to calm things down, and the Tui Nukunuku, a diminutive but confident former soldier, did so. When he finished speaking the room fell into a thick silence for a few minutes. At least two rounds of kava were served in the uncomfortable stillness. No one was enjoying the drinking session at this point, suspended in the charged and awkward moment, waiting for resolution.

Then Rev. Serewai spoke. His tone was conciliatory. He requested the forgiveness (*veivosoti*) of the vanua, and the older men of the kava circle uttered a relieved "Good, thanks" (*vinaka*). These men were sitting at the sides of the room, in the middle of the spatially ordered hierarchy—old enough to be respected elders who could speak at a difficult moment, but not high chiefs themselves. Rev. Serewai also spoke performatively (per Austin 1962), declaring that the matter was "finished" and "clean" (*oti, savasava*). In other words, the matter was now dropped because Rev. Serewai said so; the Tui Tavuki was right, and the Church did not protest. Lotu deferred to vanua after all; the call to the collection plate would revert to the original practice. Rev. Serewai explained that Ratu Qara was still learning in his new position.

After this conciliatory speech the tension began to dissipate, but the affair was not over yet. Ratu Qara, chastened, left the hall. A short while later he came back in, bearing a large bundle of kava. He presented the kava as an *ibulubulu* ("burial," with a meaning similar to "burying the hatchet" in English) to atone for his transgression. In his speech he was visibly emotional. The Roko Tui Kadavu accepted the kava on behalf of the Tui Tavuki,[21] and then, after an intermediary round or two of kava drinking, the Tui Tavuki gave a final speech. The affair was now truly finished.

This condensed story of a conflict illustrates local power dynamics. In Tavuki, Church and chiefs often work in harmony, just as John Wesley would have wanted them to, but the vanua is the dominant force. A critical fact, however, is that by publicly deferring to chiefly power Rev. Serewai earned the gratitude and respect of villagers who were thus inclined to support the Church. Evidently Rev. Serewai understood what many European and Australian missionaries failed to understand during Methodism's early years in Fiji. In 1860 an observer "criticized missionaries for not appreciating the basic aristocratic character of the chiefly class and claimed that the demeanour of the missionaries towards the chiefs would not generally encourage great loyalty to the church" (Thornley 2002: 225; see also Carey 1867–1874: 199). Rev. Serewai, in contrast, apparently knew that by supporting the Tavuki chiefs and deferring to them he was fostering people's loyalty to Methodism as well. He was an effective lotu authority precisely because he recognized the ultimate authority of the vanua in village life.

But the dispute might still seem opaque to the reader. Why did it take the form it did? Why did the Church want people to contribute money by village, after all, and why did the paramount chief object to this plan, preferring that people contribute by subclan affiliation? The answers to these questions will become clear through a consideration of church services.

CHRISTIAN RITUAL ACTION

Although *ritual* is a problematic term for many contemporary scholars (Scott 1994; cf. Kelly and Kaplan 1990), Methodist services fit most well-known anthropological definitions. They are formalized, repeated events that help foster certain sensibilities and motivations in the participants; they follow a particular order of service and involve communication with invisible powers (Jesus, Jehovah); they are performative, public ceremonies that effect change in the world and creatively index the social order (Tambiah 1985).

Three of the five weekly Methodist services are prayer services (*lotu masumasu*), which take place on Wednesday, Saturday, and Sunday mornings. In Tavuki the congregation might be as small as twenty people or as large as forty-five for these events. The service leader chooses several hymns, reads from the Bible, discusses the passage briefly (this is not a full sermon), and asks people to volunteer prayers on several topics. Although service leaders can use the Church calendar's daily Bible verses as a source for their reading, they often take the opportunity to select a passage of their own choosing. What is most notable about prayer services is that these are the only events at which congregation members are asked to pray aloud individually and voluntarily. The prayer topics chosen by service leaders usually include the welfare of the lotu and the vanua, treated as separate topics, and also youth and the provincial government. In other words, the standard metacultural division of Fijian society into three units—Church, chiefs and people, and government—is replicated in prayer service topics, with youth added as a unit of its own. After the service leader announces the topics, there is a pause of several seconds, and then someone begins praying aloud on the first topic. The first prayer giver finishes, another pause of several seconds ensues, then someone else begins praying aloud on the second topic; and so the prayers continue. Rarely do two people begin praying at the same time, and no one ever competes for the floor, trying to pray louder than someone else. This raises the question of how people know who is "supposed" to pray, and part of the answer is simply that a small group of self-selected people dominate the prayer giving. In a sample I took from May to July 1999 thirty-four separate prayers at *lotu masumasu* were given by only twelve people. Significantly, eight of these twelve prayer givers were women. This suggests that prayer giving, unlike preaching, is a genre in which women feel relatively comfortable speaking publicly in a mixed-sex group.[22]

On Sunday two full church services take place, one around 10 o'clock in the morning and the other around 3 o'clock in the afternoon. Religious education (Sunday school, lit. "Sunday book reading," *wili vola Sigatabu*) is held for young children between the two main services. The morning service might draw around one hundred people in Tavuki. The afternoon service is the biggest communal affair of the week, drawing people from the seven villages in Tavuki Bay. It is held at one of the large churches, often the one in Tavuki village, and can draw a crowd in the low hundreds. At these two Sunday services, chiefly speeches are made, money is collected, the choir sings— sometimes different village choirs have a competition—and formal sermons are delivered.

Specially designated services in the Tavuki Bay area include *lotu ni vula vou* (new-month services) on the first Sunday of every month and *lotu ni vanua* (services for the vanua) on the third Sunday of the month. New-month services take place at both 10:00 A.M. and 3:00 P.M., whereas *lotu ni vanua* occur only in the afternoon. Each of the full Sunday services is supported (*viqaravi*) by a kin group, meaning that the group is supposed to provide a preacher if one is not already listed on the preaching plan, give the speech of welcome to visitors, give the chiefly speech, and provide the kava for the after-service drinking session.[23] At *lotu ni vanua* responsibilities for support are usually divided three ways, based on the subclans of Tavuki village: Nadurusolo, Naocovonu, and Vunikarawa. Each of the other villages—politically subordinate to Tavuki—are affiliated with one of these three subclans. For example, Baidamudamu village members belong to their own clan, Viniuniu, but at these church services they are affiliated with Tavuki's subclan Naocovonu. Subclans are major segments of the vanua, part of the traditional order, and the fact that they are given responsibility for the organization and performance of these Church services and the subsequent kava drinking shows how the vanua sets the boundaries of discourse and practice within which the Church acts and abides in Tavuki.

Some Sunday afternoon services are special ones in honor of women, men, or children, or special occasions such as the first-fruits (new harvest) service held on the first Sunday in March. The service in honor of women is led by women, but a man usually delivers the sermon. Attendance at these services is not limited to the group responsible for running the service; for example, men can go to the women's and children's services, and vice versa.

The structure of all Sunday services is generally the same. The typical order of service is this:

1. As people arrive, the catechism is read from the hymnbook in a call-and-response pattern; the call (question) is given by an adult woman, and the response (answer) is given by women and children.

2. The entrance song (*sere ni curu*) is sung by the choir as the minister enters.

3. The service leader welcomes everyone and announces the order of service.

4. The first hymn is sung by all.

5. A short prayer is given by the service leader, followed by the congregation's recitation of the Lord's Prayer (a standard formulaic Christian prayer, commonly beginning in English with "Our father who art in heaven, hallowed be thy name").

6. The anthem (*sere ni tacake*) is sung by the choir.

7. The lesson (*lesoni*), a short passage from the Bible on which the sermon is often based, is read; often the reader is neither the service leader nor the day's preacher, but a third person.

8. A speech of welcome (*vosa ni vikidavaki*) is given to visitors and is often responded to with a speech from one of the visitors.

9. A money contribution (*soli*) is taken under the direction of the steward; a short prayer is offered immediately afterward.

10. The song of thanks (*sere ni vakavinavinaka*) is sung by all.

11. The sermon is given.

12. The recessional (*sere ni suka*) is sung by all.

13. The prayer of benediction (*masu ni vivakalougatataki*) is offered, usually by the highest ranking religious authority present, finishing the service.

Within this basic structure, services sometimes have additional features such as short drama performances or choir competitions. Every so often communion is given and baptisms are performed as part of the service, at the minister's discretion.

Two elements within Sunday church services deserve special mention for the ways they highlight the vanua's presence within the lotu's ritual space: speeches of welcome and money collections. Speeches of welcome (*vosa ni vikidavaki*) are notable for the way chiefs' authority is affirmed. Consider the beginning of such a speech from September 1998, when the steward from the Ravitaki circuit formally welcomed Rev. Serewai to the village of Nasegai. Rev. Serewai was traveling around Kadavu at the time, conducting quarterly meetings in different circuits:

Sir, it is I. [Respectful opening.] Here is the gentleman, the leader of the great [Church] district of Kadavu, the appointment of the Conference in Fiji and Rotuma. Also sitting here is the Vunisa Levu, the honorable Tui Tavuki. I am standing on behalf of the gentleman the Tui Ravitaki, on behalf of the leader of the circuit, the gentleman the minister, the gentlemen and ladies, members of the Quarterly Meeting, so I can speak a few words to welcome you gentlemen.

The Tui Tavuki was formally recognized and welcomed in this speech ("Also sitting here is the Vunisa Levu [an honorific title], the honorable Tui Tavuki"), but he was not actually present in the church at the time. Nor was he present in the village. Nor did the orator think he was. It is simply standard politeness to recognize the visiting party by welcoming their chief in this way. Although speeches of welcome often greet particular guests, sometimes they are given to greet the congregation as a whole. A second speaker then usually responds, thanking the hosts for their welcome.

Monetary contributions to the Church are notable for how they display Fijian concerns with the public recognition of social identity. "The idea of an anonymous donation," Christina Toren (1999: 31) points out, "is absurd in Fiji where all instances of giving mark the fulfilment of a recognised obligation to one's kin and incur obligations from the receivers." When contributions are called for during a service, they are solicited according to kin group membership. For example, at a service that only Tavuki and Nagonedau villagers are attending, Tavukians will be asked to contribute money by subclan (Nadurusolo, Naocovonu, Vunikawara), and Nagonedauans will be asked to contribute money as Nukunawa clan. The point is that, in Fijian practice, money must be tied to a social location, and the size of the contribution can indicate a group's cohesion, which is morally valued. Contributions are never anonymous, never private; they are always socially made and recognized. For example, after the collection at the new-month service on June 6, 1999, the catechist announced:

Now that your new-month offering is attended to, gentlemen and ladies, congregants of Nacolase and Nukunawa, the groups give their different offerings this afternoon: Noble group of Nadurusolo, ten dollars, thirty-seven cents.

[Audience: "Good, thanks."] Ten dollars, thirty-seven cents. Noble group of Naocovonu, twenty-two dollars, four cents. [Audience: "Good, thanks."] Twenty-two dollars, four cents. Vunikarawa, seven dollars, eighty-nine. [Audience: "Good, thanks."] Seven dollars, eighty-nine. Noble group of Nukunawa, thirteen dollars, thirty-six cents. [Audience: "Good, thanks."] Thirteen dollars, thirty-six cents. You gentlemen and ladies have given the total amount [at] our new-month service this afternoon, fifty-three dollars, sixty-two cents. [Audience: "Good, thanks."][24] Fifty-three dollars, sixty-two cents. [I] ask that we serve God [now] in prayer.

Sometimes people choose to contribute on behalf of groups that they are not members of themselves, but with which they have a social connection. As in the example just quoted, collections are always followed with a prayer.

I have described and quoted from these two parts of a typical church service to show how the vanua plays a central role in the lotu's practices. The crux of the dispute at the July 1999 *lotu ni vanua* service should now be slightly clearer. When the Tui Tavuki objected to the call for contributions by village rather than by subclan, he was probably doing so because it was a change in the traditional order that denied the subordination of other groups to Tavuki. The Church leaders had not designed their plan to be politically subversive, however; I believe they had done it simply to make more money. Creating more divisions and emphasizing smaller localities lead to higher expectations for each division. But the Tui Tavuki apparently perceived the realignment of contributing groups as a political challenge. He objected to it, and the Church acquiesced.

Projects of boundary drawing necessarily raise the possibility of transgression, and even invite it; recognition of transgression motivates new attempts at boundary drawing. Competition between lotu and vanua is the main factor, I argue, in generating the Fijian sense of loss. In the next section of the book, I examine the metacultural shaping and expression of this sense of loss in church services, kava sessions, and chain prayers. In the final section I analyze the ways that a sense of loss motivates attempts at recuperation. As Dan Jorgensen (1981: 237) has argued in a different context, ideas of entropy, belief in "the world's tendency towards loss, contingency, dissolution, and chaos," can spur people to regenerate or recapture what they think is disappearing: people embark on new "attempts to order society or their lives [carrying] with them the sense that they are bucking the trend." I argue that Christianity plays a decisive role in both processes, creating entropy and order as weakness becomes strength, loss becomes gain, curse becomes blessing.

PART TWO

Lamentation

Early during fieldwork, I noticed that people referred relatively frequently to the Bible verse Genesis 1:26. In the King James Version, it begins, "And God said, Let us make man in our image, after our likeness." The Fijian version is, "A sa kaya na Kalou, Me datou bulia na tamata mei tovo vata kei kedatou, ka me ucui kedatou." People do not repeat this verbatim, but paraphrase part of it idiomatically and poetically as "Tou ia tou bulia na tamata" (We are making humanity). It is a moment of creation, a moment when God decides on humanity's existence and form. Genesis 1:26 "means that God intends that our customs and habits and all our works are holy and correct just like His," according to the Fijian hymnal's section on doctrine (Methodist Overseas Missions Trust Association 1981: 247; my translation).

Over the course of fieldwork I heard this verse used in a variety of contexts. For example, a friend of mine from Solodamu village once used the verse to criticize people who got drunk often; clearly, they were not living up to a divine image. Another time, a friend was telling me that he had once belonged to a gang in Lautoka but was now hoping to become a Methodist minister. I asked why he had changed his ways, and he said that he had read Genesis 1:26. Thus, like my friend from Solodamu, he used the verse as a negative example—it depicted a situation contrary to the one he had been in—and he had decided to try to become more godly. Besides these examples from casual conversations, I heard Genesis 1:26 referred to in sermons, a prayer during a church service, and a government minister's speech, and the theologian Ilaitia Tuwere (2002: 122–123) offers an intriguing interpretation of the verse in his work.

Genesis 1:26 was not the only Bible text I encountered repeatedly. Another prominent verse was Philippians 4:13, "I can do all things through Christ which strengtheneth me." It was impossible to miss this verse when watching rugby videos in the late 1990s, for the Fiji national sevens team had "Phil 4:13" emblazoned on the front of their uniforms at the time. When I was preparing to return home after fieldwork in 2003, the catechist Sevanaia Takotavuki advised me to begin my farewell speech in church with this verse. Several ethnographers of Fiji have noted the popularity of other Bible verses as well, including Psalms 127:1 (Miyazaki 2004: 111) and Ecclesiastes 10:8 (Tippett 1960: 90). Alan Tippett writes, "The whole field of Biblical parable and allegory has been taken over and is in use daily, especially from the Old Testament Book of Proverbs and the sayings of Jesus. However the particular sayings used most frequently by Fijians are not those most frequently used by Westerners" (90). The verses that are heard relatively frequently, and prominently, challenge the old truism that the Bible can be used to prove anything; it can, semantically, but it isn't, practically. People choose specific passages to focus on and, comparatively speaking, ignore thousands of others. Verses such as Genesis 1:26, Philippians 4:13, Psalms 127:1, and Ecclesiastes 10:8 circulate with notable success in Fiji, suggesting that as texts they are particularly amenable to recontextualization.

Intrigued by the circulation of Genesis 1:26, I asked Rev. Setareki Tuilovoni about its use. He and his wife, Ana, said that people could not be quite like God but should strive to be as good as possible. Such an interpretation shows that Genesis 1:26 offers a model of perfection. Crucially, it offers a model of perfection that is often invoked critically: people in Tavuki use the verse to call attention to people's failure to conform to it. People are evidently not godly at present. In this regard, Fijian Methodism shares the common religious theme of humanity's divergence from a powerful spiritual being (or beings) long ago, but it puts Fijian Methodism at odds with some newer forms of Christianity, such as Faith Christianity (Coleman 2000). Faith Christians emphasize the second half of Genesis 1:26: "and let them have dominion over the fish of the sea, and over the fowl of the air, and over the cattle, and over all the earth, and over every creeping thing that creepeth upon the earth." Humankind's godly creation, according to Faith Christians and members of similar movements, is a warrant for humanity's supreme power in the world today, not for the lamentation of lost power.

By referring to divine perfection in human creation, Genesis 1:26 intratextually sets up the story of humanity's fall; by referring to the verse's standard of original perfection, Fijian speakers set up the story of contemporary decline and loss. The speakers I heard did not make distinctions between the loss of will and the loss of reason, as some theologians do; instead, their emphasis was on lost power, as I show in chapter 2.

Here I want to pose two pivotal questions: If people are not like God but were supposed to be, what went wrong? And how do they respond?

For indigenous Fijians, ideas of lost power and declining morality are united in the sense that social order is breaking down. Social unity is a sign of good morality and practical strength. Social unity means that everyone knows his or her place: commoners fulfill their traditional obligations in service to chiefs, and chiefs act in appropriate chiefly style, providing "good speech, good water, good cooking pot" (*vosa vinaka, wai vinaka, kuro vinaka*), meaning they speak well and make sure that people have good kava to drink and good food to eat. If chiefs are effective in these ways, people should be able to work well for them, and society will be strong as a result (see Milner 1952). The image that many indigenous Fijians have of present-day society, however, is one in which properly unified relationships are breaking down, or are already broken, and as a result people's mana is diminished or lost.

CHAPTER 2

Signs of the Golden Age

In the book of Genesis, God creates the original man from dust, breathing into him so that he becomes "a living soul" (2:7). The Hebrew translation of "human," *adam,* is used in the King James Version as the name of this first man. Adam is placed by God in "a garden eastward in Eden" (2:8), where the creator has put "every tree that is pleasant to the sight, and good for food" (2:9). Eve, created from Adam's body, is with him in the Garden of Eden, where they are naked but "not ashamed" (2:25), living in both physical comfort and social ease. Then a snake comes and tempts Eve, who persuades her partner to eat the only fruit that God has forbidden them.

Upon learning of the transgression, God curses women and men. To Eve, the creator says, "I will greatly multiply thy sorrow and thy conception; in sorrow thou shalt bring forth children; and thy desire shall be to thy husband, and he shall rule over thee" (3:16), inflicting women with the physical pain of childbirth and the social pain of subordination. To Adam, the creator declares: "Cursed is the ground for thy sake; in sorrow shalt thou eat of it all the days of thy life; Thorns also and thistles shall it bring forth to thee; and thou shalt eat the herb of the field; In the sweat of thy face shalt thou eat bread, till thou return unto the ground; for out of it wast thou taken: for dust thou art, and unto dust shalt thou return" (3:17–19). Thus God punishes men with the physical pain of labor and inflicts all of humankind with the painful loss of death.

The Garden of Eden myth is a narrative of loss and suffering. Read in the context of the whole Christian Bible, it gestures toward a more encompassing story of loss, one spanning human history: the final book in the Bible, Revelation, describes chaos, famine, and war before the return of God's son Jesus. In other words, Genesis begins humanity's story with paradise as order imposed on chaos; Revelation wraps humanity in violent chaos just before the ultimate conclusion, a new paradise. The loss of order and the resultant suffering are not a perfectly consistent pattern in this history. Christians believe that two thousand years ago, Jesus came as God on earth; this was a dramatically positive moment. However, when Jesus was rejected by most and crucified, a new era of decline and loss began. Thus perhaps it is most accurate to write of general Christian conceptions of history as periods of decline interrupted by relatively brief cosmic upturns. Many Christians do not believe that they are living during a period of upturn; for them the world keeps getting worse.[1]

In the introduction to this section, I described how Fijians refer to Genesis 1:26 to trace an arc of decline. When they refer to creation, it is the ground against which the figure of contemporary loss stands out. I will discuss this further in chapter 3, but here let me note that Fijian symbols of decline and loss are significantly different from those in the Genesis story. In Genesis humankind is cursed by the need to sweat, the obligation to work vigorously in order to survive. For many Fijians, however, the admirable thing about the past was that people did sweat, did work vigorously with the soil in order to eat its fruit; there was "pleasure, honour, and food to be gained from heavy labour" (Scarr 1984: 90; see also Hocart 1929: 152–153). For Fijian Methodists, the story of humankind's fall is profoundly influential, but the present-day signs of loss that it encourages people to see are distinctly Fijian signs.

My data come from Kadavu, but ethnographic reports from the four corners of Fiji confirm that the theme of decline and loss is widespread. From the nation's eastern Lau Islands, Andrew Arno (1993: 76, 79) reports a spirited conversation among five men about "why the 'kinship way of life,' *na bula vakaveiwekani,* was becoming weaker," with one of the participants adding that "things are less orderly now" than in the old days "and people ignore communal work." Moving west to the Ra district of Vitilevu, the nation's largest and most populous island, Karen Brison (2007: 24–25) summarizes the views of one teenage girl as follows: "Ema . . . voiced the common view that Fijian villagers no longer conformed to the sacred, time-honored order at all. People had lost respect for tradition and hierarchy; villages were now just hotbeds of gossip and drunkenness. . . . People no longer had respect for rank; they did not know how they were related to each other. They did not know traditional Fijian kinship practices. What was left was just an empty shell without any real knowledge of, or respect for, Fijian traditions. She explicitly connected the need to preserve tradition with maintaining Fijian power and pride."

I have already quoted several of Buell Quain's observations from Vanualevu in northern Fiji, where in the old days "all chiefs were miracle-workers" (1948: 200). From southern Fiji, the work of Richard Katz augments my own findings. Katz (1993: 91, 63, 17), who studied traditional healing on an island (which he keeps pseudonymous) near Kadavu, quotes informants delivering the following pithy metacultural summaries: "As the real Fijian life weakens, so does the *mana*"; "The *mana* is getting weaker in Fiji because people are not now following ancient customs"; and "Today we have almost nothing left." Based on these examples and others (e.g., Colchester 2005: 45; Hocart 1912a; Macnaught 1977; Thomas 1997: 63; Toren 1990: 102), it is safe to say that decline and loss are prominent themes throughout indigenous Fiji and have been for some time.

Sources of Decline and Loss

Precolonial Fijian chiefs asserted "that Fijian customs had degraded in the last few generations" (Thornley 2000: 330; see also Macnaught 1977), and this claim resonated with early Methodist missionary discourse about "fallen and depraved" humankind. The missionary James Calvert, in describing Fijian society, referred to the first chapter of Romans, where Paul wrote that humankind had become "filled with all unrighteousness, fornication, wickedness, covetousness, maliciousness; full of envy, murder, debate, deceit, malignity; whisperers, Backbiters, haters of God, despiteful, proud, boasters, inventors of evil things, disobedient to parents, Without understanding, covenantbreakers, without natural affection, implacable, unmerciful" (Romans 1:29–31). Calvert lamented that "the state of the Fijians confirmed the sad picture of fallen and depraved human nature given" there (cited in Thornley 2000: 72; Romans was one of the first books translated into Fijian).

Different Christian traditions frame decline and loss in different ways, however, with some choosing to emphasize humanity's ultimate salvation at the end of history rather than its present degradation. Moreover, the theme of humanity's decline is not found exclusively in the Judeo-Christian tradition, as shown by countless ethnographic examples of non-Christian societies valorizing their mythic pasts of power and glory. Other forces are at work in Fiji, including experiences of colonial and postcolonial subjugation. In Fiji, as in many places, the colonial era featured humiliations of political subjugation and forced changes in social categories.[2]

The British did not invent the Fijian chiefly system but did help to institutionalize it, turning chieftainship into a fixed position of privilege rather than a local recognition of ability. In addition, they froze relatively fluid social units into rigid hierarchical forms—chiefdoms encompassing clans encompassing subclans—regardless of what the local dynamics of social organization had been. Martha Kaplan (2004: 161) has noted that "the British authorized chiefs from the top down" while downplaying the rights of certain commoners to install chiefs in the first place. The British project drove changes in the jural sphere, specifically landownership laws, beginning with the establishment of the Native Lands Commission in 1880. As Peter France explains in his pathbreaking study, *The Charter of the Land* (1969), the colonial government imposed a label of "traditionality" on a diverse set of flexible land tenure practices and, using such supposed traditionality as a basis for the process of indirect rule, codified landownership and tenure in ways that were unfamiliar to many indigenous Fijians (see also Clammer 1973; Kaplan 1995, 2004; Kelly and Kaplan 2001; Lal 1992; Miyazaki 2004; Nayacakalou 1975). The Fijian sentiment that the colonial Native Lands Commission got its facts wrong about land and chiefly titles—either through error or informants' duplicity—is common today and contributes to a sense of disorder.

Besides introducing Christianity and co-opting tradition, the British also imported a large population from South Asia to work as indentured laborers, introduced devastating new diseases, and circulated commentary on the decline and imminent disappearance of Fijians, especially around the turn of the twentieth century: "The notion that the Fijians were fast on their way to extinction and that the process could not be arrested, was . . . firmly embedded in the thinking" of colonists (Tippett 1974b: 20). Sometimes Fijians' imminent demise was celebrated, as when a Melbourne journalist wrote, "As Fijians withered away, so their islands could be expected to pass altogether into European hands" (quoted in Scarr 1984: 45). Often it was decried by administrators, who proposed measures to help Fijians regain their health and prosperity (Colony of Fiji 1896). When the indigenous population did begin to grow again, around the 1920s and 1930s, this demographic recovery did not halt the circulation of discourse about decline and loss.

A British official's report from 1883 movingly evokes sentiments of loss. Describing the prophet Navosavakadua's religious movement, he wrote, "By treading the ground . . . and filing through every house in the village, they [the prophet's 'soldiers'] gave immortality to the inhabitants and the promise of the resurrection of their ancestors. The latter is greatly desired by all the old Natives, as it is by it they hope to regain what they consider their ancient power and prestige" (quoted in Kaplan 1995: 112). Already by 1883—when Fiji had been a British colony for less than ten years, Indians had been immigrating to the islands for less than five years, and the indigenous population had been largely Christianized for less than thirty—some indigenous Fijians lamented the loss of "ancient power and prestige," hoping to recapture it before it vanished into the ever-receding past.

Colonial subjugation cannot be the only explanation for the prominence of a decline-and-loss theme in contemporary Fijian discourse, however. There are many societies without histories of colonization in which this kind of thinking is equally widespread (see Pick 1989; Williams 1973). In this regard, I would like to consider the specifically local dynamic whose analysis is the core of this book: competition between Methodist Church authorities and traditional chiefs. As I explained in part 1, friction between lotu and vanua is often subdued. Indeed, it is often sublimated into other expressions, such as anti–Indo-Fijian sentiment. Yet its generative force cannot be overstated, and I argue that conflict between lotu and vanua is the most important factor shaping Fijian visions of historical decline. Chiefs are guardians of tradition. They are expected to lead people effectively into the future, but their legitimacy and efficacy must come from the past. The Methodist Church, however, demonizes the past and sets itself up as the defender of living people from ancestral curses. People's discussions about the proper roles of lotu and vanua, and about the degradation of society, are metacultural statements about Fijian social processes that generate the tensions to which they point.

Such tensions are worked out—but perpetuated too—in ritual. For example, Christina Toren (2004) has argued that funerals and related death ceremonies are influential moments for children, in which they "learn to be Christians" but also learn about mana, the non-Christian ancestors, and chiefliness. This learning process is tinged or even suffused with fear: "sorrow and fear . . . are intrinsic" to Fijian death ceremonies, as the recently deceased haunt the land and "terrify the living" (233–234). Besides producing anxiety, death rituals can help produce a permanent sense of loss, as funerals are paradigmatic ritual markers of separation and absence. (The dead do not disappear completely, however, because Fijians tell ghost stories and can see dead people in dreams.)

As I demonstrate in chapters 3 and 5, Fijian Methodist ritual often foregrounds language as a consequential form of action; the Fijian language itself, however, is framed by an ideology of disorder. Many Fijians consider their language to be "inferior" to English and claim that it has "no grammar" (Cook 1975: 95 n. 67; see also chapter 3). In Tavuki I heard people complain that the local word for "no," *mino,* was just a borrowing of the English phrase "me no," suggesting an inappropriate mixing of old and new, local and foreign—although Waterhouse (1866: 429) noted in the mid-nineteenth century that *mino* is a Kaduvuan word. More subtly, speech's ephemeral nature—its character as palpable but instantly vanishing object—becomes a focus of people's concern. Many societies, not only Fiji, combine an anxious need to remember fading voices with the sorrowful certainty that transmission is always imperfect and something is always lost.

In addition, the pragmatics of performance can help create a sense of decline and loss. "A good story," Mary Steedly (1993: 29) points out, "is one that surprises its audience, transgressing or temporarily exceeding the givenness of its form." Audiences are hooked by exaggeration—and exaggerated versions, once told, become new standards. For example, I found myself a character in such stories in Kadavu, and I couldn't help but notice the process of inflation at work. When I returned to the field in 1998 and 2003, I was told that I had previously spoken Fijian well but had evidently lost my skills while away. With due respect to my friends in Kadavu, I had not really lost any speaking skills; they were not very good to begin with, and definitely not as good as they became in stories told afterward. Imagine the process: an outsider with a funny accent and mangled syntax comes to the village, telling everyone he wants to learn about Fijian culture and proving it by attending church regularly and drinking kava enthusiastically. Once he's gone, he becomes an archetype, not only of strange outsiders and their difficulty fitting in, but also of a kind of efficacy. It turns out I had been able to speak the Fijian language well after all, and I could speak it better and better with each retelling. By the time I actually showed up again in Kadavu, my narrative character was fluent even though I was still burdened with a funny accent and mangled syntax. I became a living sign of decline. These stories get told because they are, per Steedly, good ones; they are a bit surprising and imaginatively involving. I heard similar tales about Peace Corps volunteers from past decades, how perfectly they had adapted to local life and how they brought Fijian customs back to their homes overseas. Exaggeration is a technique by which stories get better, and therefore increasingly worth telling and listening to. Stories of decline, so commonly heard, are injected with vigor and made more interesting when they take up new signs as evidence and emphasize the precariousness of the present.

Lost Mana

In Tavuki, people's sense of past strength and present weakness is expressed in many ways. Perhaps the most vivid sign of lost power is the human body and the landscape it has transformed. Ancestors are described as bigger and stronger than present-day people.[3] They were able to accomplish impressive feats quickly. As I noted in the introduction, when human remains were accidentally unearthed in Tavuki in 1999, one man commented on how big the decedent must have been, although to my eyes the size of the bone and skull fragments seemed unremarkable. This suggests that the equation "older=bigger" influenced his perception, or at least his commentary. Similarly, when an ancient burial site in Vitilevu was exposed by winds in 1988 "reports of 'giant' skeletons were advanced as archaeological proof of the modern decline of Fijian physiognomy" (Becker 1995: 16). Working in Vanualevu in the mid-1930s, Buell Quain (1948: 200) wrote, "A generation past, chiefs could uproot great trees with their bare hands."[4]

During the colonial period of epidemic disease and population decline, Fijians observed the loss of strength in individual bodies and wider society. For example, a Fijian man working for the colonial government was quoted in 1910 asking, "How is it that notwithstanding the British peace, we decrease in numbers. In the old pagan days there were more villages, fenced and at war, honouring the greatest murderer, and having more difficulty in producing food. Why were they stronger than we are today? I am not an old man, but I have seen it going on" (quoted in Tippett 1974b: 20). Note the man's apparently double-tiered notion of strength: the ancestors were individually strong—as warriors, murderers—and they were communally strong too, before the decline in population. The individual body and the social body were linked in a relationship of unity, strength, and effectiveness. Communal strength was demonstrated not only by population numbers, but also in the ability to work together on labor projects. In other words, the supposed diminution in body size was a sign of society's own encroaching weakness.[5]

In the old days, I was told, people worked together in their gardens and on building projects. For example, a man from Nagonedau and a Public Works Department employee from Soso village told me about the impressive construction feats still visible in Soso. They said that one earthen house foundation there, bordered by large standing stones, was made by men using only *balotu,* the thick shovel-like ends of coconut palm leaves; each man hauled one stone, which could be six feet long. Nowadays, people work together in large groups only when commanded to do so by chiefs or the village headman or when requested to do so by the Church—and sometimes these calls are not heeded.

A key factor in the fragmentation of communal labor power is the lost mana of chiefs. As noted in chapter 1, chiefs' mana comes from formal installation, and no Tui Tavuki has been installed within living memory. Buell Quain's observations from 1930s Vanualevu are worth quoting at length here, for his description of lost power resonates with discourse from Kadavu in the late twentieth century and early twenty-first:

[The] sacredness of chiefs has degenerated far below old standards. They say that in former times one who had accidentally touched an object which had been infected with old-fashioned chiefliness would cut off a finger to propitiate the chief's offended dignity. Now begging forgiveness is usually sufficient; but, if an angered ancestor sends misfortune as a punishment, then the offender knows that he must make more elaborate amends. . . . Before the advent of the Wesleyans and the British, which was followed by widespread negligence in "re-membering" ancestors and chiefly tradition, all chiefs were miracle-workers. Bu-lisivo's father could put a lighted cigarette in a safe place for the night; in the morning it would still be burning, and the tobacco would not yet be con-sumed[.] When he dug wild yams in the bush, one could hear the steam hissing out through the holes his digging-stick made; when he unearthed the yams, they would be already cooked. (Quain 1948: 200)

Two important facts emerge here. First, the nexus of chiefly and an-cestral power was severely disrupted by the Wesleyans. Second, when people lament the loss of chiefs' power, they do not imagine that a chiefly standard has evaporated. A popular complaint about the pres-ent age is that commoners who earn money think they are chiefly too and begin to act—inappropriately—like chiefs. But money cannot buy chiefliness; education cannot buy chiefliness; presumption cannot

FIGURE 5. Semi Cawa, a ceremonial guard, stands watch at the sacred burial ground in 2003. In the old days, the club would not have been just for show.

buy chiefliness. In a speech to the people of Nadroga explaining his first coup in 1987, Sitiveni Rabuka said, "Let not our thoughts . . . be led astray so that we say to ourselves, since we have studied we can be chiefs. It's wrong, if we study we are wise, if we are chiefs, we are chiefs; they the chiefs are chiefs only from God, as the Apostle Paul says" (quoted in Kaplan 1990a: 141). Rabuka's point, which would be endorsed by many people in Tavuki, is that nowadays too many people illegitimately pretend to be chiefs. This is considered gross misconduct. But even real chiefs fall short of past chiefs in terms of mana. No one enjoys perpetually lit cigarettes these days.

Beliefs about lost mana are often expressed with a sort of wistfulness toward the violence that chiefs once commanded. If you walked across the middle of the village green inappropriately in the old days, you would be imprisoned. If you tried to enter the sacred graveyard during a chief's burial and you weren't welcome, you would be clubbed on the spot. Such assertions are made with just a hint of longing, a sense of lost justice and discipline.

Drinking kava at Waisomo village in July 2003, I heard a seventy-year-old man using the word *mana* as a noun. As described in the introduction, mana is canonically a verb in Fijian, but now it often gets used as a noun; mana has become a thing, a kind of invisible substance, in the classical Polynesian mold. Because I had been paying close attention to people's descriptions of power and history, I took the opportunity to ask the old man my key question: If chiefs got their mana from being formally installed, and they are not installed anymore, where is mana now? He answered without hesitation that there was not any mana now. A few weeks earlier the catechist had said something similar as we worked in his garden: "There is no *sau*" (*Na sau sa mino; sau* is supernatural power, and is a term sometimes used in parallel construction with mana). But then he said that *sau* was with Jehovah. In other words, his gut reaction was to lament the loss of power just as the elderly Waisomo man had done, but then he realized that power must logically reside with God.

On another occasion the catechist told me a story about Christian authorities having the power that chiefs had lost. Intrigued when I first heard him tell the tale, I later asked him to retell it so that I could record and transcribe it. He did, as follows:

One story I heard, ah, Ratu Sukuna [a paramount chief and statesman] was standing with a church minister. It's a story, okay? There was a gathering, and the rain was falling. The rain was falling like this, and Ratu Sukuna said, "Ooh, look at my *sau*—the rain isn't falling on us." And then the minister said, "Right. Please take a step forward." So then Ratu Sukuna stepped forward, and the rain fell on him. Then Ratu Sukuna knew it was a truly godly person who was more *sau* [spiritually powerful] than him. Because God gives all the mana, the *sau*. The one who was standing up there [i.e., the minister], he was an image of God, a messenger of God. It was just as if God had been there then. When there's a person of God, a messenger of God—receive them, take good care of them because they're standing in for God. Jesus isn't with us [bodily], but you can see his face [in the person of Church officials]. If you're with one of them, take care of them so that you can be blessed. It was confirmed then [in the story] that mana and *sau* is with the people of God. Less is with the chiefs of the land of Fiji.

If Jehovah now has the power that Fiji's traditional chiefs once had, it makes logical sense that Jehovah's representatives have the best chance of wielding that power in human affairs. In fact, however, as shown by people's declarations that mana is gone—and as shown by the overt respect paid to chiefs at kava sessions and traditional ceremonies—Christianity has not appropriated the power of chiefs. It may be common knowledge that chiefly power is no longer what it was, but Christianity has not been able to balance the equation. Lost power is just that: lost.

A sense of decline and loss is often based in a belief that disorder now reigns. Kinship and associated political titles are two sites of contemporary disorder. The anthropologist Rusiate Nayacakalou (1957: 55) argued that as capitalism penetrated Fiji, "a certain degree of individualism" became necessary. As a result, he wrote, "Kinship ties get attenuated and the intensity of kinship unity is rendered less" (56). With weakening traditional authority and the lure—and perceived necessity—of money, younger people leave the villages. In the process of urban drift, Nayacakalou argued:

Even kinship attitudes seem to have become attenuated. In cases where brothers and sisters are continually in contact with town life, for instance, it is particularly noticeable that the rule of brother-sister taboo is not followed to the letter: they talk to each other more freely now than they would have been permitted to do in the past, and the respect and reverence in which they traditionally held each other are in many cases almost absent. In a similar manner, the norms of attitude and conduct formerly expected between kin of every other description are nowadays becoming something of a mere reflection of their past reality. (57–58; see also Rivers 1968: 291)

Ratu Irinale Soqeta, Tavuki's oldest man during the period of my fieldwork (he was born on January 7, 1920), echoed Nayacakalou's claim about the loss of the traditional brother-sister taboo of respectful avoidance. He claimed, furthermore, that some younger people today did not know their kinship connections because their fathers had not explained the connections to them. This second criticism encapsulates a double loss: not only the loss of proper social conduct, but loss of the knowledge that makes that proper social conduct possible (cf. Dureau 2001: 150).

As kinship norms are suspected of changing for the worse, so are political titles suspected of changing hands illegitimately. With the disruption of proper kinship and title holding comes a challenge to proper landholding, because kin and land are inseparable in indigenous Fiji. In this regard, consider a remarkable passage from a sermon that Ratu Josaia Veibataki preached in Namuana village's Methodist church in October 1998. I quote Veibataki at length because he weaves together ideas of indiscipline and loss and concludes with an assertion about the loss of knowledge of landownership:

Look at the present age. There are many problems [*leqa*] in the present age in our land because life isn't disciplined. We see the life of soldiers. They are told to do something; it's quick [lit., "its quickness," i.e., they follow orders promptly]. If we look back at the life our ancestors lived, gentlemen and ladies, sometimes, before—we have heard storytelling, we hear life was still good because life was still just a word.[6] They lived a disciplined life. . . . It is proper, gentlemen and ladies, that we tell the truth to our children. Tell them our land was dark once upon a time. The God we are serving today enlightened our land in the present age. . . . Tell them what is theirs and what is not theirs. . . . Look at the present age. Our children overstep their bounds a lot. They overstep their bounds a lot. Why? Because you and I are not telling them correctly the things pertaining to children. A question we should ask: Who should be accused about our children's going about selfishly? Who will be accused? It is proper that we accuse only ourselves, proper that we tell the truth about them [the children]. Tell them, "This is yours, this thing here is not yours." I say on the other side [i.e., in Tavuki Bay, which is on the other side of an escarpment from Namuana] the land is not owned. It is not known what is whose because people do not know it.

Veibataki is tracing an arc of decline. Life "was still good" in the old days, when villagers acted like soldiers: quick, disciplined, responsible. Proper organization and effective action were intrinsically related. He then encourages his audience to take charge of their children, to teach them to stop being selfish, to draw proper boundaries around what they do and do not own. He concludes with a condensed lament, "The land is not owned," which is a deeply disturbing notion to indigenous Fijians who take great pride in being true *itaukei,* "owners of the land."[7] By claiming that people do not know what land they really own, Veibataki is saying that people do not know where they belong and have no base for effective action. The sense that land is now in the wrong hands is common in Fiji and has led to many disputes, some violent. In chapters 5 and 6 I discuss some nationally known disruptions caused by anxious (and sometimes opportunistic) landowners.

The disordered nexus of kin, titles, and land is a source of anxiety in Fiji, and signs of decline and loss are read in people's everyday actions. The breakdown of proper relationships drives people to interpret many unfolding actions as proof of deterioration: nothing is good enough anymore, and certainly not as good as it once was. Again, I quote at length a speaker who compellingly weaves together various strands, multiple manifestations of the fall from a golden age. The speaker is the head steward, Ratu Meli Qaravanua, who delivered this litany of complaint at a Tavuki village meeting (*ova*) in January 1999:

This is bad trash: singing songs, drinking too much kava. You youth are not getting married much these days. Communal garden work is announced, communal garden work doesn't happen. . . . Today, we went today, there were only thirteen of us [doing communal garden work]. That's the authority of the noble land of Nacolase [sarcastic, disapproving]. You are unable to follow things because you are not entering the meeting house [on Monday mornings]. . . . I am requesting we should begin to revive and pass on the proper way it is performed or done so our land and our people will live on doing this. Gentlemen, ladies, forgive [me] if some words are strong. This is the house where we discuss things so that our vanua prospers. If we discuss with worthless words it won't work, it will really be useless. Our religion will be useless, [it] will just be wasted. . . . Sir, I now see a different behavior, a new way of doing things in our village. The haircuts we see on each of the children is something else. Some want to decide to cut themselves bald, their skulls are cut bald. That is not the haircut of the noble land of Nacolase.

Ratu Qara's harangue is short but comprehensive. He touches on several commonly heard assertions: people do not work together anymore; marriage customs are falling apart because of sexually irresponsible youth; and people drink too much kava these days. He also turns to a seemingly trivial subject: haircuts. In a contemporary spin on the Samson story, Ratu Qara implicitly posits a link between lack of hair ("their skulls are cut bald") and weakness—in this case, social weakness. "The haircut of the noble land of Nacolase" is presumably a *buiniga,* a thick, bushy head of hair that many Americans would call an Afro. Few people wear *buiniga* anymore. (I believe that one of the hairstyles that village youth wanted to imitate at the time was that of the Tongan rugby star Jonah Lomu.)[8]

This harangue suggests that the fall-from-a-golden-age theme has become dominant in Kadavu. Ratu Qara refers to all of these problems in a row, swiftly, as if they are common knowledge rather than disputable historical assertions. Many Fijians, not only Kadavuans, would nod in agreement at his checklist. One of the most explicit statements about the fall from a golden age was spoken to me by a man from Tailevu who had married into a chiefly family in Tavuki. He explained to me, "The cause of problems in the present day is that people forget or don't follow their true customs, their true traditional methods" (*Na vu ni leqa e na gauna nikua, na tamata sa guilecava se sa sega ni muria na nona itovo dina, nona ivakarau dina, vakavanua*). Such a statement resonates with Ratu Qara's complaints at the village meeting, focusing on the loss or forgetting of proper custom.

Local certainty of social decline is sometimes echoed back to people in outsiders' voices. In the late 1990s the government's Fijian Affairs division conducted local workshops full of metacultural talk about problems in Fiji and how to honor tradition appropriately. At the event I attended (in Yawe district, west of Tavuki) various Fijian-language documents were circulated. The main workbook was prepared by the Hanns-Seidel Foundation, a German firm that sponsors international development projects. The workbook contains a striking visual representation of the decline-and-loss theme. Its title, "The Problems Affecting Contemporary Fiji" ("Na Leqa e Tarai Viti Tu Nikua"), features the commonly heard word *leqa,* meaning "trouble, difficulty" (Dixon 1988: 363; see also Arno 1993: 10).[9]

The chart is a map of degradation. Despite the German name on the cover, the diagram has a strong Fijian imprint, as shown by the designation of the metacultural categories of lotu, vanua, and matanitu as the three main columns near the top of the page. Perhaps the most telling characteristic is the placement of "individualism" as a social problem near the base and center, an overlapping zone between material problems (poverty and unemployment) and spiritual ones (lack of faith and understanding in God). Other elements in the chart do not match dominant Fijian expectations, however, such as the identification of subsistence farming as a baseline problem, something fostering insecurity, poor educational achievements, and poor health. The chart, in its black-and-white simplicity, is a fantasy—a single-minded projection of an ideal, although a negative one. It is a portrait of the fall from a golden age done up in boxes and arrows. In a presumably unintended historical irony, it inverts the suggestions of a well-known report commissioned four decades earlier, which argued, "The future for the Fijians lies in a turn from communalism towards individualism" (Spate 1959: 97; see also Burns, Watson, and Peacock 1960).

When understandings of decline and loss are keyed to a past that had mana, the result is not just nostalgia for the old days but fear of the damage that ancestors can still inflict on living people. One day, when I was conversing with a friend, he described a village near Tavuki as *sauji.* *Sauji* is an adjectival form of *sau,* so it might be translated as "suffering from supernatural retribution because of a misdeed"—in a word, "cursed." I was intrigued, for here was an opportunity to learn how one reads the signs of supernatural affliction. How did my friend know that this particular village near Tavuki was cursed? And why was it cursed?

The reason the villagers were cursed, it turned out, was because long ago they had participated in the misappropriation of a hereditary title. The proof of their accursedness, my friend explained, was that "they only have young people in that village."[10] He named the village's oldest man and noted, "He's not very old." Ancestral misdeeds haunted the present in a specific and evident way: the village lacked mature elders.

"But your village is doing well," I remarked, thinking of their elders.
"No," he lamented, "we have a lot of old people."

There are two ways to interpret his assertions. One is that an ideal social balance exists between old and young, as well as between chiefs and commoners, men and women, and so forth. Another interpretation, however, which I think is more revealing, is that the balance will never be achieved because of the dominance of the initial assumption that curses exist and are afflicting people. Like the ideal of a life without sin, it is an attractive impossibility. Most signs will be read as supporting the notion of ongoing affliction—or, to phrase it in reverse, people will not perceive their village as blessed because the dominant theme is the fall from a golden age. All evidence will tend to show curses at work.

The missionary Wallace Deane wrote in 1921, "The memory of a solemn vow, request, or curse would be exceedingly vivid in the Fijians' imagination, and, indeed, would become almost a voice to intimidate them, sounding from the other world. A very real conviction sprang up in their minds that, if they did not attend to the will of the dead man, the latter would assuredly be able to make the survivors suffer for their negligence" (42). Curses frighten people because ancestors still have power to act in the world. One man in Natokalau village, Yawe district, described curses to me as if they were genetic. A man and his family might be entirely free of curses, he suggested, but if that man's wife's grandfather had caused her family to be cursed, the couple's children might inherit the malediction despite their father's freedom from it. Sickness, poverty, or lack of education may be interpreted as the result of something a non-Christian ancestor did long ago. One of the most well-known Fijian stories of a cursed place concerns the village that killed and perhaps devoured the Methodist missionary Thomas Baker and his Fijian assistants in 1867: "The superstitious mountaineers felt that they were under a curse because of what had happened, and the odium lingered until in 1903 a son of the chief who had sent the fatal whale's tooth [to request Baker's murder] presented another tooth to the [Methodist] Synod that met at Rewa that year" (Wood 1978: 163–164). However, the villagers' formal apologies to the Church failed to remove the curse. "The grass in that river valley village is said to be stained red with the dead clergyman's blood as an indelible souvenir of their misdeed" (Becker 1995: 112). In November 2003 a new ritual apology was made in yet another attempt to lift the curse for Baker's murder, which, like degradationist narratives generally, has become a permanent state of affairs.

As the Baker example suggests, some curses come from Jehovah rather than Fijian ancestors. When officials of the Methodist Church wanted the new constitution to declare Fiji a Christian state, they wrote to the constitutional review commission, "We are . . . of the view that if this is not recognized now then this nation is under a Divine curse" (quoted in Ryle 2005: 70). Such a claim is remarkable, not only because of the implicit political threat, but also because of the taken-for-granted, matter-of-fact manner of its expression. The existence of curses is not in dispute either locally or nationally, and much circulating discourse is predicated on the assumption of their existence.

The overarching theme to which all of these claims contribute is that people and society in the past were unified, proper, and powerful; the present is fragmented, improper, and relatively powerless by contrast. The past has an aura of danger that bleeds into the present when ancestors express their malice through curses—or are invoked, by kava sorcery, for example. Methodists are not defenseless against the dangers of the past, as I describe at length in chapter 5; but a sense of decline and loss is prominent and consequential.

QUALIFICATIONS AND CLARIFICATIONS

People in Tavuki do not always speak in terms of decline and loss, however. For example, in December 1998 Ratu Qara told me that custom (*itovo*) was not being followed correctly by many people. He noted two recent examples of customary violation in Kadavu. In one village a woman had been allowed to give a formal speech of greeting, although the task should have been given to a man. In another village villagers had gathered coconuts on a Sunday, violating the day's taboo on work. (I suspect that the coconut-gathering group was composed of Seventh-day Adventists, whose sabbath is Saturday, not Sunday.) Ratu Qara mentioned that people from elsewhere thought that Kadavuans still honored custom, but he argued that only certain villages did. I asked about Tavuki, and he said that Tavuki was doing relatively well overall in terms of custom, but that there were a few folks who did not follow it properly. In other words, he grudgingly allowed that Tavuki had not fallen as far as other places had. More sunnily, Sevanaia Tako-tavuki from Waisomo told me in July 2003, as a group of us relaxed at a beach picnic following a lagoon fishing expedition, that we were enjoying the real Fijian life. He explained that we had not purchased anything, the food was free, and we were able to rest. In other words, we were living up to Fijians' own romantic ideals of Fijian village life. In focused and short-term comparisons, Kadavuans can judge a present situation to be superior to a past one. One notable example was how Rev. Serewai, the superintendent minister of Kadavu from 1995 through 1999, was considered to be a much better Church leader than his predecessor.

Nor does the theme of decline and loss cast an elegiac pall over social life. Although the theme's prominent, durable circulation has profound consequences, including the motivation of sympathy for political violence (as I argue in chapter 6), daily life in Tavuki is hardly sorrowful. In fact, it is often exuberant, especially at nightly kava sessions, with their riotous laughter and joking. I focus on discourse about decline and loss because I was surprised by how often I heard it expressed, and in how many varied forms, and was intrigued by its political consequences. But I do not mean to reduce social life in Tavuki to this single dimension.

In addition, the fall-from-a-golden-age theme may be more prominent in Tavuki than elsewhere in Kadavu because Tavuki is the island's paramount chiefly village. As chiefs stand to lose status from the effects of new religious movements (muted though they are at the moment), capitalist economic relations (even though chiefs have an advantage here, being considered legitimate points of economic redistribution), and other forces of globalization, they may be more vigorous in circulating messages about the powerful old days.

Finally, when the theme of decline and loss is expressed, it may be marked geographically rather than temporally. As already noted, Ratu Qara distinguished between places that were holding onto proper custom and those that were not. One of the most prominent signs of degradation in local discourse is the capital city, Suva. As the seat of government it is a focal point for tensions between indigenous Fijians and Indo-Fijians. But to understand Suva as a site of violence, one needs to understand it not just as a government center but also as an index of wealth and hazard. For people in Tavuki, Suva marks opportunity and risk, desire and danger. Sometimes it signifies material progress, as when the Roko Tui Kadavu told men at a kava session that another chief's house was rather impressive with all its furnishings from Suva (*mai Suva*). Here Suva served as a code for aesthetically and technologically non-Kadavuan things. However, the flip side is that Suva can become a sort of metaphorical hell where bad things happen. I noticed during research that bad things that happened off-island were sometimes said to have happened "in Suva" even when it turned out they really took place elsewhere on Vitilevu. In addition, new, evangelical Christian sects were based in Suva, so Kadavuans who saw new denominations as culturally disruptive forces were given another reason to see the city as a source of breakdown and loss (cf. Lal 2001: 83–84).

CHAPTER 3

Sermons

Preached this afternoon on Adam's primeval innocence, and enumerated a few of the deplorable ravages which sin has made on the souls and bodies of his posterity.

David Cargill, journal entry, May 11, 1836

Fijian Methodist sermons are performances in which a sense of decline and loss is made intelligible. In sermons, as Hirokazu Miyazaki (2000: 37) has written, "a critical picture of village life as a *problem*" is often presented, and "early Fijians' manner of worship [is given] as the *solution* to these contemporary problems"(emphases in original). Sermons are metacultural forms in which culture is described, reflected upon, and potentially reshaped. They express themes of decline and loss in the sanctified setting of church with the textual support of the Bible, which is held to be the word of God. Moreover, sermons are delivered in a performance space where feedback is minimal, providing a sense of the univocal declaration of truth. They are metaculture with a negative cast: the present is described as powerless and disorganized compared with the past, and so a return to forms of the past is considered desirable, even necessary. Preachers shape social categories, including lotu and vanua, by delineating their boundaries, contours, and trajectories, setting them within histories of decline, where everything is falling but nothing is beyond redemption.

Sermons are preached by Church officers such as ministers and catechists and by lay congregants who have been approved for the task. To become a lay preacher (*dauvunau*), one must begin as a trial preacher (*dauvunau vakatovolei*); when one's performance is judged adequate by the local catechist, one will be nominated and confirmed as an accredited preacher (*dauvunau yaco*) at a quarterly meeting. Only a small percentage of villagers become preachers, and most of them are men.

There is no formal course of study to become a preacher, but ministers sometimes give advice and guidance. For example, in July 1996 Rev. Serewai was apparently dissatisfied with a sermon he had heard, so he called a meeting of local preachers. He explained to them that one must prepare for a preaching assignment by reading the topical Bible passage repeatedly, thinking about it, praying, and even fasting. Later he explained to me that congregations were "very wise" and knew their Bible stories well, so preachers had to "be well prepared." To evoke a sure, confident performance, he said, "Pu pu pu pu pu," sounding like a machine gun, as if a preacher was firing verbal bullets at the congregation. As another example, in January 1999 he met with preachers in Baidamudamu village and quoted Ephesians 6:10–14 to emphasize the need for proper preparation: "Finally, my brethren, be strong in the Lord, and in the power of his might. Put on the whole armour of God, that ye may be able to stand against the wiles of the devil. For we wrestle not against flesh and blood, but against principalities, against powers, against the rulers of the darkness of this world, against spiritual wickedness in high places. Wherefore take unto you the whole armour of God, that ye may be able to withstand in the evil day, and having done all, to stand. Stand therefore, having your loins girt about with truth, and having on the breastplate of righteousness." In using these verses, Rev. Serewai was suggesting that preachers "put on the whole armour of God" by getting ready both intellectually and spiritually to explain the word of God to a congregation. Preaching, in other words, was not an obligation to be taken lightly, but one to be treated metaphorically like a military campaign.

To deliver a sermon, then, is not a casual task. It is a distinctive responsibility, something to be approached diligently and seriously. And, to recall the old cliché, people should practice what they preach. As the catechist's wife explained to me in July 2003, it would be very bad if someone preached a message but did not live up to it in his or her own life.[1] Intrigued by statements such as this, I asked two men who were church members in good standing why they were not lay preachers. Their answers were instructive. One, a man around my own age (early thirties at the time), gave two reasons. First, he explained that heaven was a place of singing and that singing hymns was thus the same act as praying. He was the head of the Tavuki choir, so he was positioning himself as a central religious "speaker," the man in charge of giving praise to God through song. His second reason was that if everyone was a preacher, no one would be the audience. He was happy, he said, to be part of the audience, to be one of the listeners. A middle-aged man, a carpenter and a mechanic, told me that Jesus had preached both indoors and outdoors. In his own manual labor, the man suggested, he was "preaching" outdoors; that is, when people saw the good work he did as a carpenter and mechanic, it was a good example on public view, like Jesus' preaching from a mountain. Both men therefore portrayed themselves as the functional equivalents of preachers, and neither wanted the additional responsibility of standing in the pulpit.

People who are scheduled to preach may decide that they are not adequately prepared—for example, because of excessive kava drinking the day before—and request that the catechist take their place. Traditional social obligations can also interfere with one's preaching assignment. For example, a middle-aged man from Nukunuku village, Sitiveni (this is a pseudonym), had been scheduled to preach at the village of Solodamu, but asked to be relieved of his duties. A few days earlier, an elderly man from Solodamu had passed away and Sitiveni had not attended the funeral. If he had attended, he would have been expected to bring *ireguregu,* gifts for the dead such as whale's teeth and woven mats (Capell 1991: 172). Because he had not attended, however, he was under the obligation to present *boka,* another class of gift, the next time he set foot in Solodamu. *Boka* are gifts given after an absence and include such items as woven mats and drums of kerosene (see Nayacakalou 1975: 155 n. 6). At that moment, however, Sitiveni did not have anything to offer as *boka,* which, I suspect, is the reason he did not attend the funeral in the first place, since presumably he would not have had much to offer as *ireguregu* either. With his lack of resources, the well-intentioned but impoverished man decided that the honorable course was not to preach. Weighing his obligations to the lotu and his obligations to the vanua, Sitiveni found that the obligations to the vanua took precedence.

Standing in the Pulpit

The Fijian model of good preaching is shaped partly by British Wesleyanism, especially John Wesley's ideal of speaking plainly: to "keep to plain texts, avoid 'rambling,' be sparing in allegorizing, eschew quaint words" (Rack 1989: 344). Some expectations, however, bear the imprint of markedly Fijian influences. For example, one young man who hoped to become a minister told me that if a person got in the pulpit to preach but did not do garden work, people would believe that he did not know anything. In other words, a person had to be a good manual laborer to be a respected textual authority. Working the earth and preaching the Word: one granted legitimacy to the other.

Sermons are a rare opportunity for Fijian men to shout in public, making the sermon a distinctive performance genre. Some preachers imitate Western evangelists' wavelike contours, raising their voices to a yell and then dropping their volume dramatically. Some preachers are less artful and shout most of the time. In 1921 Rev. Wallace Deane noted drily, "All have volubility in preaching" (114). The tone of preaching contrasts strongly with that of chiefly speech, which is "relatively slow, almost halting in some cases. . . . The pitch register is even and low" (Arno 1990: 254). An implicit rule seems to be that chiefs do not need to expend effort to capture people's attention; the audience is expected to listen automatically. When delivering short speeches during Methodist services, chiefs speak in "chiefly" style, relatively quietly and steadily, and do not imitate preachers' surging tone and volume. Because the congregation sits for the duration of the sermon and their feedback is limited to an occasional affirmation, such as "Good, thanks" (*vinaka*), preachers have a captive audience, yet their speaking style is evidently designed to hold people's attention in ways that chiefly speech is not. Buell Quain (1948: 410) noted, "Wesleyan services, which permit men of low status . . . to speak presumptuously from the dais in the church, amuse most chiefs."

Generally speaking, texts and speakers are not tied together too tightly: a preacher might prepare his own notes for the sermon, he might borrow someone else's notes, or he might build on a sermon he has heard previously.[2] For example, I once noticed that Nagonedau's steward had borrowed preaching notes from Rev. Serewai (I thought the sermon sounded rather familiar), and on another occasion, Tavuki's catechist gave a sermon that was based partly on feedback he had gotten from Baidamudamu villagers on a sermon that Rev. Serewai had preached there. A preacher might also refer to other people's sermons within his own, as the catechist Sevanaia Takotavuki did at a service in Tavuki in 2003:

We heard the sermon of, of Tuikilakīla, Reverend Tuikilakila. He said, said about the high chief who died [recently], "He's going home." This means, it's not our place, it's impossible for you to rest in this world. You want to follow Jesus. Our place, our house, awaits us in heaven.

Takotavuki was referring to a recent sermon in Tavuki given by Tuikila-kila Waqairatu, a prominent figure in the national Church organization who was the principal of the Davuilevu Theological College at the time. By referring to this well-known preacher and his recent performance at a chief's funeral, Takotavuki was not only developing his own unfolding sermon, but also making a claim to authority—positioning himself as an interpreter, representing Waqairatu's words (which were quoted in English to the congregation), and then explaining what they meant.

The preaching notes that I have seen are simple outlines—telegraphic talking points, not fully fleshed-out scripts—which perhaps facilitates their circulation (cf. Besnier 1995). Here, for example, is a translated excerpt of the preaching notes that Rev. Setareki Tuilovoni drew up for a sermon he delivered on May 24, 1998, in honor of the 260th anniversary of the date on which John Wesley famously felt his "heart strangely warmed" by God:

Today we are remembering the life of Rev. John Wesley
* May 24th, 1738 (8:45 P.M.)
We're at the 260th anniversary
NOTE: It's the day John Wesley's life and belief were confirmed
Stress: Best of all is, God is with us
* Today we declare our belief
* And it's the foundation of our lives
    a) Father
    b) Son
    c) Holy Spirit
NOTE: Our declarations will be meaningful when they're [made] visible in our lives
    Topic: True Faith
    I will point out a few things in which True Faith is revealed [or, I will point out a few things which are manifestations of True Faith]
1. Your cleansing yourself [spiritually]
    a. Your cleansing your life
    b. Your offering up your life [to God]. . . .
    c. *Matt. 5:3:* Those with clean spirits are blessed. . . .
2. Your taking care of the purpose for which you were created
    a. You were created for a purpose
    b. It's today's purpose too
* Gen. 1:26—We are making humanity. . . .
* Life will be new and clean. . . .
* That is also true faith.

This text shows that Fijian Methodist sermon notes are partial scripts for oral performance: the minister would be able to glance at each short line and extend it in performance to a fully developed theme with a coherent structure.

Rev. Tuilovoni used many English words in his notes. This is not surprising considering the language's prestige and association with pedagogy.[3] Once when I asked Rev. Serewai about the English words in his preaching notes, he explained that English words were shorter; for example, he pointed out that *forgive* has only seven letters, whereas *dauveivosoti* (*veivosoti* ["forgive"] plus the habitual prefix *dau*) has twelve letters. The belief in the superiority of English runs deeper than this, though, for as Barbara Cook (1975: 95 n. 67) puts it, "Most Fijians are thoroughly convinced that their language is inferior to English. I was told, both by villagers and by urbanites, that 'Fijian has no grammar' " (see also Arms 1984; Geraghty 1989). Fijian, of course, is as grammatical as any other language, but the conviction that it suffers from disorder—like Fijian culture generally—is a particularly noteworthy expression of a sense of entropy.

Sermons are preached in the Kadavuan dialect or in Standard Fijian.[4] Higher level Church officials such as ministers and superintendent ministers, who tend to be outsiders in the villages they serve, usually use Standard. Lay preachers and local officials such as catechists, in contrast, are likely to preach in Kadavuan. When speakers codeswitch—to explain a translation, to indicate the foreign nature of something they are describing, to display their expertise, or simply to call attention to a theme in the sermon—they use English, or, if they are preaching in Kadavuan, they might switch into Standard Fijian. In the following example, note how Rev. Serewai first translates the word *iapositolo* (the Fijian version of "apostle") by referring casually to the Greek version, stating, "We all know its meaning." Then, having made both a claim to authority and a claim to solidarity with his audience, he displays his erudition by switching into English (italicized text):

There are a few things I want to point out; first, in this lesson Paul is an apostle. "Apostle" is a Greek word, we all know its meaning. There one is sent, one agrees to be sent, one who is submitting his or her body, his or her willpower, going down to be an emissary for the sake of his or her vanua, for the sake of his or her lotu, for the sake of his or her god. *The one who is sent*. It's not possible that someone will be sent if he or she does not humble himself or herself.

As I have argued elsewhere (Tomlinson 2006a), preachers sometimes metasemantically "flag" their translations and explanations by using the formulaic phrase *kena ibalebale*, which means "Its meaning is" (or, more loosely, "That means"). The phrase, which can be heard in other speech genres besides sermons, acts as a pivot between something that is to be explained and its explanation, and thus often serves as a claim to authority: in deploying *kena ibalebale,* the speaker presents himself or herself as one who is able to give an interpretation that might not be available to the listener otherwise. Sermons can be considered performances of *kena ibalebale* writ large, for in applying Bible passages to contemporary Fijian social life, preachers are pragmatically pivoting between textual representations and their application to daily life, making interpretations both semantically meaningful and practically useful.

Once a sermon has been delivered, people may discuss it informally at kava sessions, although I heard such discussion only rarely. Alan Tippett (1974c: 331) wrote that after he preached in a Fijian church, people discussed his sermon as they shared a meal; he described this as "a humiliating custom they have" (cf. Besnier 1995: 127). I did not hear such free commentary. However, I do not see sermons as a genre entirely set apart from others, for they resonate with themes that are culturally prominent. That is, sermons echo widely circulating public discourse, but in a sanctified ritual setting. I argue that it is the combination of resonant, commonly heard themes and the sacred performance space that makes preaching a particularly effective kind of metaculture.

Sermons as Metaculture

Sermons are metacultural performances. Broadly speaking, they take on culture along two axes: a temporal axis and a social axis. Temporally, sermons depict Fijian culture as a phenomenon marked by historical decline, a view of culture as something that was owned and performed *better* by the ancestors. Socially, sermons draw boundaries around the terms *lotu* and *vanua,* and occasionally *matanitu.* In describing histories of decline and loss and defining the proper roles of lotu and vanua in social life, preachers are not only reflecting on Fijian culture but are also actively attempting to reshape it. Fijian metacultural emphasis often cants toward tradition, toward fortifying the ever-crumbling foundation of an imagined past.

In sermons present-day Fijian culture is rarely portrayed positively: preachers never say that everything's fine and people should keep doing what they're doing. Portrayals of the past are more complicated in terms of morality and strength. Local Fijian histories have at least two moral-temporal levels: the remote past was a time when the ancestors are said to have lived like the ancient Israelites; the more recent past was a time of war, cannibalism, and resistance to Christian conversion. These pasts resonate in different ways with the present, but on the meta-cultural plane Fijian histories always suffer a basic rupture: the past was "dark" without Christianity, but it had (or was) mana; the present is "enlightened" by Christianity but lacks (or is not) mana. Thus in the same sermon Ratu Josaia Veibataki could both insist that his listeners tell their children "our land was dark once upon a time" (*na noda vanua ma butobuto tu ina dua na gauna*) and also complain that children were "going about indulgently" nowadays (*lako vaveitalia*), a stern criticism in Fijian terms. Veibataki was thus able to describe the present as an age of both enlightenment and decline.

Hirokazu Miyazaki notes that for many preachers, the historical moment of Christian conversion serves as a focal point for comparative criticism. He aptly summarizes the moral-temporal dynamic that is generated in preachers' performances: "The predominant theme of Methodist sermons concerned the relationship of the present to the past. Methodist preachers frequently used stories about early Fijian chiefs' encounters with Christianity . . . as vehicles for criticizing the congregation's sinful practices. In these sermons, early Fijians' conversion to Christianity and manner of worship was presented as a *model* for present-day Fijians, whose life had lost its strength and vigor" (2004: 93–94, emphasis in original). Preachers not only criticize, as Miyazaki notes; they can also present models of a better present and future. The hoped-for present and future, however, are grounded firmly in images of the ordered, powerful past. As described in the previous chapter, Ratu Josaia Veibataki preached a sermon in which he declared, "There are many problems in the present age in our land," and explained that this was "because [present-day] life isn't disciplined," in contrast to the lives of the ancestors. The solution, he implied, was for people to follow the example of soldiers, who quickly do as they are told.

Lost discipline, and the sense of encroaching social weakness, was a theme in a sermon of Rev. Serewai's that I recorded in Nasegai village in September 1998. He focused on the problem of children's willfulness, arguing that adults need to assert their authority over children so that the Church will have a "straight" journey into a proper future. After mentioning "the arrival of Churches still going on in our land" (*na vaka-cabe lotu se lako tikoga e na noda vanua;* that is, newer Christian sects who challenge Methodism's dominance), he preached:

We receive some of the teachings of the [Methodist] Church and many teach-
ings get twisted. It is useful that we consider Paul's thoughts again to confirm
our journey. . . . I will put into words ten thoughts that Paul emphasized to the
Galatians. I very strongly urge you elders: be firm, do not waver, [by] your [tak-
ing the] proper position the children of the future will take the proper position.
The word he [i.e., Paul] uses in this lesson: you are spiritually mature in the
Church. We are in a time [that is] beginning to come up very quickly in Fiji.
Our youth's lotu is strong. Many families get twisted [turned around] suddenly
and very quickly in the strength of the youths' movement. And the youth see it.
And the youth like it. They bring it into their families. This turns the backbone
and the heart and the spine of a family. Paul confirms tonight: you elders, you
are spiritual, you are mature. Stand properly. Stand firm. Because when you are
straight and stand firm the journey of the Methodist Church in Fiji and Rotuma
[to the] children of the future will thereby be straight.

The lesson that served as the basis for this sermon was Galatians
6:1–10, which begins, "Brethren, if a man be overtaken in a fault, ye which
are spiritual, restore such an one in the spirit of meekness." In this part
of his sermon, Rev. Serewai contrasted children's impetuous willfulness
with elders' maturity and noted that youth seemed to be winning the
battle. He characterized "our youth's lotu" negatively, presumably referring to newer evangelical groups, which have a more significant presence in urban Fiji than on Kadavu. Rev. Serewai cast the onus of change
on "time" itself when he claimed, "We are in a time [that is] beginning
to come up very quickly in Fiji." It was not just children who were
twisting the backbones and hearts of families, then, but the new time
and new forms of authority that it represents. The future will not be ir-
redeemably bleak, however, if adults intervene and set children and
Church on their straight and proper paths.

If a single Bible passage can be said to shadow most sermons, dappling
them in the light and dark patterns of a history seen in reflections of divinity and loss, it is Genesis 1:26: "And God said, Let us make man in our
image, after our likeness." For many Fijians, this verse shows that humanity was once on a divine level but has evidently fallen far from that original
state. The earlier example of Rev. Tuilovoni's preaching notes includes a
reference to the verse. A good example of a preacher using Genesis 1:26 in
a sermon comes from the catechist Tomasi Laveasiga's performance at
Tavuki's morning service on February 7, 1999:

One thought I can pick up on this morning, I think that we should hear it together. . . . The morning's thought is begun, begun in Genesis, chapter one,
verse 26. [God] declares, "We are making humanity in our image and after our

likeness." That information is really very clear, and growing up, anyone [lit., "a gentleman (or) lady"] can use the Bible to read this passage. It's very clear that life should be like that. The Creator declared, "We are making humanity in our image and after our likeness." We were not made to resemble anything else.

Laveasiga presents Genesis 1:26 as having an obvious interpretation, and one that should already be known by his whole audience. He argues that anyone growing up in Fiji can read the Bible and encounter this verse, whose meaning is "really very clear" (*matata vavinaka tu sara ga*). He leaves the social criticism implicit—he does not come right out and say that people are failing to live up to Genesis 1:26—but his message is impossible to misunderstand, especially as he concludes with the negatively phrased restatement, "We were not made to resemble anything else," a strong suggestion that this is, in fact, the problem of the present situation.

Negative comparisons of the present with the past can have immediate points of reference. During the national elections of May 1999 many people in Tavuki grew increasingly distressed at the poll results indicating that the Indo-Fijian–led Labour Party would win. With the village astir, Laveasiga preached a sermon on Pentecost Sunday in which he compared the nervous anxiety of that moment with the confident unity of Jesus' disciples as described in the book of Acts:

Our Bible reading tells us "they were all with one accord" [Acts 2:1]. Opinion is divided on this newly elected government. One big division of—we landowners [i.e., indigenous Fijians], they're saying the Prime Minister shouldn't be an Indian. Difference and division is happening. I want to confirm to us this Sunday, Pentecost Sunday has only one purpose: for us to be united. All united.

In contrast to the disciples who were united and thus blessed by the Holy Spirit, as described in the second chapter of Acts, present-day Fijians were rent by "difference and division." Here is an example of social decline presented with perhaps uncomfortable clarity and immediacy: people who were agitated because of the election, the catechist seemed to suggest, were failing to live up to the perfect example of the disciples, who were "all with one accord." Later in this same sermon, he repeated the ideal of unity, but with a negative cast: "Nothing can be fulfilled in our traditional life if we are different. [If] difference exists—difference of spirit, different thoughts, different judgments—it's impossible to build a good Nacolase [clan] or a good Nukunawa [clan] for tomorrow." Like other preachers, Laveasiga referred to a hoped-for future in terms of a perfect past. But, as Hannah Arendt (1969) pointed out, "The ancient notion of a Golden Age . . . implies the rather unpleasant certainty of continuous decline," and Laveasiga returned to the theme of loss, emphasizing how distant people are from receiving the blessings of the Holy Spirit:

Something is very impoverished in our lives, in being traditional, village life: the dearth of kindly love, dearth of unity, dearth of working together, the fruit of the Holy Spirit in the world. The Holy Spirit does not cause division and difference.

The preacher's vision of disunity and distance was coherent and strongly argued. It coexisted in tension with the possibility of unity and nearness to God; but the possibility, he preached, remained unrealized.[5]

In tracing these histories of decline, Fijian preachers refer frequently to the metacultural categories of lotu and vanua, and sometimes also to the category of matanitu. Some of the most evocative statements I heard about what the lotu is came from Rev. Serewai's sermons. He was a gifted preacher with a knack for parallelism and dramatic intonation, and his subjects were usually clearly stated and boldly argued. For example, in a sermon at Namalata in March 1999, he declared:

The lotu is a thing for individuals. Don't make it a thing of the whole household, don't make it a thing of the clan, thing of the group, or thing of denominations, or thing of gatherings. . . . The lotu is a thing for individuals. Because each of us will receive the fruit of the lotu. Each of us will also return to God [i.e., when we are dead]. We will also go alone in the face of God in the future.

Rev. Serewai was challenging his listeners' expectations about who should be considered proper, responsible social actors. Individual effort is usually considered good if it conforms to social role expectations and if it serves the interest of larger groups. Here, however, Rev. Serewai subverted cultural norms by placing responsibility on all individuals equally, and explicitly denying the importance of social groups such as the clan (cf. Robbins 2004). He then presented an image of spiritual power that contradicted Fijian communal expectations—indeed, contradicted one of his own previous sermons (see below)—by depicting individuals as sources of effectiveness and responsibility:

It is important for you always to try, to try hard for your lotu, to achieve first of all the spiritual life in your lotu and your soul by yourself. And it will flow through and touch all parts of life: family, vanua, subclan, clan, or the whole world.

In this vision, the lotu depends for its strength on individuals, and if that strength is generated it can be uniquely transformative, shaping the vanua and indeed "the whole world" in its terms. Conversely, the vanua depends on this flow of power channeled through the Church. The minister then referred to the day's Bible reading, Acts 2:42–47—in which the apostles perform miracles, praise God, and sell what they own to help people in need—and stated that the author, Luke, was saying, "The lotu should not build you [up]; each person should build up the lotu" (*Me kua ni tarai iko na lotu; na tamata yadua me tara cake jiko na lotu*).

Rev. Serewai then shifted gears rhetorically and used the well-known Christian metaphor of the Church as the body of Christ (see 1 Corinthians 12:12ff.; Colossians 1:18). In this part of his sermon, he recast the lotu as something separate from humanity:

I emphasized this to the pastors at the Quarterly Meeting in Galoa: The lotu, many times, we take it. We take it like we lead it. We say it is ours. We say the lotu is just me. The lotu is just us. But the Bible says the lotu is the living body of Christ. It is a taboo thing, clean thing, very right thing. Its meaning is our lives should be tools for building up the lotu in the land we are in. The lotu cannot [build us up] because the lotu is the body of Christ. It is a very important thing. It is a taboo thing. When [the lotu] is worked against or damaged or destroyed or whatever else happens to it, if it is the body of Christ it is a living thing, it is a breathing thing, a seeing thing. There is also a place where it breathes.

Describing the Church as the body of Christ, Rev. Serewai explored the related metaphorical possibilities. As he explained it to me later, the "breathing thing" meant the lungs and throat, the "seeing thing" was the eyes, and the "place where it breathes" was the nose. The Church, in other words, was a fully living body with organically interconnected parts.

But what effect does such a description have? In depicting the Church as Christ's body, surely the minister was not actually reshaping the institution in any way; he was simply using a vivid and well-known metaphor. However, I argue that Rev. Serewai's performance is more creative than that. First, his emphasis on individuals' responsibility was a challenge to chiefly authority. In his vision, at least as presented in this particular sermon, chiefly authority plays a small role in contemporary Fijian society; it simply receives its potential from individuals working through the Church. This was a challenge to which chiefs could not respond directly, as it was spoken from the pulpit. Second, by speaking of the lotu abstractly and metaphorically, Rev. Serewai cut it loose from the immediate referent of the Namalata church and its congregation. Verbally he was turning the lotu into something much larger than the here-and-now body of Christian believers in a village in Kadavu. This might not sound surprising to a Western reader who is familiar with the discourse of global Christianity, but in Fijian terms it sets the lotu sharply against the vanua, which always has integral and permanent ties to locality. In making such rhetorical moves, the minister was attempting to accomplish something practical: to define a sphere of legitimate authority for the Methodist Church, one that is notably expansive.[6]

The vanua is spoken of more frequently than the lotu, even in Church contexts. That is, during church services, one is more likely to speak explicitly about chiefs and people, land, and tradition than to speak of the Church or worship. Moreover, vanua is often possessed pronominally, usually as "our" or "my," whereas lotu usually is not (Tomlinson 2002: 136–137). However, lotu and vanua are often spoken of in conjunction, suggesting that they are complementary entities that define each other. An example of lotu and vanua being brought into tandem comes from Rev. Serewai's sermon at Nasegai in September 1998. Note how he described the two entities as ideally complementary but potentially rivalrous:

The lotu should very strongly help the vanua. The vanua [should] very strongly help the lotu. The province should help the government. The government should help the province. We should emphasize this sort of help because individualism is beginning to rise very quickly in our land. When I see Kadavu, in the four years I have been here it is easy for me to see the lotu here, the vanua here [i.e., in different places] because they are separated very often. . . . Who leads? The lotu or the vanua? Who should be leading? The lotu or the vanua? I should confirm one thing: forget the word "lotu"; forget the word "vanua." We can say the lotu is behind; the vanua is behind; God alone leads. He built this world. Forget the vanua. Forget the lotu. Because when we pronounce the vanua we remember the high chiefs of our land.[7] When we pronounce the lotu we remember the Church's leaders. . . . [We] narrow our vision.

In this part of his sermon, Rev. Serewai poetically brought lotu and vanua into equivalence, grammatically and semantically. He depicted them as separate but complementary groups—groups that were also, to a degree, competitive. Crucially, he depicted this competition with reference to a perceived problem: increasing individualism. In contrast to his sermon at Namalata, here Rev. Serewai portrayed individualism as a foreign idea and practice that threaten the Church. He suggested that individualism can be defeated, ideally, by total indigenous Fijian unity.

To achieve such unity, he was arguing, Fijians need to go beyond their standard division of lotu and vanua. Both are subordinate to God. After the minister spoke the line "He built this world," several members of the congregation acknowledged his argument by saying "Good, thanks" (*vinaka*). Then he immediately made a bold rhetorical move, commanding his audience to "forget the vanua" (*guilecava na vanua*)— a shocking statement, but one that Rev. Serewai immediately took the sting out of by adding, "Forget the lotu." Still, one can detect a challenge in his polite words, because by proclaiming "God alone leads," he was claiming an authoritative position for himself. For Rev. Serewai, the lotu should indeed take precedence over the vanua, but it is a mark of his sensitivity and discretion that he never came out and said this explicitly, for to do so would alienate many Kadavuans.

Sermons are especially notable for their sanctified context of performance. Words from the pulpit are not subject to immediate criticism, and they are fraught with particular responsibility because the preacher is interpreting and explicating the words of God. The themes expressed in sermons are not unique to that context, however, as discourse bleeds through generic boundaries. People in Tavuki spoke of lotu and vanua frequently, and often as a pair. Rev. Serewai's sermons made sense in local terms because, whether or not people agreed with his vision of the lotu as the source of the vanua's potential, they would understand the oppositions and categories that he set up. These oppositions and categories, by being delineated in multiple performance contexts, can become consequential in social life.

A Christmas Sermon

On Christmas day 1998 Ratu Josaia Veibataki preached at the morning service in Tavuki's Methodist church. Slightly more than seventy people attended. This was not a particularly large crowd, but, unlike for many Christian congregations in the West, the Christmas morning service was not considered especially important. During the service the congregation recited the Lord's Prayer and part of the Te Deum. The three hymns sung before the sermon were "Cradled in a Manger, Meanly," a Fijian hymn written by A. J. Small to the tune of "Wheatfields," and "O Come All Ye Faithful"; after the sermon, the hymn was "Brightest and Best of the Sons of the Morning." The Bible reading was Galatians 4:1–11, verses from St. Paul in which he describes Jesus' birth in the

FIGURE 6. Ratu Josaia Veibataki preaches in the Tavuki
church.

famous lines "But when the fulness of the time was come, God sent forth
his Son, made of a woman, made under the law." As will soon become evident, Genesis 1:26 was the subtext for much of Veibataki's sermon.

Veibataki began by relating the well-known Christmas story of Jesus'
birth in a manger, and quickly moved to interpret this in terms of decline: Jesus came to earth because Adam and Eve had failed in regard to
God's purpose for humanity.

This week we hear the story[8] about this day [Christmas]. Most of the time we hear
Matthew's story together with Luke's about this day. This tells of the birth of

Jesus. I want to look back, please, on some stories we have heard this week. In two books Matthew and Luke . . . emphasize the Lord and the purpose of Jesus' birth. One to straighten us out,[9] to straighten us out. God sees that his word of creation was mistaken by Adam and Eve. God was planning for a time that our lives would be straightened out again, gentlemen, ladies. We are living in His world. First [topic]: we should please straighten ourselves out again. The purpose of Jesus' birth was that our lives would be straightened out again, gentlemen, ladies.

Veibataki begins in a simple and straightforward manner, mentioning the congregation's common experience of hearing the Christmas narrative in the gospels of Matthew and Luke. In the story, Jesus, who is to be the spiritual savior of humankind, is born in a humble stable: Mary, his mother, "brought forth her firstborn son, and wrapped him in swaddling clothes, and laid him in a manger; because there was no room for them in the inn" (Luke 2:7). Veibataki claims that Jesus was sent "to straighten us out," to save humanity from the error it had fallen into from the very beginning, when Adam and Eve sinned in the Garden of Eden.

Having appealed to this well-known Bible story, Veibataki then sketches in a few details and makes an explicit connection to the Fijian holiday season, a time when many people return to their home villages:

We see what is said in Matthew and Luke. Mary and Joseph's journey to go to Bethlehem, to go confirm again or to renew again their written entry in the book of descendants of their land. We see our day of—today, some of our relatives are arriving. Some of our children are arriving. They are staying elsewhere. They want to confirm themselves again in their land. They want to straighten themselves out again in this, their true land. That was also the journey Joseph and Mary went on [when] the time came for our Lord whom we serve today to be born.

Here, the preacher draws a parallel between the trips taken by Jesus' earthly parents and the journeys of modern-day Fijians. Mary and Joseph were in Bethlehem because the Roman emperor had commanded a census. Veibataki refers to the census with the phrase "their written entry in the book of descendants of their land" (*nodru volai ki na ivola ni kawa ni nodru vanua*). For indigenous Fijians, such a "book of descendants" exists, and literally in book form: the *Vola ni Kawa Bula* is the master publication of indigenous Fijians' birth dates and kin affiliations.

Veibataki appeals to the symbolic importance of a holiday trip home, when people may "confirm themselves again in their land." By making this appeal, stoking Fijian emotions and expectations of what a trip home means, he is emphasizing the importance of Jesus' birth in a real earthly vanua. That is, the story of Jesus' birth is a story of how the Son of God was born as a human among humans in a particular place. He then mentions another sermon, given the night before by a Baidamu-damu villager, Lepani Qalomaiwasa, to confirm that Jesus "was born in the world." Qalomaiwasa is understood to have legitimate knowledge of this because, having served as a soldier in the United Nations peace-keeping forces years earlier, he had been to the Near East—the land of the Bible (cf. Ryle 2005: 68).

The Lord Jesus Christ was born in the world. We heard last night the, the sermon last night, that the preacher who preached to us last night has been to the land where He was born. He testified to us that the Lord was truly born here in the world. Its meaning is the Lord was born in the world. Its meaning for us is in this age do not misapprehend this world because the God we are serving, Jesus Christ, was born in this world. Many of us focus only on heaven and do not see clearly his or her life in this world. Therefore today it should be clear to you and me, to us all, our lives in this world should be like the Lord Jesus Christ's birth on earth. If you don't understand what you're doing on earth, as [I] said above, one saying is "It is extremely difficult for you to gain eternal life."

By mentioning Qalomaiwasa's sermon—"He testified to us that the Lord was truly born here in the world"—Veibataki emphasizes how important this mortal life on earth is. "Many of us," he chides, "focus only on heaven, and do not see clearly [our] life in this world." He sees this as a profound mistake and argues that one needs to pay attention to life on earth in order to gain future admission to heaven. The fact that Jesus came to earth to be born as a human being, he insists, should indicate just how important "what you're doing on earth" is.

Third. The two lessons say gold, frankincense, myrrh were presented to the Lord, were presented to the Lord. If it is desired that our land prosper, if it is desired that our noble families live, let us try not to have wealth, our rank in our families or in our lives, lead us because the Three Wise Men already presented the precious wealth of this world. They presented it to God. Bethlehem, the land where the Lord went to be born, it was said it was a bakery. It was already presented. It was already weakened. It is also said Bethlehem is the first Adam. True, it was a stable, but it is the land where the first person was created. Many of us will disrespect his top of the foundation. Many of us will disrespect his top of the foundation. The Lord's birth here confirms for us [that God] blessed the soil where the first person was created. This is an important thing, our respecting our top of the foundation.

After a strong, clear start to the sermon, this section is slightly more difficult to follow, and not only because Veibataki begins by saying "Third" when he is only on his second point. The preacher states that Bethlehem "was a bakery. It was already presented. It was already weakened." When working on the translation of this sermon, I asked him what he meant by comparing Bethlehem to a bakery, and he explained that he had gotten this part from Rev. Serewai, who could give a better explanation. So when he preaches these lines, Veibataki is relying on Rev. Serewai's authorship of them—or at least his use of them—to judge them worthy of inclusion, even though the preacher himself is perhaps unsure of what they mean.[10] It is also not entirely clear what Veibataki means by saying that "Bethlehem is the first Adam" immediately afterward, although the following line, "It is the land where the first person was created," offers a reasonable gloss.

At this point he turns in a new direction, claiming, "Many of us will disrespect his top of the foundation." The phrase "top of the foundation" (*dela ni yavu*) strongly connotes the locus of tradition in village life. The reference is to the earthen foundations on which older houses, as well as some newer ones, stand. The phrase can be used to indicate something like "one's true and permanent home." Here Veibataki seems to be stretching the phrase to encompass Jesus' humanity and to resonate with the story of the first human's creation from dust in Genesis 2:7. Past and present, Jesus and humanity, Bethlehem and Kadavu: all are tied together through reference to the top of the foundation. It is a foundation that suffers disrespect, however.

It is also said [in] the, the story of the land of Bethlehem, there was a town in Judah around five miles to the south of Jerusalem which was also known by the name Ephrath. In the land also where Benjamin was born, that was also the land where the woman Rachel died. Bethlehem was also the village where David was born and also the village where Samuel anointed David to be the Israelites' king. In that same land Jesus Christ was born, whose arrival in the world we commemorate today.

When Veibataki mentions Ephrath, an alternative name for Bethlehem, he gains surer footing. He quickly mentions Benjamin, Rachel, and Samuel's anointing of David (see Genesis 35:16–20; 1 Samuel 16:11–13), showing his familiarity with the Bible and bringing his sermon back to the anchor point of Jesus' birth.

In the following section, he turns to the darker story of King Herod, with another comparison to contemporary life in Kadavu. King Herod's story is entwined with that of the Three Wise Men, who, as Veibataki has already mentioned, "presented the precious wealth of this world," giving gifts of gold, frankincense, and myrrh (gum resins) to the infant Jesus. The wise men, claiming "We have seen his star in the east" (Matthew 2:2), announced the birth of the "King of the Jews" in Bethlehem. The tyrant Herod, disturbed at the news, asked that the baby be brought to him, "that I may come and worship him also" (Matthew 2:8). His real intention was to kill the child. After the wise men found Jesus and presented their gifts, they had a dream telling them not to go back to Herod, so they returned to their own lands instead. Joseph, who also had a dream warning about Herod, fled with Mary and Jesus into Egypt. "Then Herod, when he saw that he was mocked of the wise men, was exceeding wroth, and sent forth, and slew all the children that were in Bethlehem, and in all the coasts thereof, from two years old and under" (Matthew 2:16).

In this part of his sermon, Veibataki challenges his audience by comparing them to the evil king:

Gentlemen and ladies, Matthew and Luke say the shepherds on their journey met with Herod and [he] told them, If you see the Lord you tell me too so I can go bow to him. We, gentlemen and ladies, our living in God's world, many of us are [living] like Herod's life. Many of us are [living] like Herod's life. [I] confirm to us, if your life's journey is difficult, God told the shepherds: You [shepherds should] follow a new path. Because Herod had bad intentions toward the Lord. They wanted to go present gifts to Him. This is why I am saying many of us are like Herod. Many of us want to harm the way our vanua is progressing.

The preacher argues that many people "want to harm the way our vanua is progressing."[11] This is one of those statements that at first sounds potentially offensive, but actually cloaks responsibility for harming the vanua in the phrase "many of us." Many listeners, I believe, would agree wholeheartedly that *other* people, not they, are indeed harming the vanua, for the vanua is always considered threatened. Just as mana is always diminishing, the vanua is always in peril of being taken away, although most people would not blame themselves for this state of affairs.[12]

After drawing this critical comparison, Veibataki makes two points in quick succession: first, that Jesus offers "a new path," and second, that "God has already appointed the time" for Jesus' transformation of humanity, his rescuing people from their sins and errors.

God tells us if the life we are living now is difficult, if the way we are progressing is difficult in this age [there is] a new path we should follow so we can have life. But the point I want to explain to us this afternoon from the Bible reading, first thought: God has already appointed the time. God has already appointed the time.

The reference to "a new path" comes from John 14:6, in which Jesus tells the apostle Thomas, "I am the way, the truth, and the life: no man cometh unto the Father, but by me." In the Fijian Bible, "I am the way" is translated *Oi au na sala,* which literally means "I am the path."

Now Veibataki deftly looks backward in time to the story of Jesus' birth and forward to Jesus' second coming ("it will come"). The path from past to present is overgrown by the disorder, decline, and loss summarized for many indigenous Fijians in Genesis 1:26. Veibataki uses the verse's standard paraphrase (*Tou ia tou bulia na tamata*) and offers the standard interpretation: "We are not in the image, we are not after the likeness of Him." The meaning of Genesis 1:26, in other words, was thwarted by Adam and Eve when they sinned and fell short of God's perfection, and people living in the present also fall short of the original divine model. The response to such failure, for the preacher and his audience, is the standard Christian claim that one needs to accept Jesus as one's own savior.

Its meaning is as I already said before: God sees that his word of creation is not being realized. He declared, "We are making humanity in our image and likeness." God intended there to be an appointed time for His only son to be given to live here and make [us] follow the things God wants us to follow. Gentlemen, ladies, we are living [in] His world here. God has already appointed the time and it will come, and it will come, the right time. God sent his son here. Today we are commemorating the day that our Lord was born to buy you and me [i.e., with his blood]. Today. Its meaning is: the Lord's birth wasn't a mistake. It wasn't a mistake that the Lord went to be born in a stable. It wasn't a mistake that the Lord was born here in this world because God saw the purpose of our human lives was not being realized. We are not in the image, we are not after the likeness of Him. That is why I said God has already appointed the time. God has already appointed [it].

Veibataki, like other artful preachers, uses parallelism to appeal to his audience, and his use of this technique is particularly notable in this section: "and it will come, and it will come"; "It wasn't a mistake. . . . It wasn't a mistake"; "God has already appointed the time. God has already appointed [it]." He is creating a cadence that is aesthetically appealing and also underscoring his major claims. His statement that "our Lord was born to buy you and me" refers to such verses as 1 Corinthians 6:20, in which Paul writes, "Ye are bought with a price," meaning that humanity is saved by Jesus' sacrificial act of dying on the cross.

At this point, Veibataki begins a new line of argument, telling the congregation that Jesus himself was subservient to the "law." The word he uses is *vunau,* which literally means "preaching"; the translation of *vunau* as "law," with echoes of Mosaic divine lawgiving, is used in the Fijian Bible.

Second thought. He was made under the law.[13] Jesus was made under the law. Its meaning is: when Jesus was born he did not just do things that were his will. The Lord was born to work [according to] the law. For us, gentlemen and ladies, we are born, the law comes down to us, to father and mother. Let us ask today: Are we still following that law? When Jesus was born here to follow the law, why do we not follow the law today? Questions we should ask: Why are we not following the law? The Lord we serve today was made under the law. He wasn't born here to work with his own authority. Hebrews chapter two, verse fourteen to eighteen, tells us "For as—"

The sense of "law" as God's word, not government legislation, is crucial here. Veibataki is haranguing his audience, asking people why they are disobeying God. Implicitly, he is making the strong accusation that people are willful, following their own desires. Even Jesus had responsibilities, Veibataki is arguing, and he honored them, unlike people in the present. When I was translating this sermon I asked him about his statement that Jesus was "made under the law," and he explained that Jesus was an "obedient messenger" (*talai rawarawa,* lit., "easily sent"). To be an obedient messenger is highly virtuous in the Fijian ethos: it means knowing one's place, fulfilling one's responsibilities.

The preacher then reads Hebrews 2:14–18, verses that emphasize Jesus' humanity: "In all things it behoved him to be made like unto his brethren" (2:17). After finishing this passage, Veibataki offers a brief interpretation:

It points out to us this noon our Lord Jesus Christ's birth made under the law. He did not fear death and made reconciliation for the sins of the people so it was possible for them to overcome the tempter.

Having explained that Jesus, although human, "did not fear death" and gave people the power to resist the devil's persuasions ("it was possible for them to overcome the tempter"), he returns to the metaphor of Jesus as a "price" paid for humanity's sins. He expresses the hope that Jesus will "buy us again"—that is, that Jesus will provide salvation, eternal life in heaven—and then makes a comparison to shopping in Fiji's capital city.

The third thought. May God buy us again so we can know Him well again. May Jesus buy us again so we can know God well again. See the present age in the big stores in Suva. It's something, their lowering their prices, the stores' competition, the reduction of their prices. To make buying easy, to finish off the old stock, to be able to bring in some new stock. Our Lord Jesus Christ's birth is to buy you and me today. He wants to buy life there and life here [i.e., your life and my life]. And it's proper for us not to make our lives cost too much. Because if you cost too much you can not be bought. Its meaning is: a gentle spirit makes it easy for you to make today meaningful. To make our Lord's birth meaningful. To be able to buy you again so you return to God.

Vividly comparing Jesus' metaphorical purchase of humanity's salvation with the price wars of megastores in Suva, the preacher revives his earlier criticism that people are too willful. Here he argues that "if you cost too much," Jesus will not buy you, and the whole lesson of Christmas that he has been developing—that Jesus was born as a human in the world to save everyone—will be made meaningless. Just as Jesus was obedient and dutiful, the preacher is suggesting, Kadavuans should be obedient and dutiful so their salvation can be easily "bought."

He extends the metaphor of salvation as a purchase by discussing what it means to be a "stranger":

If you can't be bought, we can say you act like a stranger. Its meaning is: a stranger is in a vanua [where] he has no permanence to be able to be strong in a vanua. And when we also see the story of the temple at Jerusalem we see its blueprint. The, the place for strangers is way down low. Its meaning is: a stranger has no real permanence there for himself. That is very important for us, gentlemen and ladies. Let us try today for our Lord Jesus Christ to buy us again. That is the great purpose, his being born to carry us again to our heavenly Father.

Veibataki mentions the vanua again, now to point out that the vanua is a person's site of "permanence." He makes this claim negatively, by defining a stranger as a person who "has no permanence" in a land (cf. Mauss 1972: 31). This is an appeal to the congregation's emotions: no single Fijian term generates as much sentiment as *vanua,* with its connotations of home, tradition, and unity, the strengths of Fijian village life that are continually threatened. In these lines Veibataki brings together many of the topics he has been discussing so far: Jesus' birth, the Holy Land, the Fijian vanua, and the purchase of one's salvation.

However, he is not finished preaching, and his next statement is an intriguing new approach to his previous themes. Veibataki says that we "should not return to the things we depended on before," implying that tradition is something that God needed to correct, something that God needed to change in order to put humanity back on the right path.

Fourth thought. We should not return to the things we depended on before. We should not return to the things we depended on before. God saw that the vanua depended a lot . . . at that time on worldly things and so He gave His son to be born to enable us people to return [to God], so we return to Him. Let us not depend a lot on worldly things.

This could be interpreted as contradicting his own previous assertion, "This is an important thing, our respecting our top of the foundation." I do not believe that most of the congregation would hear this as a contradiction, however, because of Fijian history's inherent polysemy: the past was both better and worse, a time of strength but also of warlike depredations, a time of ancestral honor but also ancestral sin. This polysemy, as I mentioned earlier, is structured on a temporal split between the remote past and the near past; that is, the ancient ancestors lived like the Israelites of the Old Testament, and it is the more recent ancestors (who resisted Christian missionaries) who threaten current well-being. Here Veibataki seems to be referring obliquely to the sentiment that the recent past was a time of "darkness" that Christianity enlightened. He does not explain this assertion further, however.

Having said that people should not "depend a lot on worldly things," Veibataki turns to his conclusion. He refers to Galatians 4:10, a verse from the service's Bible reading: "Ye observe days, and months, and times, and years." For the preacher, Christmas is a day demanding commemoration, and he implores the congregation "not to be doing other things today."

Final thought. Our Bible tells us "Ye observe days, and months, and years." We sanctify this day to be God's alone. We sanctify this month to be God's alone. Thank you very much, gentlemen, ladies, you, our children, for trying to keep this day. Let us try to sanctify this day for us to serve Him alone. The Bible said "Try—ye observe days, and months, and times." The meaning of that is: our Church plans the days, it's not a mistake. Our God has already planned [them]. The Bible said, gentlemen, ladies, if we want Christmas to be good for us, to be meaningful for us, our serving our God, our arriving at this day today, let us try to commemorate the great purpose of our Lord's birth. As we have heard the word the Bible tells us let us try to sanctify the days to serve Him alone. It is greatly appreciated not to be doing, not to be doing other things today, the day to serve God alone.

With this exhortation "to sanctify the days, to serve Him alone," Veibataki moves to the end of his sermon. He has accomplished the preacher's task of applying text to context, Bible passage to contemporary indigenous Fijian life—Bethlehem to Kadavu, as it were. At the very end, he makes a quick return to the words of Genesis 1:26, encouraging people again to live up to the divine ideal.

That will lift up our land because today is the day for us to give thanks to God alone. We commemorate only our Lord Jesus Christ's being born to buy that life and this life [i.e., your life and my life] so that today we can return to him as he wants us to return, so his word of creation is confirmed: "We are making humanity in our image and likeness." And we ask God to bless for us the short thoughts we have been able to hear today.

With these closing lines the sermon is over, having lasted less than eighteen minutes. Overall, Veibataki's performance is remarkably vigorous and lucid, with artful moments of parallelism and a consistent interlacing of Bible passages and references to contemporary indigenous Fijian social life and values. Even though the sermon's lesson was Galatians 4:1–11, the subtext of the performance was Genesis 1:26, read as a criticism: people were created in God's image and likeness but have lost or lessened this resemblance to divinity.

Fijian Methodist sermons, like the Catholic sermons in Papua New Guinea discussed by Bruce Knauft (2002: 142), "braid the rope of Christianity through repetition and pull it tight through exhortation." Veibataki's performance is recognizable as a generic Christian sermon because the topic is Jesus' salvation of humanity, but many of the details are specific to Fijian cultural contexts. His descriptions of the vanua being threatened and his references to the "top of the foundation," for example, presuppose certain knowledge among his audience and an expectation that these examples will resonate emotionally. As I noted earlier, preaching is not a task to be taken lightly, and people sometimes ask to be relieved of the responsibility when they are not adequately prepared. Veibataki, however, is confident, delivering his points crisply and developing his themes over the course of his performance. Many of his topics and themes—"straightening ourselves out," "respecting our top of the foundation," guarding the vanua, and interpreting Genesis 1:26 as a lament of humanity's present state—are easily recontextualizable for many indigenous Fijians, expressed in many contexts. Veibataki's skill is displayed in the way he weaves these themes together, declaring them surely and confidently from the pulpit and supporting them with references to Bible passages.

CHAPTER 4

Kava

Fijian kava-drinking sessions are sites at which people's sense of decline and loss is made both intelligible and palpable. In talking about kava while drinking it, people engage with themes of decline and loss in a particularly dynamic way: kava sedates people's bodies in a context wherein weakness becomes an emblem of lost power. Kava is wrapped up in narratives of the fall from a golden age: people say the beverage was drunk properly in the past as opposed to the present. Despite this negative commentary, kava drinking is the center of men's social life in Tavuki, and almost all adult men drink it for hours each night. Women also drink, often in mixed-sex groups, but not with the everyday regularity of men.

Kava is a pepper plant, *Piper methysticum*, cultivated in Fiji and much of the western Pacific. Both plant and drink are called *yaqona* in Fijian. An evocative name for kava, *wai ni vanua* (water of the vanua), expresses its connections to chiefly tradition and village life, although when referring to it in English people often just call it "grog." It "is a mild narcotic, a soporific, a diuretic, and a major muscle relaxant" (Lebot, Merlin, and Lindstrom 1997: 1), relaxing people while promoting feelings of sociability. Unlike alcohol, it does not severely alter one's emotions, and the mind of the drinker remains clear (Cronheim et al. 1967: 175; Gajdusek 1967: 121). Because one's mind remains sharp during drinking, the fact of consumption remains accessible to contemplation. That is, unlike alcohol, consuming a great deal of kava does not alter one's perceptions of the fact of consumption; even during the drinking, one is aware of the social milieu, the amount that one is drinking, and the conversation that takes place.[1] Kava is not physiologically addictive, although it can seem socially addictive.

The taste has been described unkindly by popular writers. James Michener (1951: 169) characterized kava as "slimy to the tongue, earthy-tasting and mildly tingling at the gums." Paul Theroux (1992: 248–249), drinking a cup in Vanualevu, wrote, "It had a revolting taste. It was lukewarm, and it had the slightly medicinal flavor of mouthwash to which some mud had been added. . . . There was a mild afterburn and a hint of licorice." I think these judgments are harsh. To my palate, it tastes dusty and bitter, but if prepared properly there should be no muddiness; Clellan Ford (1967: 164–165) wrote evocatively of kava tasting "like the smell of a cedar lead pencil when it is sharpened." Many people in Tavuki would agree, however, that taste is not kava's main appeal. Indeed, when joking around, men sometimes declare that another person must suffer punishment (*itotogi*) for a misdeed and present the offender with a gigantic coconut shell full of kava. The offender often protests and pleads quietly, but ultimately must drink the shellful — and such a great volume is difficult for anyone to swallow all at once without becoming nauseated.

A mature kava plant is ready for harvesting after at least three years of growth. After being washed and chopped up, the roots and stems are dried in the sun for several days. These crisp bits are pounded into a powder, which is then infused in water.[2] In Tavuki and much of western Kadavu, where people adhere more strictly to traditional preparation methods than in eastern Kadavu, the kava is strained through the stringy inner bark of a hibiscus tree. In eastern Kadavu, as in many parts of Fiji, the powder is put into a cloth bag instead of a bark strainer.

The mixer, often a young man, wraps the strainer around the powder that has been placed in the bowl. An assistant pours fresh water into the bowl, and the mixer massages the powder-filled strainer for several minutes, dissolving most of the kava into the water; the liquid turns beige. After mixing the kava, he then repeatedly pulls the strainer through the liquid, sweeping it clean of bits too big to be dissolved. The mixer shakes these dregs out onto a small mat or tarpaulin, and then, toward the end of the preparation, wipes the lip of the bowl clean with the moist strainer. To mix a large bowl of strong but not gritty kava might take as long as ten minutes of focused activity. The dregs are gathered up and can be pounded and remixed several times over the course of an evening, though with diminishing potency.

FIGURE 7. Alivereti Sivo mixes kava with a hibiscus-bark strainer in the Nagonedau village hall.

FIGURE 8. The Kadavuan five-pulse rhythm
clapped by the kava mixer.

The preparation is ritualized. After the kava has been pounded but before the water has been poured into the bowl, someone calls out, "The
kava has been pounded" (*Sa vutu kora tu na yaqona*); the *o* in *yaqona* is
drawn out as "yaqooona." The task of calling out this phrase is not assigned formally, so someone in the vicinity of the bowl simply takes it
upon himself to say it. If few people are present at that point, the mixer
may make the announcement himself. At this point, the *matanivanua*
(vanua's representative, often translated in English as "herald"), who
functions as the master of ceremonies, says "Mix" (*Bali*).[3] When the mixing is finished and the kava is fully strained, the mixer sometimes dips a
coconut shell into the bowl and pours the kava back so the matanivanua
can see its color. If the matanivanua thinks it looks too strong, he will say
"Water" (*Wai*), and the mixer will dilute the kava until the matanivanua
approves of its appearance. When this process is finished and the beverage is ready to be served, the person who announced that the kava was
pounded calls out "The kava is clear" (*Sa darama tu na yaqona*), and the
matanivanua responds "Clap" (*Obo*). The mixer then claps in the distinctive Kadavuan five-pulse rhythm, diagrammed in figure 8.[4]

Finally, when the session is to be formally declared over—whether or
not most people are ready to stop drinking—a third announcement is
made: "The kava is empty" (*Sa maca tu na yaqona*). After the matanivanua responds "Obo," everyone who is sitting in the vicinity of the
kava bowl and "below" it claps together in the five-pulse rhythm.

The symbolism of kava drinking emphasizes the unity of the vanua.
Many people drink from the same coconut shell cup; most drinkers
clap once before receiving it from the cupbearer; people do not sip, but
quaff the beverage in one go; and all drinkers at the session have one
cupful each round. The exceptions to these rules are for chiefs, who often do not clap and use their own cups—but this is for the spiritual

protection of commoners, who would suffer a backlash from ancestral spirits if they drank from a chief's vessel. Christina Toren (1990: 106) writes, "To refuse to drink is an act of rudeness, a denial of social relations, and a rejection of the status quo," and although she is referring to behavior in the drinking circle, where it is rude not to take a cup offered to you, her claim can be read more broadly: it is antisocial not to go to kava sessions. Not to drink kava is not to acknowledge others, not to recognize the value of social relationships that are affirmed in the kava circle.[5]

Sessions usually begin in the late afternoon, when men have finished working, and continue for hours into the night. Suppers are eaten late, after drinking has finished. Bad weather will never cancel a kava session. Once, when a small group of us was drinking in the church social hall, rain was pouring so heavily that it was impossible to go outdoors to pound the dregs. So someone took a hammer and pounded them there and then, indoors, keeping the dregs in a folded tarpaulin so the bits would not fly all over the place. As far as I recall, this was not a special occasion where a guest was being hosted; the drinkers, especially the Methodist minister, just wanted to keep drinking and weren't going to let an insignificant detail like cataclysmic weather get in the way.

Every drinking session, formal or informal, follows an order of service. Kava sessions' formality can be graded both by the "increased structuring and predictability of discourse" and the "prevailing affective tone . . . [of] seriousness, politeness, and respect" (Irvine 1979: 774). Highly formal sessions are diagnosed by what Judith Irvine calls increased code structuring (wearing appropriate dress, comporting one's body in a "respectful" manner, refraining from conversation); code consistency (humor of any sort is inappropriate); the invocation of positional identities (chiefliness is highly evident at a formal kava ceremony, where the focus is on serving authority figures); and the emergence of a central situational focus (no distractions to the ceremony are allowed). In addition, kava marks certain events as important and lends gravity to formal discussion: if a large group of Fijians are gathered to commemorate, celebrate, or mourn, the event is marked as a significant occasion by including kava drinking as part of the proceedings (Ford 1967: 170; Quain 1948: 44 n. 45; see also Toren 1990: 99).

In this chapter, however, I am focusing on informal nightly sessions where protocol is looser but still always observed. On any given night in Tavuki village, several groups meet to drink kava, but the membership of each group is fluid. As Andrew Arno (1993: 103) writes, "*Yaqona* drinking is not a matter of cliques that are exclusive in character." Sometimes groups are composed of people who worked together during the day on a project; sometimes people meet for entertainment such as listening to the radio or watching a video (Tavuki does not have television broadcast reception); sometimes the gathering is just a comfortable circle of friends and relatives. On Sundays many men drink together following the afternoon church service, and sometimes the drinking session is held in the Methodist social hall.

The seating pattern around the kava bowl is hierarchical, with higher rank the farther "above" (in front of) the bowl one sits. In Tavuki, the first and second cups are drunk by the highest ranked person present and the matanivanua, respectively. In other words, the "chief" (whether or not the first drinker is really of chiefly status) and the herald form a dyad of chiefs and people represented in the first two cups of kava drunk in each round. Beginning with the third cup, drinkers are generally served in order of descending social rank based on characteristics including heredity, age, sex, and marital status. Reflecting this pattern of declension, there is often decreasing formality in serving and drinking as one goes down the line of drinkers.

Even the most informal kava sessions evince the division into sides that A. M. Hocart (1936, 1952) described as pervasive in Fijian culture (see also Milner 1952: 377). These sides are linked by the concept and practice of service (*viqaravi*). Broadly speaking, in any kava session there is a division between the servers and those who are served. Chiefs are always supposed to be served. Toren (1990: 117) argues that the pattern of service in kava-drinking sessions transforms reciprocal relationships into hierarchical ones and legitimizes hierarchy in general: "The centrality and significance of [kava] ritual are such that people's disposition in space when they gather to drink [kava] provides an image of social relations as properly hierarchical" (see also Toren 1988, 1994, 1999). If distinctions between server and served are blurred, the blurring can become a new sign of present-day disorder in contrast to past regimes of order.[6] Besides chiefs, the focus of service sometimes includes visitors, such as public works employees, medical personnel, politicians, or Church officials passing through the village. Kava drinking is an act emblematic of tradition, and thus it is in a sense also service to the ancestors. This is one reason why Methodists, who drink large amounts of kava in the church social hall, never actually drink kava within the church building itself.

Kava Talk

Conversations at casual kava sessions are, in many ways, the raison d'être of the sessions. Katz (1993: 191) reminisces of his time in Fiji, "No matter how many [bowls] we mix, we seem to talk about important things. The talk and the *yaqona* are intimately paired. The *yaqona* stimulates good talk and good talk demands that we keep drinking *yaqona*" (see also Turner 1986: 207). Vigorous discussion can ebb over the course of the evening as people grow tired; conversely, some taboo topics can be raised only late at night, when the audience thins out and people feel very relaxed.

Discussion flows easily and widely: storytelling, joking, reporting on the day's events, recounting one's travels, questioning visitors, and commenting on ongoing work projects are all common. Conversational constraints do exist, however. For example, I did not generally hear people openly discuss national politics. In fact, once when two men were having a hushed discussion in a kava circle, a friend jokingly told me to admonish them, "Don't gossip" (*Kua ni kakase*); playing along, I did so, and one of the men responded that they were discussing politics. He knew that one shouldn't talk about such things out loud. Generally, the privilege of commanding an audience is correlated with one's social position, so when a high-seated drinker begins to talk, lower drinkers tend to fall silent and listen. Thus the liveliest conversation with the most frequent change of speakers takes place among the drinkers sitting "low" near the kava bowl. When chiefs participate in casual kava-drinking sessions, conversations may be less bawdy and freewheeling than when no chiefs are present; young men told me occasionally how fun it was to drink kava when chiefs were not present.

Joking is prominent at informal kava sessions because people are often relaxed and in a mood to banter and laugh. People in certain relationship categories are expected to joke with each other, cross-cousins particularly. As an outsider learning the language, I was the ideal mouthpiece for many people's jokes: someone would tell me to say something outrageous to someone else at a kava session—"Matthew, tell Seru, 'Hey Seru, have you returned from preaching at Vunimoli?' "—and I was usually willing to do so. (This is a made-up example based on similar real ones. It would be funny to people in Tavuki because it would hint at Seru's doings in another village; perhaps he had a girlfriend there, or perhaps the people of Vunimoli are of mixed Fijian and English heritage and Seru is notably light-skinned himself.) Because I was directly involved in these exchanges, it was particularly easy for me to remember the details of these jokes and record them in my field notes.

Some jokes are earthy and sexual, often prompted by the handing out of cigarettes and sweets.[7] A related but more subtle kind of humor is based on the subversion of proper recognition, in which people are called by the wrong name, kin term, or other social designator. One reliable joke is to address a man by referring to his girlfriend or wife, but such joking should be relatively indirect. For example, a friend once told me to call a man *naita* since the man's wife was from Lomaiviti, the central chain of Fijian islands. *Naita,* short for *na itabani* (the sides), is a term used between people from different regions that were former enemies in battle; Kadavu and Lomaiviti share a *naita* relationship. In other words, I was to address the man as if he were from Lomaiviti—but he wasn't; his wife was. This joke is analogous to calling a man by his father-in-law's name, which, of course, I was also told to do, and which invariably got big laughs.

Other jokes fall well outside the domain of kinship and sexuality. Some humor is specifically language-focused. "One sure way to get a laugh when speaking Fijian," writes Siegel (1995: 95), "is to switch into Hindi, the language of the Indian population of Fiji." His observation is valid for Tavuki, where substituting *kai se* for Fijian *bula* (hello) or *accha* for Fijian *vinaka* (good, thanks) always makes people laugh. Some people were occasionally called by Indian names. Other codeswitching jokes, however, depend on real ancestral ties, as when I was told to say a Rotuman phrase to a man from Nukunuku village who had a Rotuman grandparent. Another man from Nukunuku was the subject of jokes because, due to a speech impediment, he could not pronounce /r/. But as the village headman (*turaga ni koro*), it was his responsibility to serve as town crier and make the public announcements that typically begin *"Turaga kei na marama!"* (Gentlemen and ladies!). To get around his predicament, he substituted words without /r/ in his announcement, and the result was odd-sounding proclamations beginning *"Tagane kei na yalewa!"* (Males and females!).

Kava itself can become a subject of jokes. For example, when I first stayed in Tavuki, in 1996, I naïvely asked about ancestral gods in Kadavu, a question people were not eager to answer directly, so they responded by joking that kava was their god. Similarly, around Christmastime 1998 I was drinking kava in Nagonedau village's communal hall when I asked an elderly man about who had left Tavuki to go elsewhere for the holidays. After naming names, he drew an implicit parallel with the story of Jesus'

birth by saying that different people, in going to various villages to celebrate the holiday, were following different stars. But we, he said, had followed one star. Then he gave the punch line by pointing to the kava bowl.
That was our Star of Bethlehem: the kava bowl, guiding us to itself.

A specific genre of performance at kava sessions is the joking debate
(see Arno 1985, 1990, 1993). As mentioned earlier, I rarely heard public
discussion of national politics in Tavuki, but that changed after the
elections of 1999, when poll results caused a great deal of tension.
Kadavuans voted strongly for the party of the former coup leader and
incumbent prime minister Sitiveni Rabuka, the SVT (Soqosoqo ni
Vakavulewa ni Taukei, Fijian Political Party). The SVT was considered
the party of chiefly interests (Robertson and Sutherland 2001: 125). Indigenous Fijians' voting patterns were fragmented nationally, however,
with their votes going to many different parties, including a nationalist
Christian party (see chapter 6). Indo-Fijians, in contrast, mostly voted
for one of two Indo-Fijian–led parties, Labour and the National Federation Party, and as a result, Labour pulled off a shocking victory. Labour's
triumph bore an ominous resemblance to the election results of April
1987, the elections that spurred Fiji's first coup by Rabuka. The SVT's
big loss nationwide was made more distressing for Tavukians by the fact
that Mahendra Chaudhry, Labour's leader, decided to take over as prime
minister himself rather than hand the position to an indigenous Fijian in
his own party.

After the election, in May 1999, rumors began circulating in Tavuki:
Fijians and Indo-Fijians were said to be fighting on the western side of
Vitilevu; the prime minister's office was burned down. These rumors
turned out to be false, but they expressed a sense of the chaotic: social
breakdown had begun. But this was not necessarily a feared chaos; in
fact, it might be desirable. A coup could mean the reassertion of Fijian
strength. The atmosphere was electric with anxiety and frustration. The
prevailing mood, grim and tense, was expressed most succinctly by
a friend who told me over kava that this was a "difficult time for Fiji"
(*gauna dredre vei Viti*), explaining that it is wrong for Indians to want
to be considered Fijian and that God gave this vanua and this kind of life
to indigenous Fijians.

Then came the joking debate in Tavuki's church social hall on June 2,
1999, a serious event that dissipated tensions through comedy. The three
main participants were Rev. Isikeli Serewai, Isikeli Rogo, and Kameli
Vuadreu. Rev. Serewai spoke as the representative of the lotu, and his
opinions were echoed by those of Isikeli, a carpenter and mechanic, who

argued calmly by analogy. Both of these men articulated a position that can be described as resigned to the situation and looking for the positive aspects. On the other side was Kameli, who played the comic figure brilliantly, acting as the humorous and volatile voice of the Fijian ethnonationalist id.

During the debate, Kameli repeatedly crossed boundaries of propriety, and the audience laughed appreciatively: this was a carnivalesque event, a temporary site where certain norms can be inverted. Arno (1990: 242) calls the Fijian joking debate "a verbal game—a well-defined, playful form of interaction in which serious issues might nonetheless be ventilated," and his description is apt for the event I witnessed. Certain norms remained unchallenged, however, most significantly the men's right to speak in public in the first place. All three were respected, middle-aged men who were not chiefs. They sat neither very "high" nor very "low" at drinking sessions, but in the long columns of men at the sides, positioned between the foci of service (the chiefs) and the servants (the young men). No women were present at this joking debate, and though some other men added their voices now and then, most stayed quiet except to laugh when Kameli said something particularly funny.

Isikeli the carpenter said that when the Israelites were in their Babylonian exile, they cried out to God, asking why they were in such a plight. God, said Isikeli, told them they were getting what they deserved. Isikeli then claimed that Labour's victory would get Fijians back on the right track, in analogy with the Jews coming out of the desert. Now Fijians would pay appropriate attention to the pillars of their society: lotu, vanua, and matanitu.

Kameli would have none of it. Instead of recognizing parallels to ancient Israel, he called up other exoticisms; for example, he joked of *kalou matakau* (wooden-faced gods), a disparaging reference to non-Christian religions such as Hinduism, the dominant religion among Indo-Fijians. As the foil for Rev. Serewai and Isikeli, Kameli kept people laughing with his energetic, outrageous responses. Rev. Serewai repeated an assertion he had made earlier: that it was wrong for people to pray for a particular party's victory because doing so was an attempt to influence God. Better, he said, simply to pray about the elections and not to request that a particular party win. On other occasions, people did not challenge this advice since it was from the local authority on such matters. At this debate, however, Kameli asserted that he *had* prayed to God for the SVT to win. People laughed, for here was a mere member of the congregation declaring that he had not followed the minister's advice—and, I suspect, many people sympathized with his desire. At another moment, Rev. Serewai recounted how, drinking kava the previous night, he had challenged people to explain why Ratu Mara had persuaded the leader of the Fijian Association Party to support Chaudhry. The minister said that when he had posed this question (with its implication, I believe, that Ratu Mara must have had good reasons for his disturbing action), no one could answer it, but Kameli kept chirping "I answered it!" (*Au ma sauma!*). When Rev. Serewai used the English word "corruption" in criticizing the SVT, Kameli responded "Speak Fijian" (*Vosa Vaviti;* he used the nonpolite phrasing). When Rev. Serewai mentioned that the national budget would be presented by Chaudhry's government in September, Kameli suggested an alternative occupation for the Indo-Fijian politician: he could take his knife, file, and shovel and go to his village to farm.

At the time, what struck me most about the debate was the laughter it generated. People worried deeply about the election results, and here were two respected men arguing that forbearance was the best course. Kameli's voice-of-the-people responses, irreverent and pointed, made people laugh. Gone was the guarded, nervous, upset, and angry tone of earlier discussions about the election. During the debate Rev. Serewai said emphatically to the audience several times, "This is the relish [or topping] for kava drinking" (*Oqo na icoi ni gunu yaqona*). In other words, the minister was saying that vigorous discussion is the perfect complement to kava drinking.

A good comparison to the joking debate is a serious conversation that took place at a kava session in the village of Nabouwalu in March 1999. Rev. Serewai had gone there to conduct the Methodist Church's quarterly meeting for the Ono circuit. After the church service and meeting, approximately fifty to sixty people, mostly men, gathered in the social hall to drink kava and converse. A man named Tomasi from the village of Vabea posed a question to Rev. Serewai about whether it was acceptable to vote for a new political party, the Veitokani ni Lewenivanua Vakarisito (called the Christian Democratic Alliance in English). Tomasi asked his question obliquely and deferentially, requesting that his "thoughts . . . be made proper." As this conversation unfolded, people were drinking kava and chatting in the background. Tomasi began:

Something you said, sir, about this Christian political party. [You] are emphasizing praying about the election. What, sir, . . . I ask for my thoughts to be made proper.

The minister responded "Yes" (*Io*), and Tomasi explained a bit more:

It isn't wrong if we just pray for the Christian party? Because of our beliefs, our hopes.

Tomasi framed the issue in terms of Christian expectations: surely a Christian should vote according to his or her faith? In response, the minister explained his own belief that praying for a particular party to win was presumptuous, an imposition of humans' will against the divine plan:

Yes, in the, when we, if we turn entirely [and] keep praying for the Christian Alliance Party, to me, it looks like we are telling God what we want.

Tomasi answered "Oh" (*Oi*), and the minister continued:

We really want, we just tell Him we want the VLV to win because—I reject that generally. We just pray about the elections and He decides who wins.

In response to Rev. Serewai's argument that God would decide the election, and that people should pray generally about the election but not specifically about which party should win, Tomasi could only muster another soft single-syllable response (*Mm.*) Then the minister concluded:

That's the foundation I'm on. I already said, everything that is in our hearts, we truly want that thing. But let us just leave it to Him to decide. If it's right, [if] it's the time for [the VLV] to win, we give it to Him. When we keep pronouncing the party's name like that we answer our own prayer. That is my thought [on] my giving a general request. Is that okay, Tom?

The last line was a gentle quip, a joking request for Tomasi to admit his error. After a few seconds, Tomasi said something that is inaudible on the tape, there was some laughter, and Rev. Serewai continued speaking, changing the topic. Throughout the conversation, both men's voices were quiet and somewhat hesitant; the tone was the polar opposite of the fast-paced, subversive joking debate at Tavuki. At Nabouwalu, Rev. Serewai's authority was unchallenged. Tomasi's question was more of an invitation to a monologue than the beginning of a dialogue. Direct questions on religious doctrine and practice are relatively rare at kava sessions, but because this was a kava session held after a Church quarterly meeting, such questions were expected.

These events show how kava sessions can be the site of joking and argumentation and, presumably, the unification of opinion, although there is no standard metadiscursive strategy for uniting opinion such as the overt exclusion of disagreement at the Indo-Fijian *pancayat* (dispute mediation session; Brenneis 1990; see also Brenneis 1984a, 1984b) or the depersonalization of discourse at the Xavante *warã* (men's council meetings; Graham 1993). Most kava-drinking sessions do not feature dramatic debates or formal question-and-answer sessions like the examples I have given here, but they are still primary sites of discourse circulation in the village. Kava sessions are not only places to drink, they are also places to talk—and, sometimes, to talk about drinking kava, and how it is a sign of the fall from a golden age.

Sedated Bodies and Enervated Histories

In drinking kava and talking about drinking kava, Tavukians reproduce a key sign of loss, for excessive kava drinking is considered to be a sign of the loss of proper custom. Many people say that the ancestors did not drink so much kava, and that today people drink too much.

In June 1999 the Fijian Affairs Board held a workshop in Naqalotu village, Yawe district, just west of Tavuki. Each day for five days, people gathered to discuss issues of social unity. Kava was drunk frequently at the workshop. Copies of a photocopied document titled "Proposed 'Tikina [District] and Village Orders' " were handed out, offering many proposals for village law. Three of the suggestions were the following: "Youths under age 16 are forbidden to drink kava"; "It is forbidden to drink kava purposelessly after one o'clock in the morning"; and "When there is a village meeting, it is forbidden to drink kava purposelessly and without meaning [i.e., without a social justification]."[8]

People needed to be gathered in a single place where this document could be distributed and discussed, and the proper and effective forum for such discourse circulation was a kava session; in fact, the workshop's success depended on the fact that kava was being drunk there. The kava bowl not only brought people together and provided a central situational focus; it also lent gravity to the formal discussion. Without kava drinking, the event would not be considered important and the discussion would not be valid or effective.

In Kadavu I heard several public complaints about the overconsumption of kava. One was another instance at the workshop, when the Fijian Affairs representative asked different village groups to criticize each other constructively. The women's group was asked to criticize the Methodist

Church. All of the criticisms were written on oversized white paper and posted on a wall in the village's communal hall, where the government official proceeded to read and discuss them. The women's group offered three criticisms of the Church: Church leaders do not listen to the chiefs; preachers do not practice what they preach; and people are drinking too much kava the night before going to church or instead of going to church. This third criticism was also the thrust of a specific complaint in July 1999, when a small group of men, including myself, were drinking kava in the communal hall of the subclan Vunikarawa in Tavuki. The session had begun as a farewell (*vitalatala*) for guests who had attended a funeral in the village. Long after the guests departed we sat drinking and conversing. An older woman came in and objected that we were still drinking when the work of preparing for Sunday remained; because no work is supposed to be done on Sunday, preparations for meals are supposed to be made on Saturday.

Another complaint was the one mentioned in chapter 2, Ratu Qara's harangue at a Tavuki village meeting (*ova*) in January 1999. In his speech, Ratu Qara criticized the present state of affairs in the village, and specifically mentioned the excessive consumption of kava: "This is bad trash: singing songs, drinking too much kava. You youth are not getting married much these days. Communal garden work is announced, communal garden work doesn't happen." Along with boisterous singing, casual sexual relationships ("You youth are not getting married"), and the lack of communal work effort, the speaker listed "too much kava" as something going wrong in social life. As with the workshop, the effective way to circulate this message was to deliver it at a meeting where kava drinking was part of the proceedings. In other words, Ratu Qara's litany of complaints gained its audience and its forcefulness precisely because it was delivered at a meeting where kava was being consumed.

These criticisms about excessive kava drinking show how themes of decline and loss are made intelligible. Kava drinking is criticized as an excessive activity, as something that is too often "meaningless" nowadays. One man put it to me explicitly when he stated that kava should be drunk "so it has a meaning [i.e., a purpose]" (*me jiko i dua na kena ibalebale*). On another occasion I heard a man from Natumua express the same sentiment but phrased negatively, when he complained that nowadays people drink kava when "it's not meaningful" (*mino ni vaibalebale*).[9] Such negative evaluations of casual kava drinking—of drinking just to drink—and characterizations of drinking and social decline are not exclusively local. For example, the *Fiji Times* propagated this message in a *Weekend* magazine feature from 1996 titled "Yaqona: Is It Getting the Nation Doped?," which presented such articles as "Is It a Social Drug?" and "Dreaded Relaxant Here, Sought After Overseas."[10]

Kava sessions also make themes of loss palpable, turning discourse into embodied certainty. Perhaps the most effective way they do so is by sedating the drinker's body while his or her mind remains sharp. Kava drinking is a pleasant, gradual loss of power over one's body: the severely drunk grow tired, stare vacantly, and eventually get wobbly legs. "When consumption is excessive . . . the limbs become tired, the muscles seem no longer to respond to the orders and control of the mind, walking becomes slow and unsteady" (L. Lewin quoted in Lebot, Merlin, and Lindstrom 1997: 58). Men are said to lose the desire and ability to have sex. In addition, people who stay up late drinking kava are likely to awaken late the next day and thus not get work done. In short, excessive kava consumption drains one of physical power. Turner (1986: 213) refers to kava drinking as "a symbolic forfeiture of vitality," but it is a symbol that is keenly felt.

In an article in the *Fiji Times* a journalist noted that kava

goes down at sporting fixtures, festivals, movie houses, weddings, funerals, 13 and 100 night [ritual] functions, shops, offices, market stalls, roadsides and meetings, not to mention at any social gathering and on any excuse.

. . . Although [kava] has been banned during working hours in many workplaces, in many others the first task of the day is to mix a bowl.

. . . Dr. [Davendra] Nandan said [kava] also took its toll on family life.

"A man who goes out drinking probably spends $4–$5 by the time he's bought his grog and cigarettes," he said.[11]

"He doesn't see his children growing up, or take any interest in his wife."[12]

In short, people who consume too much kava cannot be effective actors. They cannot work, tend their garden, have sex, or go to church. However, because drinking a lot of kava is macho, some men lament overconsumption with a smile. People occasionally say, "There's too much kava drinking," adding the question tag "Eh?" (*Sa sivia na somi yaqona . . . e?*). The question is asked as if one is mildly chagrined, yet the speakers are often not chagrined, but fondly recalling pleasurable excess while acknowledging the condemnatory public discourse about it.

Another way in which kava-drinking sessions make participants feel a sense of decline, and not only know it intellectually, is in the order of service. As mentioned earlier, people drink in descending order of relative social status. This pattern resonates meaningfully with history itself as imagined in Tavuki, which begins with powerful people—mythic voyagers, strong warrior heroes, conquering chiefs—and proceeds downward from there. In addition, as drinking proceeds from "high" to "low," strict order dissolves. Whereas everyone is silent while the first few cups are drunk, calling out *"Maca!"* (Empty!) and clapping when cups are drained, they start paying less attention when lower-seated drinkers take their turns. People start holding side conversations and stop clapping and calling out. When I served as cupbearer, I would ask about the serving order when it was unclear to me who should be served next. If I asked this question after having served the first few drinkers, people sometimes said that the sequence didn't matter at that point. The impression I got from these responses was that chiefs and high authorities such as ministers had to be served in the proper order, but once the cup was reaching regular folks strict order was unnecessary. Even then, however, the serving never in fact became random: it generally followed a basic geometric pattern from high to low and increasing proximity to the kava bowl, with the mixer being the last person to drink during a round. The hierarchical serving of kava, then, can be seen as a diagrammatic icon of decreasing social power, and to some extent of decreasing order.

Crucially, when alcohol parties are held by men, they are almost always held after kava sessions have ended. If a group of men wants to meet for a "washdown" over a bottle of rum, they will do so once the evening's kava drinking is finished. Partly, this is simply a practical way to avoid other people's judgmental gazes. Practicality is not the only reason, however, because one can imagine plenty of other ways to avoid detection. The fundamental reason is that the diagram of decline puts alcohol consumption in its proper place, at the very bottom and the bitter end, when power is almost gone. Toren (1994) observes that although Fijian men of all ages occasionally drink alcohol, only young men are accused of drunkenness. This makes sense according to ideologies of decline. Alcohol, drunk after the evening's last bowl of kava is empty, is a resonant symbol of powerlessness and disorder, with its multiple indexical links: to young men with relatively little social influence; to the inability of Fijian society to resist this product (which is often translated as "foreigner's kava," *yaqona ni vavalagi*); and to the lack of control over one's actions, which leads to outrageous, rowdy behavior, fighting, and "uncontrolled sexuality" (Toren 1994: 164; see also Arno 1993: 89–95).[13]

Kava's numbing effect on the body is projected onto the social level, as excessive drinking is interpreted as a sign of social weakness. Reading through the historical and ethnographic record, one consistently finds claims from both Fijians and non-Fijian observers that can be summarized as "People used to drink less kava than they do today, and today they drink too much." Such statements suggest that people in the past did not weaken themselves through excess. A typical claim of this kind comes from Basil Thomson, who wrote in 1908, "In the old days, it was not drunk in every house nor on every night, but only in chiefs' houses by the chief and his retainers, and on the occasion of special feasts and ceremonies. Now, however, it is drunk in the houses of the common people whenever they can obtain a supply of the root" (346–347). In Tavuki a hundred years after Thomson wrote this, I heard the same kind of discourse. I was told that people did not drink so much kava previously—that the exuberant consumption I observed was a recent phenomenon.[14]

Yet the thematic consistency and historical longevity of the discourse suggests that overconsumption has been occurring for a long time. That is, people have evidently drunk a lot of kava in Fiji for a long time, and this practice is often accompanied by the commentary that something new is going on. As early as 1827 a French observer stated, "Drinking kava to excess is commonplace. . . . When Fijians have nothing to eat, which happens occasionally, they get by with kava."[15] In the mid-1860s Rev. Joseph Waterhouse (1866: 339–340) wrote, "There is every reason to conclude that originally the Fijians were a sober people. A hundred years ago, there were but two grog-bowls in Rewa, a town then containing a population of three or four thousand people. These bowls were in the houses of the principal chiefs; and the drum was beaten to assemble those who wished to partake of liquor. Within the last thirty years, however, intoxication has become fearfully prevalent, by the use of both alcoholic and *kava* mixtures" (see also Clunie 1986: 80; Endicott 1923: 44–45; Reeves 1898: 118; Thomas 1997: 182–183; Thornley 1979: 128; Williams 1982: 141–146).

Even if Rev. Waterhouse was a biased observer, consider the fact that in 1885 the colonial government passed a regulation that kava "should not be drunk indiscriminately or immoderately," suggesting that overconsumption was considered a problem by British colonial authorities, both secular and religious, at that time (Roth 1973: 127). It is evident that in decrying kava drinking, these authorities were not merely voicing conventional Victorian stereotypes about disordered and dissolute natives, but were repeating statements made by indigenous Fijians. Only Fijians, for example, would have known how many kava bowls were in Rewa in the middle of the eighteenth century.

Like Thomson and Waterhouse, many ethnographers have taken informants' statements at face value and assumed that people really did drink less in the past. Consider the case of kava drinking by women. Turner (1986: 205) writes, "It is only in recent times that Fijian women have also drunk *yaqona*"; however, Lester (1941: 98) said exactly the same thing forty-five years earlier, declaring, "The custom of permitting women to drink it at all dates from comparatively recent times when kava drinking ceased to be purely a religious rite and became a social ceremony where all and sundry might join in." Going back further, Fijian women's kava consumption was considered "a new danger" as early as 1896 (Wood 1978: 262; see also Cook 1996: 145; Thomson 1908: 346). In short, Fijians and outside observers have often believed that discourse about past propriety and present overindulgence is historically true, whereas the written record suggests that people have long drunk a great deal of kava while lamenting the fact that they were drinking a great deal of kava.

Kava and Christianity

Fijian Methodists' love of kava is well known. In January 1999 the *Fiji Times* reported that the Church president, Ilaitia Tuwere, "said yaqona was a gift from God and people were morally obliged to consume it."[16] In contrast, in an August 1999 article in the *Post,* the Catholic former prime minister Ratu Mara criticized Methodist Church leaders' overindulgence in kava.[17]

Because adult Methodists in Tavuki drink a lot of kava and drink it seven days a week, sometimes holding sessions in the Methodist social hall, one might suspect that the beverage could be incorporated into Church ritual, specifically communion, as has happened in Samoan Catholicism (von Hoerschelmann 1995: 195). Kava drinking and Methodist ritual do not fit together neatly, however. In fact, there is a fundamental asymmetry between them: I never observed kava being drunk inside a Methodist church, in Tavuki or elsewhere, but people sometimes pray at kava sessions. In other words, the lotu can be brought into kava drinking, but kava drinking cannot be brought into the heart of the lotu. When I asked people if they could substitute kava for the red fruit juice drunk at communion, they said no; one respondent explained that kava is not red in color. (In the Fijian Bible, *yaqona* is the term used for the King James Bible's "strong drink"; "wine" is *waini.*)

Kava's unsuitability for Christian ritual is rooted in more than its color, however. It has a demonic underbelly that unsettles any union between kava drinking and Christianity. Drinking kava enables communication with the ancestors, who can still curse people.[18] Sometimes this kind of contact is desirable, even salutary; for example, Katz (1993) describes healers using kava benevolently as a channel to the spirits. Often, however, making contact with the ancestors is a dangerous sign of the drinker's malice, and to drink kava alone is one way to practice witchcraft. Solitary kava consumption can summon frightening non-Christian forces that might slip out of the summoner's control. Hashimoto (1989: 14) mentions a Fijian village where "an evil man . . . went to a grave to make *yaqona* and served it to a *tevoro* (ghost [or devil]) to ask him to kill someone, but was himself killed by the *tevoro* who refused the request." In other words, the man attempted to raise a spirit from the grave by pouring out kava for it, but his malicious plan backfired and the devilish ancestor killed him.

Thus to incorporate kava into the Christian sacraments would be a fiendish mixing of categories, as illustrated by a case that the *Fiji Times* reported in January 1999:

A [twenty-two-year-old indigenous Fijian] man who claimed that witchcraft and baptism with yaqona made him molest a girl was jailed for two years yesterday. . . .

"Before my grandfather died, he did witchcraft on me," he said.

"These days, the curse comes and makes me do strange things.

"When I was baptised at the age of three years, the church minister made a mistake.

"He ([the] minister) did not pour water on me to baptise but he poured a bucket of yaqona to baptise me.

"Because of this mistake by the church minister and witchcraft by my grandfather, I molested the girl."[19]

The story is an ingenious blend of occultism: witchcraft, a curse, and, most disturbingly, a baptism in kava. In Tavuki I was told that the lagoon and the wilderness, as well as gravesites, were places where one could pour a libation for spirits.[20] I was told that younger people did not do this, but concerns about such practices continued to circulate in Kadavu with potent results. In March 1999 an eighty-seven-year-old man was assaulted by five drunken youths (ages seventeen to twenty-two) in Mokoisa village, on Kadavu's south coast, for allegedly practicing "witchcraft";[21] although the news article did not state explicitly how the man was supposed to have conducted his witchcraft, it was likely through the medium of kava. People might have believed he had drunk kava by himself. Another possibility is that he surreptitiously contacted ancestral spirits while drinking communally, for example, by dipping one of his fingers into the cup as he took it, or by making sure that some of the kava dripped onto his hand. As one man explained it to me in July 2003, when a person is committed to serving a particular spirit, the person and the spirit are "covenanted" (*viyalayalaji*); thus when one drinks kava, the spirit "drinks" it too. During this same conversation, the Methodist minister explained that he often gave a prayer aloud at kava-drinking sessions because people may have been silently serving devils there.[22] Members of evangelical denominations such as Seventh-day Adventism and Assemblies of God are forbidden to drink kava, not only because it causes a kind of drunkenness but also because it has this potential demonic aspect.[23]

Despite its hazardous spiritual associations, kava is such a social force that the Fijian Methodist Church adapted over the course of the twentieth century to the cultural imperative that people must meet around the kava bowl, talk there, drink there, and decide important matters there. Early calls for total abstinence, complete with a "blue ribbon campaign" highlighting prominent figures as kava teetotalers, eventually yielded to requests for moderation in drinking (Allen 1887; Gunson 1966; Thomson 1908; Thornley 1979; Tippett 1958b; Wood 1978). In the article quoted at the beginning of this section, in which the Church president claimed that kava drinking is morally obligatory, he went on to say that the problem was not consumption itself, but overconsumption:

He said yaqona was used to hold the people and land together and save them from alienation like overseas countries.

"But the use of yaqona is too much. The Methodist Church has nothing against the use of the drink, but it should be taken in moderation. We have to look after our health and our life," Reverend Tuwere said.[24]

This statement is notable for its claim that kava should be drunk to promote unity, stability, and strength. Note how the minister framed the issue in terms of health and life, indicating that this was not simply a moral complaint—it was also a claim about power, specifically bodily power, and how it can be dissipated.

In chapter 2 I suggested that colonial histories of subjugation are one source of the common cross-cultural theme of a lost golden age. This suggestion now bears elaboration in light of Methodism's political role in Fiji. The course of Fijian history through the nineteenth and twentieth centuries was largely an uncomfortable coming to terms with the loss of political agency and slow but profound changes in perception of the unseen world and sources of power. Laments over excessive kava drinking and the resulting loss of power are metacultural commentaries on the transformations of the past two centuries affecting indigenous Fijians. At kava sessions Fijians reproduce one of the signs of a history that they lament: drinking kava heartily. They do so while circulating a discourse that criticizes the practice, explaining the supposed historical decline. In this way, kava-drinking sessions generate both an intelligible and an embodied sense of loss: understandings are felt, sensations explained. Laments about loss become perpetual, and people may occasionally feel that loss warrants political action. But the old days, always just out of reach, keep receding.

CHAPTER 5

Sacred Land and the Power of Prayer

The vanua is a constellation of people, land, and associated ideologies of chiefliness and tradition. The lotu is Christianity, its sites and practices, including worship, prayer, Bible reading, hymn singing, and preaching. Within these categories, people's identities are contextually variable. Lotu actors (my term) are those who bear the institutional authority of the Methodist Church in some measure, whether locally as prayer service leaders, lay preachers, and pastors, regionally as catechists and ministers, or nationally and internationally. Locally, lotu actors form into a body for Church-related activities such as conducting worship services, raising funds for the Church, weeding church gardens, attending conferences, and participating in special events such as helping to build a new boat for the minister. Vanua actors are the chiefs and commoners working in self-consciously traditional contexts, often ones in which the serving of kava is a ritual anchor point. Most people serve the lotu in some contexts and the vanua in others, but authorities such as Methodist ministers and high chiefs are more strongly associated with one context or the other.

Many ritual events invoke signs associated with lotu and vanua while keeping their spheres of authority distinct. In the following example from April 1999, an elderly man from Baidamudamu village gave a speech of welcome at the opening of the newly built church. He teased the guest of honor, Rev. Serewai, subverting the lotu's importance by joking about the vanua's perduring opposition to it. In giving this speech, the man was both drawing lotu and vanua together in unity and emphasizing their irreconcilable differences:

When I speak of the glory of the conference leader's being here, it is his last year [of assignment as superintendent minister] in Kadavu, this year. Yes, he is someone deep in theology, deep also in the vanua, deep in the demonic, just like us. It's shown very properly this morning. We are children of sorcerers. . . . That's the truth. That's how it was back then. A different story . . . but I should tell you only the truth. Before Christianity came here we were sons of sorcerers, possessees. Everything [that was] done was the work of strong-willed people.

After mentioning the "glory" of Rev. Serewai's presence at Baidamu-damu, the speaker, Akariva Nabati, playfully subverted the message by joking that the minister was "deep in theology, deep also in the vanua, deep in the demonic." By equating the vanua with the demonic, Nabati set it in opposition to the lotu, and identified Rev. Serewai with both realms. Nabati then sharpened his joke by adding "just like us"—in other words, acknowledging that Baidamudamu had a history of resisting Christian missionary efforts. The speech of welcome was given in honor of Rev. Serewai, but Nabati's words reminded the minister of how strong the vanua is in Kadavu and that even a paramount Methodist leader such as Rev. Serewai is tied to his own vanua.

The interconnections between lotu and vanua, articulated at the metacultural plane, are dense and resonant—and sometimes considered problematic. As I mentioned in the introduction, one man in Tavuki argued, "The vanua should be Christianized; [but] today, the lotu is being influenced by the vanua." As another example, a Church official who visited Tavuki in 2003 said during conversation (in English), "Fijians worship the vanua." But often lotu and vanua are brought into productive conjunction. On November 19, 1997, Rev. Serewai was asked to open the Kadavu provincial council meeting in Tavuki. In his speech he quoted Jeremiah 22:29, "O *earth, earth, earth,* hear the word of the LORD," which is given in the Fijian Bible as "Ko iko, Na *vanua,* na *vanua,* na *vanua,* mo rogoca na vosa i Jiova." When Rev. Serewai uttered the verse, he was speaking as a lotu authority, his subject was the vanua's relationship to God, and his audience was the matanitu (government). Thus the three prominent metacultural strands of Fijian public life were woven together in his performance. Further, the speech circulated beyond its context of performance because it was recorded on a cassette tape, and the Roko Tui Kadavu then played the tape in various villages when he traveled, including once in Solodamu and twice on a tour of inspection at the villages of Dravuni and Nukuvou. In these latter cases, the Roko Tui Kadavu, a man who conjoined both matanitu and vanua authority because he held a government appointment and also came from a traditional chiefly lineage, was replaying public speech from a lotu authority.

Lotu and vanua are mobilized as emblems of indigenous Fijian identity. They are not politically neutral. Lotu affiliation—that is, being Christian—is a politically significant marker separating indigenous Fijians from Indo-Fijians, most of whom are Hindu and Muslim. As I describe in chapter 6, coups spur the circulation of discourse about Fiji being a Christian nation where only Christians belong. Vanua is the ultimate marker of difference, however, because most indigenous Fijians are considered to have a true homeland within Fiji, a vanua that they come from based on patrilineage as well as a vanua that they are related to through their mother's patrilineage, and this distinguishes them from Indo-Fijians, who do not have ancient territorial links in the islands. One night, around the time of the joking debate described in chapter 4—a time when people were tense, expressing their frustrations with the national election results—someone referred to an Indo-Fijian politician as an "Indian from Ba" (*kai Idia mai Ba;* Ba is a province in Vitilevu). Someone else "corrected" him by responding curtly that the man was an "Indian from India" (*kai Idia mai Idia*). Indians, the joker implied, could not be recognized as being "from Fiji."

The Threatened Vanua

The vanua's permanent foundation as Fijians' homeland, given to them by God, is said to be threatened by Indian rapacity. That is, Indo-Fijians are said to be greedily looking to take over native Fijian lands. Discourse about the vanua being threatened has circulated for a long time in Fiji, however, and Indo-Fijians are not the first group to fill the role of dangerous outsider. In June 1839 the Methodist missionary John Hunt wrote grimly, "The Feejeeans are men of strong passions and exceeding proud, suspicious and covetous, their pride is seen in their Independent haughty spirit, their covetousness, in their desire to possess our property and their suspicion in their willingness to believe that we are come to possess ourselves of their land and riches" (quoted in Thornley 2000: 84). Mary Wallis (1851: 255), a trader's wife, reported in the early 1850s that Fiji's future paramount chief, Ratu Cakobau, "said that he was not willing to receive" French missionaries "because by and by they would take possession of the lands of Feejee, as they had done at Tahiti." Besides the English and French, another group considered rapacious in the

nineteenth century was the Tongans, who were conquering the Lau Islands of eastern Fiji (see Cargill 1977; France 1969; Routledge 1985;
Scarr 1984). The greedy foreigner is thus a long-standing stereotype in
Fiji. Ilaitia Tuwere (2002: 174) notes, "Fijian fear (potential or real) of
the dominance and superiority of migrant race(s) in their own land is
not new. They have lived with it since their first contact with the outside
world."

During the 1860s, when white settlers were growing in strength and
determined to nail down land claims while they had the chance, they
forcefully attempted to show Fijians that "sold" land was not recover-
able. Here it is worth quoting Peter France (1969: 41) at length:

At many plantations Fijians were unwelcome. Imported labour were drilled and
armed to protect the property of the European owners. Trespassing notices became common. The exclusive nature of European rights to land was emphasized
by the refusal to allow Fijians to tread on the soil which they had alienated.

Relations between the races worsened as segregation became more widespread. Sales of land became increasingly provocative of friction as Fijians began
to assert claims against each other and then to sell the disputed areas. This left
the purchaser with at least one group of disaffected neighbours. A state of open
hostility gradually developed in areas where chiefs sold occupied lands to
planters without the consent of the occupants; when the settler went into possession his plantations were destroyed, his cattle speared, or his house burned.
As the planters grew in strength and could call on armed support, Fijian reac-
tions became more violent.

Reading such a description, one suspects that the vanua developed as a
sacred space in such violent contexts. That is, when land became an object of violent struggle—and was characterized as something that could
be lost, perhaps permanently—it could become a resonant emblem of
traditional practices and a focus of ritual attention.

Struggles over land took new forms under British colonial policy. The
biggest challenge facing Fiji's first British governor, Sir Arthur Gordon,
was not a restless native population, but the white settlers who had
begun founding plantations more than a decade before Gordon's arrival.
In the face of settler opposition, Gordon insisted that Fijians be guarded
against economic entanglement, kept in their villages, and barred from
selling their lands (France 1969; Kelly 2004). Early settlers, generally unable to contract Fijian labor, preferred to hire Solomon Islanders or Van-
uatuans, or, "if this proved too expensive, they were careful to employ
Fijians remote from their estates so that the labour force would be free
from the influence (and lack the protection) of their relatives" (France

1969: 39; see also Derrick 1946: 168–176). Gordon succeeded in securing land ownership in the hands of subclans, and these groups retain more than 80 percent of all land in the nation inalienably to this day. Not all of this land is useful, however; Ralph Premdas (1995: 26) notes that "less than 10 per cent . . . is cultivable" (see also Lal 2004: 272; Ravuvu 1991: 77). Moreover, due to Gordon's efforts at "protecting" Fijians, they were largely excluded from the colony's sugarcane-based economic development. One result of this history of alienation and marginalization is the stereotype held by indigenous Fijians that Indo-Fijians are devoted to moneymaking and, given the opportunity, will find a way to take possession of indigenous lands.

As I showed in chapter 1, Methodist missionaries also contributed to indigenous Fijians' sense that the vanua was threatened and diminishing, for example, by displaying globes on which Fiji was as small as "the dung of a fly." Some missionaries threatened the vanua more actively than this, however. One chairman of the Fiji Methodist mission, William Moore, bought and sold land in the 1860s even though this was against the mission's own rules (see Thornley 2002: 368–374). His fellow missionary Jesse Carey (1867–1874: 273–275), riled by Moore's actions, wrote in October 1869:

We cannot help fearing that great and terrible evil, which will culminate in a war of races, is even now arising out of the Land Question here. . . . We cannot but fear that great and terrible evil is coming upon this unhappy country—evil which will have here (as it has already had elsewhere) the most disastrous effects upon the natives, upon our countrymen, upon ourselves, &, above all, upon the Cause of God. And, fully believing that among the causes which are bringing this evil to pass, & chief among those causes, is the acquisition of land by white men, we are of opinion that it is highly inexpedient for us, as Missionaries, to hold any lands in Fiji, excepting for Mission purposes.

Carey expected a "war of races" grounded in Fijians' intense anxieties about losing the vanua. In a sense, the coups d'état of 1987 and 2000 validated Carey's prediction of more than a century earlier—not because the coups were really aimed at preserving the vanua, but because much indigenous Fijian public discourse justified them in these terms.

Over the course of the nineteenth century, then, the vanua developed into something considered threatened and worth fighting to recover. Martha Kaplan (2004: 164–165) has written, "Property rights themselves—or at least ethnic-Fijian land ownership—became sacralized in ethnic Fijians' eyes through the workings of the [colonial lands] commissions," and although this is a significant part of the story, it is not the only part. The codification of social groups and landowning rights shaped people's understandings of the vanua as something powerful—something with mana—as well as something under threat; but many nongovernmental groups also acted decisively in this drama, including Tongan warriors, rapacious settlers, Methodist missionaries, and rival Fijian chiefs.

THE VANUA IN MODERN POLITICAL DISCOURSE

In the context of modern political turbulence, with indigenous Fijians vying among themselves for power while identifying Indo-Fijians as the source of national troubles, the term *vanua* appears prominently in official statements. Two examples from rather different sources illustrate the vanua's prominence in public discourse and its investiture with emotional significance.

Less than two weeks after the May 2000 coup, a document was circulated to Fijian Affairs Board officials with an introductory letter from the general manager of the Native Land Trust Board. This remarkable document, titled the "Deed of Sovereignty" in its English translation, tried to define indigenous Fijians' position in the chaotic atmosphere of postcoup Fiji. The authors borrowed the language of Fiji's Deed of Cession, which had given the islands to Queen Victoria over 125 years earlier; in 2000 they tried to reclaim the vanua rhetorically. Here are three remarkable excerpts, two from the preamble and one from the resolutions:

. . . WHEREAS we the Taukei through the concept of Vanua (the chiefs, our tribes, their land, their waters and seas and other possessions) and Veivakaturagataki (chiefly system) are by custom, tradition and practice united for a common purpose and destiny to protect and promote our rights for the benefit of the Taukei [landowners, i.e., indigenous Fijians], their future generations and other peoples.[1]

. . . WHEREAS . . . the survival of our Vanua as a unit being paramount and necessary . . .

THAT we do take back the possession of our full sovereignty and dominion of our people and Vanua wherever it may have been ceded and or assigned or exercised.[2]

Defining the vanua expansively as "the chiefs, our tribes, their land, their waters and seas and other possessions," the authors cast the vanua in the role of something both previously lost and currently threatened. They characterize the vanua's "survival" as the key to indigenous Fijian survival generally, implying that the vanua is being attacked and needs to be rescued. They also declare that they are reclaiming the vanua, adding the qualification, "wherever it may have been ceded." The document oozes anxiety: anxiety about the loss of land, the loss of tradition, the loss of power. But it is hardly a lament. In fact, it sounds like a call to arms.

The second example comes from a sermon given by Ratu Josaia Veibataki, whose Christmas sermon at Tavuki was the subject of extended analysis in chapter 3. In a sermon at Namuana village in October 1998, Veibataki spoke provocatively of the vanua not belonging to indigenous Fijians:

This vanua is not ours. The meaning of that is: we are, we are like, we are counted as the foreigners who are in our vanua [i.e., Indo-Fijians]. They lease [the land]. Its meaning is, your living in this world, you will not live forever. There is a time you will return to Him.

Veibataki's comparison of indigenous Fijians to Indo-Fijians was a daring one. Although he did not say so explicitly, his words seemed calculated to arouse anxieties about the loss of the vanua. What could be a bolder and more unsettling statement, in indigenous Fijian terms, than "This vanua is not ours"? Then, in a neat rhetorical trick, Veibataki explained that he meant that life on earth was impermanent, and every person (actually, "you") will have to leave this vanua to go to a different place in the afterworld. In this segment of his sermon, he expressed a standard Christian theme—God's judgment of the dead and assignment of them to heaven or hell—but inflected it with emotional urgency by appealing to Fijian fears of the loss of their land. Another way to deny most people's ownership of the vanua is to attribute all ownership to the ancestors and elders, as a Kadavuan man told the German anthropologist Michael Dickhardt (2000: 264; my translation): "You don't have a vanua, you don't have soil. . . . Because the owners are those who are long dead, along with those who will be there in a few years. . . . You are just using it."

The vanua is conceptually linked to soil through ideas of enduring landownership: people belonging to a place and a place belonging to people because of long and intimate connection. As Asesela Ravuvu (1983: 76) puts it, "For a vanua to be recognised, it must have people living on it and supporting and defending its rights and interests. A land without people is likened to a person without [a] soul" (see also Abramson 2000; Turner 1988; Tuwere 2002; Williksen-Bakker 1990; Young

2001). Examining texts such as the collected writings of Ratu Sukuna, Fiji's revered soldier and statesman of the first half of the twentieth century, one sees moments in which soil and vanua are essentially equated (e.g., Sukuna 1983: 204, 214).

Soil is conceptually linked to the vanua in multiple ways. Synecdochically, it can represent a larger territory and can therefore be "surrendered." An old Fijian ritual of surrender was the *soro ni qele,* or presentation of a basket of earth from the vanquished to the victor "signifying submission to the chiefs of the land" (Derrick 1946: 27; see also Deane 1921: 72; France 1969: 50; Thornley 2000: 145). An early missionary observer described it as "generally connected with war . . . presented by the weaker party, indicating the yielding up of their land to the conquerors. Sometimes, however, the ceremony may be an expression of loyalty by parties whose fealty is suspected" (Williams 1982: 31). Metonymically, soil can represent the ancestors' bodies, which spilled into the earth and returned to dust long ago. By extension, it can represent ancestors' unsavory aspects, such as their anti-Christian aggression. Thus, like the vanua generally, soil has (or is) mana. Accordingly, soil can be a site of spiritual warfare, as I describe later, in the section on chain prayers. Conversely, it can serve as a positively valued symbol of continuity or permanence. Tuwere (2002: 144) relates one man's tale of "baskets of earth taken by the people of Wailevu when they moved from their old village to the new. The earth from the old village was to ensure continuity of blessing, mana, and the presence of the gods in their new village." Sacrality is apparently easiest to recognize when it has been lost or violated, but positive instances such as Tuwere's example show how a dynamic of blessing and curse, punishment and benefit, works itself symbolically through Fijian soil.

Pursuing the topic of soil's metaphysical associations while drinking kava one night with friends, I asked a man about soil's importance. He began to say that Indo-Fijians wanted it—they wanted to own land in Fiji—and that this was both reprehensible and impossible. I wasn't surprised by his answer but sought a different line of discussion, so I asked why the minister took soil from house foundations after chain prayer rituals. He answered that taking the soil was an act of taking away the "errors" or "sins" (*cala*) of the ancestors (*qase*). This explanation resonated with what another young man, a non-Kadavuan resident in Tavuki, said at a chain prayer: that the earthen house foundation contained "devils" (*tevoro*). These devils might be ancestral figures, or perhaps nonkinsfolk who were buried in the house foundation long ago (see Tuwere 2002: 137); in either case, they were non-Christian spiritual forces, and they were dangerous.[3] When I asked Rev. Serewai about soil, he responded that it was "important" (*bibi*, lit., "heavy") because the elders are buried in it. In 2003 I asked Rev. Tuilovoni why soil needed to be cleansed ritually, and he gave a fuller answer. First, he said, humankind was made from soil, as stated in the book of Genesis. Second, in the old days, when Fiji was cannibal country, much blood was shed; spilling into the soil, the blood made it "filthy" (*dukadukali*). Third, he noted that if someone wanted to practice "witchcraft" (*vakate-voro*), he could pour kava onto the earth. Yet another explanation of soil's importance was given to me by a Nagonedau man. His first two statements were similar to the minister's: God built Adam from soil, and ancestors fought over it. (This second reason seems to be both a reflection and a cause of soil's importance.) Third, he explained, the earth was created before everything else, according to the Bible's story of creation in Genesis: before water, before animals, before humankind, land was brought into being.

When I asked directly about soil's mana, people gave broad answers. Once, when I asked a chief about soil's mana, he responded that it was "precious" (*mareqeti*), explaining, "because soil can result in death" (*baleta ni qele e rawa ni yaco ke na mate*). He meant that arguments over land could result in lethal fighting, or perhaps that stolen land would curse the thief, as suggested by what he said next: "If some [people] come and want to take someone's land just as they please, it can cause death. That's one reason I say that soil is a very heavy thing" (*Ke so i na lako mai ka via taura vakaveitalia na nona qele i dua na tamata, i na rawa ni na yaco ke na mate. Kacei i dua na ere au tukuna ni ere bibi sara ke na qele*). The same man also said that he saw in the Bible how the ancient Israelites "really cared for soil a lot" (*dau vamareqeta na qele . . . valevu sara ga*).

Because old village sites and earthen house foundations are places imbued with mana of the ancestors who lie within, they may be particularly dangerous. Such dangers are variably weighted, however; some may be dealt with cursorily, and others may be considered too daunting to deal with at all. Two examples illustrate this point. First, in April 1999 I helped a woman and a young man gather red ginger for decorations for a festive occasion. The red ginger grew in Tavuki's old village site, an uninhabited place cloaked in silence, still marked with stones at the edges of house foundations. When we arrived at the site, the woman leading us called aloud, "Good morning [polite]. We request flowers"

(*Ni sa yadra. Keimami sa kere senikacu*). In passing an old foundation, she called out "Excuse me" (*Julou*) a few times—the sort of thing one would do if living humans were sitting there. Finally, in leaving the old village site, she called out, "Thanks for the flowers" (*Vinaka na senikacu*). These simple acts of recognition presumably negated any spiritual threat we faced in treading on the earth of the ancient village and plucking flowers within its borders. However, other sites may be considered much more threatening. I once expressed an interest in visiting a different old village site, and two men in Tavuki advised me against it, even though I had the landowner's permission. (In fact, I had originally been invited to see the site by a member of the old village's descendants.) The day that I was supposed to go torrential rain poured out of the sky, so I was unable to go, and the Methodist minister interpreted this as divine intervention.

Because soil is imbued with mana, disturbing it can have bad consequences. For example, when a Tavuki man fell ill in March 1999, he believed that his illness had been caused by his digging up earth for the placement of electrical wires. In such cases, both the lotu and the vanua may be called upon to help, and indeed the man asked the Methodist minister to help rectify his violation of taboo, but he also had a feast of pork and taro prepared to mollify the ancestors. Such a conciliatory presentation of food or kava is called a *madrali* (see Spencer 1941: 57–66; Williams 1982: 230–231). The landscape's mana extends from soil to living things, especially certain trees that are considered spiritual haunts (see, e.g., Deane 1921: 33; Hashimoto 1989: 13–14; Quain 1948: 176; Tippett 1944: 293–294). In a story told to me in the late 1990s, said to have occurred a few years earlier, the Public Works Department was building the road into Tavuki. A large coconut tree stood in the proposed roadway, so the bulldozer driver rammed it repeatedly to knock it down. But the tree would not fall, and the PWD workers recognized this oddity as a spiritual problem. They asked the local landowning group to give a *madrali* to placate the ancestral deity. After the *madrali* was offered, the bulldozer went back to work. The tree promptly fell.

A similar event unfolded during my stay in Tavuki. When it came time to build an extension on the catechist's house, kava was presented to the head of the relevant landowning group so that a tree could be cut down for the house posts. The landowner accepted the kava, but at the time it was not pounded and drunk. When the tree was cut with a chainsaw, so deeply that it should have fallen, it nonetheless refused to topple over. (Although I was in the village at this time, I was not an eyewitness to these

FIGURE 9. Building an extension to the catechist's house in
Tavuki, 1999.

events.) When people saw this, I was told, they went back to the
landowner and actually drank the kava with him. In this version of the
generic tree-won't-fall tale, the consumption of kava was key to recognizing the vanua's mana—that is, the effectiveness of the landscape itself—
and, by extension, the power of the ancestors. When people returned to
the tree after drinking the kava, they tried again. Down it came.

Considering the vanua's significance—as diminished and threatened
space, object of supposed Indo-Fijian desire, sacred and taboo site,
source of effectiveness—knowledge of borders and proper ownership
has deep implications. As noted in chapter 2, the supposed loss of the

knowledge of proper landownership is one sign of the fall from a golden age. Once, when a Methodist Church–appointed estimator visited Tavuki to assess the worth of all the land the Church owned in the area (he was doing this throughout Fiji), it was discovered that in 1890 a certain patch of land in a village near Tavuki had been given to the Church. At some point this fact had become obscured, however, and now a man had his house on the land. The minister told me that two of the man's children had died. "Just my thoughts" (*Noqu vakasama ga*), he said, hedging his speculation, but there might be a connection between this man's taking Church land and his children's deaths. The irony is that landownership is such an emotional issue that when they learned that the Church owned the land, no one told the man about it; presumably it was too difficult a subject to broach.

Disagreements over landownership, and over who should receive payment for use of the land, occurred in Kadavu during my period of research. In deference to local sensitivities, I prefer not to discuss these cases here. Certain disputes from elsewhere in Fiji are known nationally, however. For example, landowners from the Suva peninsula have repeatedly but unsuccessfully requested compensation from the government for their land's alienation in the late nineteenth century (Miyazaki 2004). Another well-known case is the Nasomo landowners' protests of the Emperor Gold Mining Company's lease of their land (Emberson-Bain 1994: 207–209). Some land disputes have been encouraged or energized by the coups, such as the events at the Monasavu hydroelectric station (Robertson and Sutherland 2001) and Nadi International Airport.[4] Martha Kaplan (2004: 177), describing an attempted takeover of the Fiji Water bottling plant, writes of ethnonationalists' desires "to synchronize the national takeover and local takeovers."

Soil is thus an integral part of the vanua, and the vanua partakes in all of the rich significance of threat, curses, and loss balanced by promise, blessings, and growth that are metaphorically read into the soil. The sense that land acts *upon* people — that land is an agent that can affect humans, that land is mana — is expressed metaphorically, as reported by Michael Dickhardt from Levuka, on the south coast of Kadavu: "In my respondents' statements, [the vanua] appeared as something alive (*e dua na ere bula*, a living (*bula*) thing (*ere*)), as something possessing *mana* . . . as something with ears (*taliga*) for hearing (*rogo*) and eyes (*mata*) for vision (*rai*) . . . even as something that could bite (*katjia*) in the sense of a punishment for particular forms of transgression" (2000: 260; translation from the German by Mark Ashley).

Chain Prayers

Methodist missionaries in Fiji did not erase beliefs in ancestral spirits, but revalued these spirits as "devils" and "demons" by using the phonologically shifted words *tevoro* and *jimoni*. In doing so, they helped create a sense of historical rupture between a dangerous past and a present that has to engage with, and defuse, dangers from that past. Like the Ewe (Ghana) deliverance ritual described by Birgit Meyer (1999: 214), Fijian chain prayers are returns to the past and also ruptures with it, attempts to extinguish the past's influence on the present. They are also rituals in which soil's semiotic potential is exploited. Non-Christian ancestors lie unquietly in their graves, coming back through curses and interrupting people's lives in the present. To defeat them, people must cleanse the soil of house foundations through prayer.

In Fiji talk of ancestral spirits is quietly present. Indirection is a general feature of Fijian address—it is respectful to address people using kin terms or house-foundation names, for example, rather than their first names—and rules of indirection apply to spiritual beings as well. Richard Katz (1993: 138, 252) notes that an elderly healer referred to original ancestral figures (*vu*) as " 'someones' and 'others,' " and children called them "those things." One learns about spiritual figures, and sometimes their names, in informal contexts such as conversations at nightly kava-drinking sessions. These invisible beings become frightening when they curse living people. As I argued in chapter 2, curses frighten people because the ancestors are still effective and sometimes malicious; they have power that living people lack, but, because they are not Christian, these spirits can be dangerous sources of affliction. Spiritually caused suffering is manifest in symptoms such as sickness, poverty, lack of education, difficulty getting married or having children, and general failure to prosper.

In 1996 I observed healing rituals for a girl whose father was worried that she was possessed by a demon. The first round of healing that the Methodist minister conducted was a prayer session, and the second round was a chain prayer. In the following sections I describe the different kinds of chain prayers conducted in Tavuki and analyze the speech used in one particular case, showing how God's agency was consistently requested and invisible malefactors were referred to ambiguously. Ultimately, indeterminate presences were only jabbed at pronominally, poked with the unsteady weapon of deictic language. In casting humans as powerless actors, I argue, chain prayers perpetuate a sense of loss and give demons new life. Moreover, once unleashed, discursive demons may confound even their authors. Ambiguous language can heighten people's awareness of the risks they confront and compel future ritual practices.

A CRISIS AND ITS DEMANDS

On Wednesday, July 24, 1996, Rev. Serewai told me about a young girl from Solodamu village, fifteen or sixteen years old, who was suffering a peculiar illness. Her illness began while she was at school and was serious enough that she was taken to the island's hospital at Vunisea. The doctor found nothing wrong with her, and she was taken home. She spent the night awake, apparently hysterical, screaming and spitting. Sending the catechist to investigate, Rev. Serewai joked that if the girl's affliction was caused by a "devil," he and I would go to Solodamu to cast the devil out.

The joke grew serious in a hurry. The information Rev. Serewai received from the catechist must have been disturbing, for the next day, he and I and a young Tavukian man went to see the afflicted girl. Arriving at the house where she lay ill, we were welcomed with a round of kava. Including Rev. Serewai and me, twenty people were present: thirteen men, five women, and two children. The sick girl, Venina (this is a pseudonym), lay on a bed at the extreme "high" end of the house.

After the first round of kava drinking, Venina's father described the girl's condition: she had not slept beginning on Sunday, continuing through Monday, Tuesday, and now, late Wednesday afternoon. She had not eaten either, until the catechist prayed for her earlier that day and she drank some tea and ate some biscuits. She now lay in bed, mute and glassy-eyed. Venina's father spoke of a "demon," worried that an evil agent was afflicting his family.

After discussion and further kava drinking, Rev. Serewai devised his plan to reach Venina through her silence and haunted stare. I was told to sit on the other side of the room and say "Hello, Venina" (*Bula, Venina*). This was a simple act of recognition, and like most such acts of recognition in Fiji, needed to be recognized in return (Toren 1990: 95–96). So Venina was prompted by someone to respond "*Bula*, Matthew," and she did. Later Rev. Serewai explained to me that he saw her utterance as a "gap" in which he could operate. She was evidently cognizant, and now he could try to begin healing her.

The minister respectfully crawled on his hands and knees up to her bed. Touching Venina gently on her head, rearranging her blanket and the shoulder of her shirt, he quietly asked her several questions. One of his questions was whether she knew who he was, and she responded correctly, *"Talatala qase"* (superintendent minister). Another "gap": she recognized him personally. The chance for effective action was now at hand: Rev. Serewai asked for his special woodblock-covered Bible. The catechist pushed it toward him. Then, facing the wall by the foot of Venina's bed, the minister spoke for several minutes on James 5:13–20, passages concerning affliction and the healing effects of prayer. Because this passage asserts the authority of "the elders of the church," Rev. Serewai's discussion of it can be interpreted as a mild rebuke of Venina's parents for not asking him for help earlier. (Later that night he told me that an earlier remedy attempted for the sick girl had been a traditional leaf remedy, which he disparaged.)[5]

Then he opened the Bible, laid it on Venina's head, and prayed. People closed their eyes, and when Rev. Serewai had finished his prayer, all uttered "Amen" (*Emeni*). The minister added a formulaic second closure to the prayer, and the audience murmured "Amen" again. The ceremony ended, the minister returned on his knees to his sitting place, we all proceeded to drink kava, and within a few minutes Venina had risen from bed and gone to drink tea. The minister outlined a plan of action: Venina's parents were to pray during the upcoming week, in the early morning and in the evening, and to fast on Wednesday from 5 A.M. until noon. At noon they were to break their fast and await our arrival.

When next Wednesday arrived (July 31) Venina was still suffering. Rev. Serewai, the catechist Tomasi Laveasiga, and I returned to Solodamu to address the lingering danger. Specifically, we went to perform a chain prayer. Before the ritual began, Venina's parents explained what had happened during the past week, including a trip to the hospital they had taken the previous day, where a doctor had given Venina an injection and sleeping pills. The doctor had told the parents not to believe in the devil, but to keep praying. Then Rev. Serewai gave instructions for the ritual we were about to perform. The group was divided into four teams of prayer givers: Venina, her classificatory sister (father's brother's daughter), and the catechist; Venina's father and mother; Venina's father's younger brother and his wife; and Rev. Serewai, Solodamu's village pastor, and me. These four teams were to circulate counterclockwise among four sites, spending fifteen minutes at each site. Two sites were the extended family's houses, wherein prayers were offered; the other two were rest sites, located outdoors but still on the family's land. When teams were inside the houses, they were to pray on specific subjects: the house, the land, and all those associated with the place (including the deceased); Venina; and the education of the children of Solodamu.

These subjects were linked conceptually through notions of ancestral power's location in specific areas of soil, particularly in earthen house foundations. The demon afflicting Venina might have been one of her forebears, and its influence would be vibrant in the foundation.[6] Furthermore, one of Venina's great-grandfathers had declared that no child of Solodamu would become educated. Present-day villagers were distressed to find his words—an implicit curse?—coming true. His declaration haunted this family in an especially frightening and tragic way: not only was Venina afflicted at a time when important school exams were coming up for her, but her classificatory brother had recently died accidentally just before he was to go to England for advanced study. This was part of the reason why Venina's father feared a demon's influence on his family. Thus these prayer themes articulated tightly with each other: a force from the past was afflicting people in the present, and the malice was localized in the soil.

The night was dark and rainy, which added to the gothic atmosphere at Solodamu. The four teams circled the ring of sites twice, for a total of two hours' worth of prayer and rest segments. We prayed on the designated subjects for fifteen minutes at one site, then moved to the next site to rest for fifteen minutes, rotating along the chain. At the conclusion of the second cycle, we gathered in the grandfather's house and Rev. Serewai prepared to finish the ceremony.

An open Bible sat on the floor, and the minister laid his woodblock-covered Bible atop it. On top of the two Bibles, he placed a pink plastic bag containing soil that had been gathered from the family's burial ground and each of the four corners of the two houses we had prayed in. Kneeling with his body upright, he lifted the woodblock-covered Bible and the bag of soil atop it. Then he prayed, eyes closed. (I peeked to see if everyone followed suit. All sat cross-legged with eyes shut, except for one young man and Venina herself.) This marked the end of the chain prayer, but not the end of the evening. We drank kava, and when the drinking was finished the minister offered one last prayer for the evening. Later he explained to me (in English), "You must finish with one prayer, not finish with a grog party." We carried home food given by Venina's family in thanks for the service. Rev. Serewai also carried home the pink plastic bag of soil, kept it in his house for a week, then emptied it out.

Having witnessed this haunting event—a girl afflicted by a demon in the dark, rain-soaked night, her defenders treading the soil and praying to heal her with God's power—I was surprised to hear that Rev. Serewai had begun holding chain prayers regularly each month when I returned to Tavuki in September 1998. But, it turned out, these were chain prayers of a very different sort from the one just described. The minister explained that he had begun doing this the previous year for several reasons: the coming elections which were to be held in May 1999, the schoolchildren's coming exams, and the approaching year 2000, that great fosterer of anxieties. He did not explain further, but I interpreted his answer to mean that these future events were potential challenges to Kadavuan well-being, and that the chain prayers would build up protective power.[7]

These monthly rituals were not entirely at the minister's initiative. The Methodist Church in Fiji publishes an annual calendar, authored by a minister named Apete Toko, and in 1998 and 1999 it suggested that congregations should conduct chain prayers to prepare for the year 2000 (Lotu Wesele e Viti kei Rotuma 1998, 1999). Thus Rev. Serewai, in instituting monthly chain prayers, was following suggestions from headquarters. The institutionalized chain prayers in Tavuki took place on the last night of each month, from 6 P.M. to midnight, with different people arriving sequentially at the church to perform focused rituals at designated times. In Tavuki a list was drawn up before the chain prayers took place, specifying which household was to show up at the church at what time. If a designated household did not show up to participate in the chain prayer, it was the catechist's responsibility to pray in their place. If members of the household did arrive at their appointed time, they entered the church and prayed on the topics listed.[8] The topics at these monthly chain prayers adhered to the Methodist Church calendar's suggestions and consistently designated the lotu and the vanua as subjects for prayer.

Formally, these public monthly chain prayers resembled private chain prayers in certain respects. First, human mobility was an essential part of the ritual: people needed to move to a designated site to pray. Second, topics were written down for prayer givers to refer to. Third, prayers addressed common themes of prosperity and children's education. In other respects, however, these monthly prayers were profoundly different from chain prayers such as Venina's: they were not motivated by immediate crises; there was no capstone ceremony finalizing the event, and so soil was not dug up for devils to be expelled; and kava was not drunk at a common base point as part of the proceedings.

Because of these differences, the institutionalized chain prayers withered on the vine. In March 1999 no end-of-month chain prayer was held because March 31 was part of Easter week. But then April 30 too seems to have passed without a chain prayer; at least my field notes neglect to mention one. In early June I realized that none had been held on May 31 either, so I asked the catechist why. He said that everyone had forgotten. As institutionalized monthly rituals, chain prayers were something the entire village could forget about. The danger was not real enough; the risks were not compelling. Potential difficulties in the future might mildly unsettle people, but hazards of the past—curses from ancestors, afflictions from demons—were what made people move.

I have not been able to trace a precise historical lineage for the development of chain prayers as Methodist rituals, but the ethnographic literature suggests possible influences. The ritual practice of treading on particular patches of soil goes back at least to the nineteenth century. Consider this colonial government report, written by an assistant commissioner in 1883, describing how a Fijian prophet named Navosavakadua honored villagers' requests for immortality:

When a community desired the promised blessings they sent a messenger to beg the tuka or gift of immortality. If the request was granted a body of so-called soldiers was sent, who by treading the ground of the place and performing certain ceremonies conferred the boon.

Thus it was at Udu; by treading the ground there and filing through every house in the village, they gave immortality to the inhabitants and the promise of the resurrection of their ancestors.

The latter is greatly desired by all the old Natives, as it is by it they hope to regain what they consider their ancient power and prestige. (Quoted in Kaplan 1995: 112)

The description of entering houses, of mobilizing human bodies to engage with different points in the landscape, resonates with the chain prayers I observed. The fascinating thing about this report is that it described the actions of a prophet who explicitly cast himself in Christian terms: for Navosavakadua, the Bible was a Fijian document and Jesus and Jehovah were Fijian figures (Kaplan 1990a, 1990b, 1995). Such claims offended the British authorities, who exiled the prophet. Navosavakadua's followers were sent to Kadavu in 1891, ultimately spending ten years at Korolevu village in Naceva district before being allowed to go home.

Another likely influence on the development of chain prayers is traditional healing practice as described by Becker (1995), Katz (1993), and

Ravuvu (1983). Katz quotes a healer on his work method: "The patients bring in their [kava] then, and when they are here, I make a list of all of them and their problems. Each helper gets the list. I call out the number of the patient, and my helpers and I concentrate our thoughts on giving the patient a healing" (130). Note the three strong parallels between the healer's description of traditional curing and the form of chain prayers: anchoring the ritual around kava, formulating a list of problems or dangers that need to be addressed, and then having the ritual leaders focus their energies on removing these difficulties. In Katz's account, however, the traditional healing practice is explicitly considered non-Christian by most villagers.

A probable third influence on chain prayers is the program of "spiritual warfare" designed by American evangelicals. Spiritual warfare is one element within the Christian movement that has been called "Third Wave evangelism" (Jorgensen 2005: 446), one of whose leading figures, Benny Hinn, led a wildly successful "miracles crusade" in Suva in January 2006. Briefly, practitioners of spiritual warfare believe that particular regions of the earth are dominated by evil spirits, and they argue that aggressive prayer at specific sites can defeat these spirits. Citing a leading theologian of spiritual warfare named C. Peter Wagner, Dan Jorgensen (2005: 457 n. 7) has observed, "A striking fascination with cadastral properties is revealed in the use of spiritually-mapped 'prayer walks,' 'prayer marches,' 'prayer journeys' and 'prayer expeditions' . . . circumambulation of settlements, and 'cardinal points prayer' " (see also DeBernardi 1999: 87). Although Fijian Methodism's thoroughgoing conservatism stands in contrast to Third Wave's charismatic exuberance, spiritual warfare's resonances with chain prayers are suggestive, specifically the emphases on mobility and prayer at specific sites to defeat localized indigenous spirits.[9]

THE LANGUAGE OF CHAIN PRAYERS

On January 29, 1999, I observed and participated in a private chain prayer at the house in Tavuki standing on an earthen foundation that I will give the pseudonym Vale. This was the home of a chief. The event began at 6 P.M. when Rev. Serewai, the catechist Tomasi Laveasiga, and I walked the short distance to Vale. Outside, Rev. Serewai and the chief engaged in small talk, and their conversation continued as we entered the house and sat in the communal room. In the hierarchical seating arrangement, Rev. Serewai and the chief sat "high"; sitting lower were the catechist, the chief's wife and daughter, his son-in-law, three young children, and I.

We had come because, the week before, the chief's wife had requested the Church's help. (Hereafter, I will call her the Radini, a female title.) She was in ill health; her leg bothered her particularly. Although it was never stated, I suspect that the children's maladies also prompted her to request the Church's assistance. One of the children, the son of the chief's daughter, was sick and lying with his head on a pillow, and another had received a nasty cut on her right eye a few weeks before, when a louvered windowpane fell on her. In asking the minister for help, the Radini did not specifically request a chain prayer, but that was the form of assistance that he delivered.

In the communal room at Vale, Rev. Serewai, thinking aloud, decided that there would be two bases in the chain prayer: one prayer site and one rest site. Eventually a bedroom was designated as the prayer site, and a separate building, the nearby cookhouse, which was quite large and often used for kava-drinking sessions, was designated as the rest site. Then, still thinking aloud, Rev. Serewai formulated and wrote down four topics for the prayer givers to address; my impression was that the designation of these topics had been discussed beforehand with the Radini. When he had finished writing, Rev. Serewai read the topics aloud, and the chief approved them. Here is a translation, with minor reformatting and punctuation changes:

1. The Vale dwelling
    —house foundation
    —those who live there
    —God's glory is asked to shine on it
2. The Honorable [Radini]
    —[her] illnesses
    —request God's salvation
3. The Honorable [Chief]
    —his responsibilities
    —work appointment/assignment
4. All the descendants
    —children
    —their study and work
    —God's help is requested

After outlining these prayer topics, Rev. Serewai began the proceedings by giving a short preparatory prayer, asking God to "permit" (*veivakadonuya*) the actions to follow. Then he read Matthew 5:38–48, from the Sermon on the Mount, wherein Jesus offers advice about loving one's enemies and turning the other cheek. Rev. Serewai discussed the passage, speaking of "our enemy" (*keda meca*) and "God's love" (*loloma ni Kalou*). He read Proverbs 14:27 ("The fear of the LORD is a fountain of life, to depart from the snares of death") and Proverbs 14:30 ("A sound heart is the life of the flesh: but envy the rottenness of the bones"), and he commented, "The soul will be healthy [when] the body is healthy" (*Ena bula na yalo, sa bula na yago*). These passages, suggesting the presence of an unspecified enemy and anticipating God's healing of the Radini, were introductory statements to the ritual action. They established in people's minds the fact that a common enemy afflicted them and that appealing to the Christian God was the appropriate form of engagement with such a dangerous force.

Rev. Serewai explained that the evening's ritual would conclude with the taking of soil from the Vale foundation to his own house. Then, announcing that it was time to begin, he went into the bedroom, a taboo space for outsiders. The catechist and I brought some kava roots and a kava bowl to the cookhouse, where the chief's daughter and son-in-law were waiting.

Eight people served as prayer givers that night: Rev. Serewai, the chief, the catechist (and I with him, to record him as he prayed), and the chief's wife, sister, daughter, and son-in-law. A little before 8:30, the catechist and I walked from the cookhouse to Vale and waited in the communal room while the son-in-law finished his prayer. When he was done, we entered the bedroom to begin our contribution, our link in the chain. Whereas the son-in-law had knelt in prayer, the catechist and I sat cross-legged in front of a small table that stood about two and a half feet high. Atop this table rested two Bibles, Rev. Serewai's woodblock-covered Bible and a softcover Bible that the catechist used in his readings that night, as well as a blank piece of paper, a pen, and the list of prayer topics.

The catechist chose Proverbs 19 as the text that would bracket the sections of his prayer. It is an assortment of admonitions, including "The fear of the LORD tendeth to life: and he that hath it shall abide satisfied; he shall not be visited with evil" (19:23). His prayer session took the following form:

1. Reading Proverbs 19:1–10, giving a short introduction and conclusion typical of all Bible readings, asking for God's blessing
2. Reading of the first topic, with a short introduction and conclusion
3. Prayer on the first topic
4. Reading Proverbs 19:11–20 with a short introduction

5. Reading of the second topic with a short introduction

6. Prayer on the second topic

7. Reading Proverbs 19:22–25 with a short introduction

8. Reading of the third topic with a short introduction

9. Prayer on the third topic

10. Reading Proverbs 19:26–29 with a short introduction and conclusion

11. Reading of the fourth topic with a short introduction

12. Prayer on the fourth topic. Only after this final prayer was "Amen" (*Emeni*) said.

In his prayer, the catechist adhered to the written topics; below, I describe the substance of what he said. When he finished the last part and we emerged from the bedroom, no one was waiting to replace us, but the chief's sister soon came to do so.

Back at the kava bowl, I asked the son-in-law why we were praying for the house foundation, and he replied that it was because there were "devils" in it. A few men, not participating in the chain prayer, came by the cookhouse to join in the kava drinking, showing that although the chain prayer was private—in the sense of being unpublicized and limited to family members, the religious leaders, and the anthropologist— the kava-drinking session itself was not closed to others. The catechist and I prayed once more that evening in the bedroom; that time, he chose Proverbs 22 as the Bible text interspersed between sections of his prayer. Eventually, around midnight, when it was time to conclude the chain prayer, the group of prayer givers all left the kava bowl and went back to Vale's communal room, where the evening had begun.

In their prayers, participants engaged with the dangers that had been listed beforehand. The strategy was to refer to an invisible malicious agent in ambiguous terms and to appeal to God for help. God is considered the ultimate effective agent, whose power alone can guide and protect people who are powerless to defend themselves against ancestral malefaction. In the first part of his prayer, addressing the topic of the Vale house foundation, the catechist prayed that God would shine divine light on the things that "fill up" the foundation:

[We] pray to you for the family's foundation, Vale, ask God to shine the light of the Holy Spirit thereupon. The things which fill it up are strong, the various people from particular places [vanua] included on the noble foundation.

The catechist used the term *vanua* in its sense of "people from particular places." In other words, the "strong" things filling up the house foundation were the ancestors, who came to Tavuki from elsewhere in Fiji, and now came to the present from the past. But which ancestors were they? Their precise identity was unstated, and at this point they were not confronted directly. Instead, God was asked to deal with them.

Later in the prayer's first section, the catechist restated the prayer topic and asked explicitly that the strength of the dangerous ancestors be neutralized:

This first topic is offered to you. [These] are some contemplations, some thoughts, some different kinds of decisions and plans to completely extinguish so those who eternally inhabit the top of this foundation are defeated or disturbed.

Dangerous ancestral power, the catechist was claiming, can be neutralized only by God. People should confront dangers by asking God for help, requesting that God render the lingering spirits "defeated or disturbed" from their place in the house foundation. In the second, third, and fourth parts of his prayer, the catechist addressed the weighty issue of traditional obligations and responsibilities. As in the first part, satisfactory resolution was entrusted to God's agency, not human agency.

The chain prayer at Vale concluded with an offering of soil from the house foundation and an oration and prayer given by Rev. Serewai. Beforehand, the chief's sister had gone to the four corners of Vale and taken a handful of soil from each; the soil had been placed in a white plastic bag carried by the daughter. After speaking briefly and offering a short prayer, Rev. Serewai instructed the chief on what to do with the bag of soil:

Please get ready for us to conclude it. The soil is here and it is asked that you take it and give it [to Rev. Serewai]. Then please give a short speech: Soil of the dwelling is given into the hand of the Church. It is asked that the enemy be weakened; it is also requested that life descend to the dwelling.

Here the afflicting agents reappeared, now referred to as "the enemy" (*na meca*); Rev. Serewai used the plural pronoun *ra* in reference to them. Later, when I asked the minister whom he meant by the enemy, he mentioned "people," "kin," and "devils" (*tamata, veiwekani, tevoro*). Note the ambiguity and possible overlap: the people afflicting the chiefly family might be devilish (non-Christian) kin. Still, the malefactors were not yet confronted directly. Whoever they were, they were approached only through a complex passive grammatical construction in which the chief was instructed to say that "it is asked [of God] that the enemy be weakened."

Taking the bag of soil and speaking briefly, and very softly, the chief followed Rev. Serewai's instructions and echoed the minister's use of passive voice verbs, asking that the soil be cleansed by God so that any "bad intentions" (*inaki baci*) in the soil would be removed, and thus stop afflicting people. This was a temporary symbolic surrender of vanua to lotu, as the chief gave his foundation's sacred soil to the minister. Rev. Serewai took the bag of soil, placed it atop his woodblock-covered Bible, and held a softcover Bible just above that, reading Deuteronomy 11:13–21, passages in which God promises prosperity to the faithful and punishment to the unfaithful. After this, the minister got on his knees and went over to the Radini, placed her right foot atop the woodblock-covered Bible, and laid the bag of soil next to it so that the Radini's toes rested on the bag. Finally, he draped the open softcover Bible, pages down, over her bandaged lower right leg. The afflicting agents (represented in and by the soil), the afflicted person (the Radini, and specifically her leg), and the cure's vector (the Bible, whose nature as material token became key here) were brought into conjunction.

Then, a sudden shift. After a short oration in which he declared, "We hope that everything will be carried on, that people will continue to pray, from time to time, that God will always come first, so that the great work we have just completed tonight will be effective and permanent," Rev. Serewai prayed. Here, in his final prayer, came the remarkable moment when the minister decided to confront danger directly, if only briefly. I quote this section at length so the reader may observe how he switched from addressing God to addressing an unidentified malefactor, and then back to God again. The part that is not addressed to God is in italics.

We hope that tonight will leave its mark. We return, return like the waves on the shore to find cleanliness, prosperity, and life. Please make the words of the prayers already offered mana. Please receive this offering of soil. It is with their spirits, their hopes [of the chief's family], and their belief that these things are possible for you, God. We hope this illness will be healed. *I order you tonight to leave this place in the name of Jesus the warrior of Nazareth, to free the legs of God's maidservant to attend to her family responsibilities,* however long the binding. Yes, we depend on you, God, please be so kind, please receive it, please touch it, please breathe on it, please eradicate this illness at its root so its strength is finished today.

The shift in address was not accompanied by any change in intonation, so the only indications that something profoundly different had occurred in the italicized section were the minister's use of the second-person singular pronoun *iko* and the direct command "I order" (*Au sa vakaroti*). These words were evidently not addressed to God; a minister would never use such presumptuous language in praying to Jehovah. (In addressing God, Rev. Serewai, like almost every speaker, used the plural pronoun *kemuni,* and he would never "order" Jehovah to do anything.) These remarkable lines were bracketed by a generic prayer to God, however, with no discourse markers signaling the shift in address before or after that moment.

So who was Rev. Serewai exorcising? Later, when I asked him whom he meant by "you" in this part of the prayer, he said that it was the "sickness" (*tauvimate*). I cannot resolve the term's ambiguity, for though I do not think he meant "sickness" in the Western medical sense, he did not explicitly mention people or devils, unlike his explanation of who the enemy was in his earlier instructions to the chief. In addition, the enemy was pronominally plural, whereas the "you" of *iko* is singular. It is possible that Rev. Serewai was politely deflecting my question in a way he thought would make sense to me. It is also possible that he himself was unsure of who "you" was. Although he was addressing some entity directly, the elusiveness of its identity during the ritual performance is suggestive: it seems that discursive demons are slipping slightly out of control. In attempting to control the force afflicting the chief's wife, Rev. Serewai could not name it at the moment he ordered it away—not because of a taboo on pronouncing its name, but perhaps because the exact agent was unknown. What was most striking about his addressing this invisible malefactor as "you," then, was its combination of precision and indeterminacy: it was a deictic form that pointed nowhere in particular. There was no doubt that "you" had caused the afflictions at Vale, but it was not clear—nor should it have been—who this "you" was.[10]

In such ambiguity, discourse can gain a malignant life of its own. There is little doubt that, in future crises, "you" will reappear. People, kin, devils, sickness: all might be implicated in dangers past and present and difficult to exorcise fully and finally. Their presence in Fijian discourse spurs the circulation of the fall-from-a-golden-age theme, as these menacing forces shape present-day misfortunes. In her consideration of ambiguity in a poetic text and its explication, Margaret Trawick (1988: 317) writes provocatively, "A habit of focusing upon ambiguity—not to

FIGURE 10. Spiritually cleansed soil in the Methodist
church grounds, Tavuki, 2003.

resolve it but to articulate it further—may help people to live in a plural
and changing world without either abandoning the past or retreating
into it, and also without becoming too solipsistically sane or, at the
other extreme, going mad." Rev. Serewai's ambiguity is such a strategy.
Indeed, he was fighting the past while simultaneously keeping it alive.
Although spirits might be mentioned in casual conversations around
kava bowls, ritual performances such as chain prayers are the sites where
the powers—and the elusiveness—of spirits are made into compelling
realities. In giving ancestors these powers, which can be defeated only
by God and not by humans, chain prayers create and re-create a pervasive sense of human powerlessness.[11]

Discourse about the ancestors and the threats they pose will be circulated in the future, remaining a social force in Tavuki. It is unlikely that the chain prayer held at Vale that night will be spoken of in public, however; it would be unseemly to refer to a family's private ritual so openly. The final chain prayer I observed, in fact, was almost hidden from me. One night in February 1999 I asked Rev. Serewai why he was dressed formally, and he reluctantly said that he was about to conduct a chain prayer. Chagrined, I said that I probably should not attend if it was a sensitive matter. But the minister told me to come along, so I did. It turned out that this was the fourth consecutive night on which this family had held a chain prayer (I had been traveling outside of Tavuki the previous nights); intriguingly, the woman who had requested Rev. Serewai's leadership had drawn up the list of prayer topics herself.

The next day I asked a friend why Rev. Serewai would have kept the chain prayer a secret from me, and he replied (in English) that it was a "secret mission," because it concerned the involved family's "curse." The curse, in my friend's opinion, was manifest in the fact that the family's parents had died, three of the four young adults were unmarried, and the married daughter was childless. In this final chain prayer, then, another curse was put to rest—and preserved, unintentionally, for future use.

When I returned to Kadavu in 2003 I was told of an elaborate ceremony that had taken place the previous Christmas in which families in Tavuki and Nagonedau brought soil from their house foundations to the church. I was told that this was not conducted as a chain prayer; it was a regular Methodist church service and had been prompted by the national Church's designation of November and December 2002 as months of "cleaning" (*veivakasavasavataki*). The superintendent minister, Rev. Setareki Tuilovoni, prayed over the soil inside the church so that it would be spiritually cleansed. After this, all of the soil was placed on a spot of ground near the church where a small wooden fence was built around it. Later, a concrete marker was laid there. The whole village was thereby symbolically cleansed, strengthened for the future by wiping away the sins of the past. The dangers of the past were neutralized through prayer and kept permanently within the Church's own patch of sacred soil.

PART THREE

Recuperation

In the early 1980s, the Fiji Visitors Bureau (1983) introduced a new slogan, "Fiji: The Way the World Should Be," and Pope John Paul II used the phrase during a visit to the islands in the middle of that decade (Fijilive 2005; Lal 2004: 262). Like many tourist slogans, it is meant to be commercially appealing and bears little relationship to what locals think about their own place. As I have shown in previous chapters, a sense of possible worlds is often subverted in indigenous Fijian discourse: not even Fiji is the way Fiji should be. The tourist slogan almost has a curious critical bite.

So what should the world be like, in Fijian terms? Describing an old ritual for invulnerability, *luveniwai*, Martha Kaplan (1989: 363) notes that it "was explicitly anticolonial," and quotes a manuscript on the subject in which A. M. Hocart wrote, "X once held out his clenched hand and said, 'Fiji is like this now: by and by it will be like this,' and he opened his hand, 'Now it is weak, presently it will be strong.' " X's claim is the leitmotif of Part 3 of this book. In displacing and transforming the old gods, Methodism set up a dynamic of light and darkness, power and loss. The "dark" old days were over, and society was enlightened by Christian virtue, but the potential for effective action is now diminished.

Links between the arrival of Christianity and the loss of power are not often made explicit in indigenous Fijian discourse; I have never heard anyone in Kadavu say that Christianity's ruptures have caused social weakness or decline (cf. Toren 1990: 102). But one author made these connections unambiguously in "A Native Fijian on the Decline of His Race," the translation of an indigenous Fijian's jeremiad that Hocart published in the *Hibbert Journal* in 1912. In it, the unnamed author claims that Jehovah is a god of spirit who delegates earthly matters to other authorities. He claims that Fiji's *kalou vu*, the ancestral founding gods, are the proper objects of worship for indigenous Fijians who wish for physical prosperity. Because he was writing at a time when Fiji had been decimated by epidemics of disease, the author's Manichaean sentiments are understandable, but he acknowledges, "[People] will say that I am one of the foolishest men" (Hocart 1912a: 86).

He is worth quoting at length for the way he recognizes a link between Christianization and the loss of mana, and also for his new vision of a reinvigorated Fiji:

Argument

The decline of native population is due to our abandoning the native deities who are God's deputies in earthly matters. God is concerned only with matters spiritual and will not hearken to our prayers for earthly benefits. A return to our native deities is our only salvation.

The Essay

. . . Well, how is Fiji? Do we abide by our customs which Jehovah gave us? Do we still follow our Vu [ancestral founding] Gods whom Jehovah gave to be our leaders or not? No, we have come to follow imported maxims, maxims let fall by the various destitute lands that keep entering into Fiji, to wit those lands that surely have no Vu Gods . . . and are not like Fiji, a land beloved of Jehovah, who gave them their land and its Vu Gods to return oracles and tell his vessel [i.e., the traditional priest] what must be done to burn down a village, or what must be done to save the country. Now, the words of power [Hocart gives the word *mana* here in a footnote] or the words of truth of the Vu God are due to Jehovah having given him the sovereignty of the body; I think it were hard for the Vu God's words to have power, if Jehovah had not previously approved of him as Vu God of the Fijians.

It is not clear to me, sir, whether there are at all Vu Gods in all countries or not? If any has not, then it is a weak and destitute land, and not like Fiji. . . .

But now that Fiji has by the introducers of Christianity been placed on the same level as various foreign lands, that our Vu Gods have come to be lightly set aside as a thing of nought, or have received the name of devil, that is the only cause that has brought about the increase of disease. . . .

. . . I know . . . that if Fiji returned to its proper constitutions according to the customs with which we were endowed, then would Fiji be justified, and it would be impossible that it should decline or infant deaths be many. But if the various countries of the world do not follow this path and yet are justified, no wonder since they have no Vu Gods. But for Fiji, it is a small land which Jehovah loves exceedingly; the proof of this is that when our respective districts in Fiji were created, they were created each with its own Vu. And if the Vu were placed at our head and we then went up together to our goal, to the Great God, to wit the Spirit God (Jehovah), there would be no still births and Fiji would then be indeed a people increasing rapidly. (Quoted in Hocart 1912a: 86, 92, 96–97; see also Hocart 1952: 7–8)

These passages convey a remarkable view of mana and how it might be recuperated. For the author, worship of the ancestral gods is an integral part of proper Christianity. Note how burning down a village, an old method of warfare, is characterized as a positive act if guided by the deities. Fiji's devastation by disease, the author writes, is the product of missionaries arriving from "destitute" lands to demonize the ancestral gods—which they, the missionaries, do not themselves have or therefore recognize—and Fijians' thenceforth ignoring the gods who are actually Jehovah's representatives. The author criticizes foreigners for their ignorance and presumption (Hocart notes wryly, "Whites pity Fijians, but they find reasons to pity us"; 1912a: 97 n. 2), but he also envisions a future in which indigenous Fijians thrive again. This future is a Christian one—Jehovah will be in charge—but a distinctively Fijian Christian one, in which ancestral deities of the vanua are the mediators between humankind and the ultimate God.

Some cultural changes are more durable than others: note how the author of "A Native Fijian on the Decline of His Race" characterizes Fiji as "a small land," which, as shown in chapter 1, is a conception brought to Fiji by Wesleyan missionaries that endures today. But he follows with the phrase "which Jehovah loves exceedingly." The matter of Jehovah's favor toward Fiji is central in these last two chapters, which show how laments for a lost golden age can motivate attempts at recuperation. When individuals see themselves as newly forceful, acting with increasing mana, the standard Fijian interpretation of Genesis 1:26 is reversed. When calls are made for Fiji to be a Christian state, the three paths of lotu, vanua, and matanitu draw together in a single sharp line.

CHAPTER 6

Onward Christian Soldiers

This chapter is an exploration of Christianity's role in Fiji's recent political upheavals. Building on the argument developed so far, I show that political violence has been meaningful to many indigenous Fijians because it has seemed like an effective response to the loss of mana. Despite descriptions of conflict, violence, and exclusion, this chapter is about recuperation, that is, attempts at recovery from perceived loss. When explaining why he executed independent Fiji's first coup in 1987, Sitiveni Rabuka explained, "There is only one reason for this coup, that is my apprehension that the time might come when the rule of our land and our soil might be taken and that in such future times our descendants might therefore be impoverished" (quoted in Kaplan 1990a: 140). His explanation might be considered misleading and self-serving in many ways, but to many indigenous Fijians it was emotionally convincing. Discourse about decline and loss is so vibrant, so vigorous and durable that it is itself generative and not merely reflective of people's sensibilities. Rabuka needed only to read the fall from a golden age into the future and to frame his actions as recuperative to effectively strike a resonant cultural chord for his many indigenous supporters.[1]

Rabuka's Coups

In April 1987 national elections saw the Labour Party's Timoci Bavadra take the post of prime minister away from Ratu Sir Kamisese Mara.

Ratu Mara, one of Fiji's most revered chiefs, had led Fiji since independence in 1970. Bavadra was an indigenous commoner from the western side of Vitilevu, but his leadership was thought by many indigenous Fijians to be tainted: his multiethnic Labour Party was in alliance with the National Federation Party, a powerful Indo-Fijian institution.

A month after the elections army colonel Sitiveni Rabuka led a coup d'état. Rabuka was a charismatic soldier who quickly became a hero for indigenous Fijians who wanted a strong, decisive, and proudly Christian ethnonationalist leader. In September 1987, frustrated at the way he felt his vision was being compromised, Rabuka executed a second coup and declared Fiji a republic. This action led to the expulsion of Fiji from the British Commonwealth, although it was eventually readmitted.

For the past two decades scholars have debated the multiple causes, interests, and forces at work in the events of 1987. Most scholars agree that the discourse of "race" that was prominent at the time—statements that the coups were executed in the interests of indigenous Fijians and against the interests of Indo-Fijians—were misleading insofar as they masked important class and regional divisions among indigenous Fijians. That is, although Rabuka was not a chief, his coups were aimed at regaining power for indigenous Fiji's eastern chiefly elite—not just from Bavadra and Indo-Fijians, but from western Fijians, commoners, and democratic processes generally.

With the coups, Christianity became a sharply etched emblem of national identity for many indigenous Fijians. A member of the Great Council of Chiefs, Adi Finau Tabakaucoro, summarized the situation as she saw it: "This is not their [Indo-Fijians'] country. . . . They still speak Hindi. They still eat curry. They are not Christians."[2] A group that united Christian identity with overt militarism was the Taukei Movement, a gang that claimed it was acting for indigenous interests by planning to blow up oil tanks in Suva harbor, releasing prisoners to foment chaos, and burning Indo-Fijian temples and cane fields (Lal 1992: 274). In the days before Rabuka's first coup, they were a potent force of agitation.[3] Four thousand marchers had demonstrated in Suva on April 24, holding signs with messages such as "Fiji for Fijians" and "Noqu Kalou, Noqu Vanua," meaning "My God, My Vanua" (Lal 1992: 273); Ratuva (2002: 21) refers to the formulaic phrase "My God, My Vanua" as a "maxim [that] represents the ideological core around which Fijian ethnonationalist pride revolves" (see also Ryle 2001, 2005). The turmoil of 1987 energized many indigenous Fijians' efforts to define their land as a divine inheritance, a gift from Jehovah that was now threatened and needed protection.

Indeed, Sitiveni Rabuka claimed that his May coup was "a mission" from God. According to Rabuka, the final spur to action, the final call to overthrow the government, was a miraculous and divine sign:

> In the early hours of Thursday, May 14, as he finished writing his Operation Order [for the coup], Rabuka prayed for rain. "I prayed for rain so that the soldiers going into the Government Buildings would have good reason to be wearing rain-coats and jackets, with their weapons hidden inside."
> This was his sign that he was doing the right thing. He is convinced that the rain was a direct response to his prayers. "I asked for rain, and it rained. That really strengthened my faith in God. I believed then that everything I was doing was according to God's plan." (Dean and Ritova 1988: 67)

Although Rabuka needed this divine intervention at a crucial moment, his life had long been suffused with a sense of biblical purpose. He compared his life to those of the prophet Jeremiah and the martyr Stephen, his namesake (Dean and Ritova 1988: 162). Moreover, "his early [Methodist] religious training was reinforced by a tour of [military] duty in the Middle East," according to Rutz and Balkan (1992: 66), "where he came in contact with Biblical sites and teachings of the Old Testament, and where his early childhood upbringing predisposed him to pay attention to the Jewish themes of a promised land and a people held captive." One of the coup participants, Ratu Inoke Kubuabola, later claimed that "the final decision to mount a military coup was 'taken in [his] office at the Bible Society with Rabuka' "; later, when his rebellion was validated by support from Fiji's governor-general, Rabuka triumphantly addressed a crowd of supporters at the Suva Civic Centre as the military band played, among other tunes, "Onward Christian Soldiers" (Lal 1992: 274, 278). In late June a Fijian-language newspaper, *Nai Lalakai,* featured an advertisement from the military stating, "The Call to War is Sounded. Fight On! Fight On! In the Spirit of God!" (quoted in Ratuva 2002: 21). In July Rabuka spoke to the Great Council of Chiefs, "calling for the formation of a 'Christian democratic state' " (Howard 1991: 299).

Fiji's different Christian congregations had divergent opinions on Rabuka's coup, with Catholics tending to criticize it and Methodists ultimately supporting it: "When the [Methodists'] internal debates were over . . . the church went along with the views of the coup supporters. Fiji should be declared a Christian state, guided by Christian precepts and ideals. . . . This was a great victory for the coup supporters, for the church's stand sent a powerful signal to the bulk of the Fijian community already torn between their political conviction and their Christian beliefs" (Lal 1992: 286; see also Premdas 1995: 106–116; Ryle 2005).[4] As Lal indicates, however, there was dissent within the Methodist Church leadership. Josateki Koroi, Ilaitia Tuwere, and Akuila Yabaki were moderates and progressives, and Daniel Mastapha, an Indo-Fijian former president of the Church, refused an invitation to join the Council of Advisors formed by the governor-general soon after the May coup (Lal 1992: 279).[5] But other Methodist leaders were willing to participate in the political turmoil, notably Manasa Lasaro and Tomasi Kanailagi. Lasaro, according to Halapua (2003: 79), "systematically discouraged the Heads of the Churches from making any statement concerning the coup." Tomasi Raikivi, who was serving as the Fiji Council of Churches' general secretary, accepted an invitation to join Rabuka's interim government (Barr 2004: 9). He "endorsed Rabuka's claim that God had inspired him to undertake the coup, and became intimately associated with participants in street violence aimed at Indians and threatening the judiciary. His theological stance implied that indigenous Fijians, above all others in Fiji or the world, were God's people" (John Garrett quoted in Barr 2004: 9).

Within the Methodist Church, two impulses were exemplified at the top level of leadership: one was outward, toward ecumenism, tolerance, and democracy; the other was inward, toward isolation, intolerance, and demagogic autocracy. Manasa Lasaro was the Church's general secretary when the government was overthrown, and as a friend of Rabuka's he was determined to tie religious identity to ethnonationalism as tightly as possible. The Church's president, however, was Josateki Koroi, who complained, "In the field of religion 'Taukei-ism' [i.e., indigenous Fijian ethnonationalism] is the domination of Christianity against non-Christian religion[s]" (quoted in Ernst 1994: 208). This ideological split became crucial when Christian nationalist movements gained momentum following Rabuka's September coup and the declaration of Fiji as a republic.

The Sunday Ban, the Church Coup, and Interventions of the 1990s

On November 9, 1987, Rabuka's government issued the Sunday Observance Decree, outlawing most business and recreation on the sabbath.

Both the Pacific Conference of Churches and the Fiji Council of Churches opposed it (Premdas 1995: 112), and not all Methodist leaders supported it either. Akuila Yabaki, for example, wrote in the *Fiji Times,* "Jesus was opposed to the legalistic observance of the Sabbath. . . . The Sabbath was made for man and not man made for the Sabbath" (quoted in Dropsy 1993: 49; Yabaki was quoting Jesus from Mark 2:27). Nicholas Thomas (1997: 236 n. 1) notes that the Sunday ban "was initially directed mainly against Fiji-Indians, but the subsequent dispute was essentially intra-Fijian and did magnify old tensions between [Seventh-day] Adventists and others." When the decree was weakened in May 1988 with the allowance of picnics, agricultural work, and public transportation, three thousand Methodists protested publicly (Heinz 1993: 419).

A week before Christmas Manasa Lasaro set up roadblocks around Suva to show disapproval of the Sunday law's dilution, and, in response, the Church president, Koroi, suspended him from his position (Ernst 1994: 207–208). The roadblocks continued into January 1989 as the Methodist leadership carried on its dispute. Lasaro was tried in a special court session along with nine other ministers on January 14; he was fined five hundred dollars, and the magistrate rebuked the accused by reading 1 Timothy 2:2 ("For kings, and for all that are in authority; that we may lead a quiet and peaceable life in all godliness and honesty") and Romans 13:1–2 ("Let every soul be subject unto the higher powers. For there is no power but of God: the powers that be are ordained of God"; Heinz 1993: 420).

As Rabuka gained a firmer grip on government, the Methodist leadership dispute grew worse. In February 1989 Lasaro and his supporters literally locked President Koroi out of Epworth House, the Methodist Church's national headquarters in Suva. This was the crudest of coups, but it was effective. The rebellious ministers appointed Rev. Isireli Caucau to take over as president of the Church. When Koroi took the matter to court, he won the case—but, not surprisingly, "the Lasaro faction rejected the court ruling and refused offers of peace from Koroi, preferring to play out the Methodist schism on the political stage of [Rabuka's] military coups" (Heinz 1993: 422). Although Lasaro was jailed briefly in August 1989 on the charge of unlawful obstruction because of the roadblocks, his friend Rabuka, acting in his capacity as minister for home affairs, ordered Lasaro's release (Ernst 1994: 209). It was evident that Rabuka, the fervent lay preacher turned government leader, supported the ethnonationalist faction of the Church at this stage.

The Methodist Church's national conference was set to take place in August, so when Lasaro was freed from jail the scene was the Christian equivalent of a gunfight at high noon: time for a final showdown. Lasaro and his supporters held their own parallel conference in opposition to the official conference headed by Koroi. Soon, however, in an apparent change of heart, "Lasaro led his followers through Suva's streets to where Koroi's conference was being held. He wept as he expressed repentance for past sins, and was welcomed very emotionally" (Ernst 1994: 209). Manfred Ernst points out that Lasaro's apology was a strategic one; those were crocodile tears. But it was effective. The conjoined conferences voted by a large majority that Lasaro continue as general secretary of the Church and chose his supporter Caucau to become the new president (209). The Church coup, like the military coups, was thus legitimized after the fact by popular support and institutional recognition. What worked in Parliament also worked in Epworth House.[6]

Popular support sometimes turned violent as Methodist villagers vented their fears and frustrations against Indo-Fijians, against the perceived threat of the loss of land, and against non-Christian symbols in general. Discussing indigenous Fijian support for the Sunday ban, Tuwere (2002: 103) writes movingly of the fear behind such actions:

Fear is definite and cannot be treated lightly. Expressions of this fear can be found in sermons preached, in songs, and even in church anthems and hymns. Fear-laden thoughts often surface, such as: "*Sa qai vo ga vei keda na noda lotu. . . . Ni kau tani ga vei keda oqo sa oti vei keda*" (The *lotu* . . . is the one thing that remains with us. If this also is taken away from us, we are finished.)

This is not a simple statement of uncertainty; it is a cry of anxiety.

John Kelly (1995: 49) relates an illustrative incident that took place in western Vitilevu:

On the night of October 14, 1989, a Methodist Youth Fellowship met for all-night prayers. After praying from 8:00 P.M. to 4:00 A.M., eighteen members of the group, ten men and eight women, left church, bought benzine at a gas station, and set out to burn down all the Indo-Fijian houses of worship in Lautoka, Fiji's second-largest city. They were arrested as they regrouped after setting fire to the four largest. . . . Only one of the eighteen arsonists was a juvenile, sixteen years old; the oldest were in their twenties. A few had police records, not uncommon for urban indigenous Fijians. All confessed to the police. . . . All told the police that they acted because the Bible said to burn idols. One of the arsonists added that they wanted to make Fiji a Christian country, another that the Bible said that Indians prayed to goddesses and the idols must be destroyed.

When taken to trial half a year later, all of the arsonists except the leader "received absolute discharges after pleading guilty" (52). Their lawless aggression was legitimized judicially. Thus in government, Church headquarters, and courts of justice alike, a pattern was being set in the months after Rabuka's coups: lawbreaking was given token condemnation when it occurred, but then given a stamp of official approval afterward.

The turmoil of 1987–1989 was a historical rupture for the Fijian Methodist Church during which it turned inward, rejecting global and multicultural connections in favor of strengthened indigenous loyalties. Before Rabuka's coups "the Church's orientation [had] become more and more ecumenical, as shown by the establishment of institutions . . . like the Pacific Theological College, the Pacific Conference of Churches, the Bible Society of the South Pacific and the Fiji Council of Churches" (Dropsy 1993: 45). After the coups, however, the Church withdrew from the Pacific Conference of Churches (Srebrnik 2002: 194). Steven Ratuva (2002: 19) notes that Fijian Methodism "tends to be inward looking and locally focused," in contrast to smaller denominations that have headquarters in other nations.

During the 1990s various leaders tried to capitalize on ethnonationalism's momentum to create Methodist-oriented political parties. Manasa Lasaro joined forces with the notorious politician Sakeasi Butadroka in 1990 to create a new Fijian Christian National Party. To justify his actions, Lasaro cited Joshua 24:15 (a verse that includes the admonition and declaration "Choose you this day whom ye will serve . . . but as for me and my house, we will serve the LORD") and explained, "This [new] party is based on trusting and being loyal to God" (quoted in Kelly 1995: 57). The party then allied itself with another nationalist group, and together they constituted the Fijian National United Front. In the 1992 elections the FNUF won five seats but lost them in the 1994 elections when the Methodist Church supported the party headed by Rabuka, who had become prime minister (Srebrnik 2002: 195; Rabuka's party, the Soqosoqo ni Vakavulewa ni Taukei, had been created by the Great Council of Chiefs). However, perhaps the most vigorous bid for power during the decade came not from a religious leader bent on taking over the government, but from a high chief interested in reshaping the Methodist Church. In 1992 the wife of the former prime minister Ratu Mara, Adi Lady Lala Mara, was insulted when the Rewa division of the Methodist Church held a bazaar and invited her illegitimate half-brother to open the ceremonies when she herself failed to show up. She was offended because her half-brother was an ethnonationalist who was ideologically opposed to Ratu Mara's leadership. Adi Lady Lala Mara met privately with the Church's president at the time, Isireli Caucau, who then reassigned the Rewa superintendent minister, "ordering him to take another position before his five year term was finished" (Ernst 1994: 210). The superintendent minister, Anare Maravu, did not budge, and was physically attacked; one of Maravu's followers then killed the attacker. The dissident faction became its own church organization, the Rewa Wesleyan Mission, although there was "no difference between the teachings and practices of the breakaway church and those of the [Methodist Church]" (210), simply a refusal to let chiefs meddle in Church affairs.

Ilaitia Tuwere was elected president of the Church in 1996 and "did much to restore the credibility of the Church and helped to break down its ethnically-defined stance" (Halapua 2003: 79). However, after he finished serving his term, "there was rapid retrogression to the status quo" (79). Toward the end of the decade, Methodist ethnonationalists tried again to form a viable political party. The Veitokani ni Lewenivanua Vakarisito (VLV), called in English the Christian Democratic Alliance, was founded in March 1998 to contest the elections of May 1999. In an interview published in the *Fiji Times,* the party's spokesman described the reason he came to the nascent group: "The reason why I came to a Christian party is because I feel that the security of the country and Fijians are secure and safe in the hands of God." But in the same interview he also claimed, "You look at the [1997] Constitution [a document whose progressivism offended many ethnonationalists].[7] Fiji is no longer the Fiji it used to be. What is the future of Fijians say 100 years from now and after that? The Constitution has opened Fiji to the world. . . . We [VLV members] are just trying to hold on to whatever is left."[8]

The spokesman's rhetoric articulated the fall-from-a-golden-age theme ("just trying to hold on to whatever is left") with a profession of faith in God's protection. For the spokesman, these two themes warranted the formation of a Christian political party. Many Methodists disagreed, however. As had happened during the previous decade, the issues were clouded because national Church leaders were in dispute. Manasa Lasaro was a cofounder of the VLV, and the party "used the Methodist Church headquarters to hold the swearing-in ceremony for its candidates" (Srebrnik 2002: 195; see also Sharpham 2000: 263–266). In October 1998 the Church's president-elect, Tomasi Kanailagi, "led the dedication at the party's launch."[9] Such actions seemed to suggest that the VLV was a Church-led body, but in a speech he gave at the 1998 annual conference in Suva, reprinted in the Methodist Church's bulletin, President Tuwere (1998) forcefully denied it. His disavowal of the VLV may have affected its chances in the 1999 elections, which proved mostly unsuccessful for the new party, as it captured only three seats in Parliament. In Kadavu the VLV lost badly.

The 2000 Coup

For many indigenous Fijians, the May 1999 elections were distressing because the Labour Party won by a stunning margin. Moreover, for the first time in Fiji's history, an Indo-Fijian, Mahendra Chaudhry, became prime minister. One year later, on May 19, 2000, gunmen staged a new coup. They kidnapped Chaudhry and members of Parliament—including Ratu Mara's daughter—and held the hostages for fifty-six days, releasing some occasionally but holding Chaudhry to the end. Later he testified in court that "rebels and armed men called him and detained parliamentarians 'heathens' and forced them to convert to Christianity."[10]

The rebels' public leader, George Speight, could not form a new government, however. Ratu Mara, after briefly trying to take control, was humiliated into resignation and left for his home island in eastern Fiji. The nation was threatening to slide into anarchy when the military commander, Voreqe Bainimarama, declared martial law on May 29 and then revoked the 1997 Constitution the next day (Kelly and Kaplan 2001: 181).

Speight made ethnonationalist pronouncements, as Rabuka had done more than a decade before, and rallied many indigenous Fijians to his side as a result. But he was overtly rude to the nation's high chiefs: "Speight went much further in his disrespect than Rabuka, who always claimed to support the chiefs as the arbiters of Fijian sovereignty" (Kelly and Kaplan 2001: 184). In addition, he did not cast himself as a divinely ordained warrior as Rabuka had done. Speight, a Seventh-day Adventist, seemed to pay little attention to religion in his mission.[11] However, other speakers were willing to reinvoke typological narratives from a decade earlier, recirculating the Christian discourse that had accompanied and furthered the coups of 1987: "[A] well-known evangelical church leader, preaching to a politically hyped up crowd at the parliamentary complex where the government ministers were being held hostage . . .

said that the coup leader, George Speight, was the Fijian biblical Joshua, following in the wake of the Fijian Moses (General Sitiveni Rabuka), who staged the 1987 military coup[s] to 'liberate' the Fijians (biblical Israelites) from their 'oppressors' " (Ratuva 2002: 21).

The national Council of Churches spoke against Speight's coup (Kelly and Kaplan 2001: 183), and Akuila Yabaki, who had written boldly against the Sunday ban in the 1980s, now wrote a letter in his role as the executive director of the Fiji Citizens' Constitutional Forum in which he urged "the international community," "Condemn in the strongest possible terms the kidnapping of members of Fiji's government and the [ensuing] looting and violence in Fiji's capital city. . . . We call especially on our international partners who have contributed to the long process of democratization in Fiji . . . governments, Churches, NGOs and committed individuals—to join us in this chorus of condemnation against this 'civil coup.' "[12] Resistance to Speight was more effective than it had been to Rabuka, partly because of Speight's refusal to engage equally with the metacultural divisions of lotu, vanua, and matanitu. Where Rabuka had effectively combined the three categories by presenting a vision of Fiji as a Christian chiefdom, Speight dismissed chiefs and Church as he boasted and preened for the foreign media. Another reason is that a surprisingly large number of indigenous Fijians, dissatisfied with the nation's lack of material progress in the 1990s, had chosen to vote for the Labour Party (see Norton 2000). But as in 1987, the Methodist Church ultimately, if indirectly, supported the coup. This time it endorsed Bainimarama's military government "to clear the air with ordinary people," in the words of Tuwere (quoted in Srebrnik 2002: 196). In March 2001 the Standing Committee of the Methodist Church "unanimously passed a resolution of support for the [interim] government" that had been appointed by Bainimarama, with Manasa Lasaro commenting that the new government, dominated by indigenous Fijians, "commands the respect of the majority and should be allowed to continue" (197).

In many ways the tumult of 2000 was a replay of 1987, with calls for Fiji to be a Christian state, threats against Indo-Fijians, and aftershocks of violence and crime. In one way it was less severe than 1987: Speight was held accountable—arrested, convicted, and jailed. In another way, however, it was far more severe: in all, "at least 20 people died violently as a direct result of Speight's folly," many of them indigenous Fijian soldiers shot during an internal military mutiny in November (Field, Baba, and Nabobo-Baba 2005: 261). Rather than confront the violence as it occurred, the Methodist Church legitimized it after the fact. Referring to the burning and stealing that had taken place in Suva, an Agence France-Presse article from the seventh week of the hostage situation noted wryly, "Churches have forgiven their looting congregations en masse."[13]

The VLV's electoral failure in 1999 did not mean that the Church was banished from politics. In fact, after Speight's coup certain leaders of the Methodist Church positioned themselves as power brokers for the August 2001 elections under the banner of indigenous Fijian unity.[14] Rev. Kanailagi eventually supported a new political confederation, the Conservative Alliance, "which stated that Fiji [should] be declared a Christian state" (Srebrnik 2002: 198). In the 2001 elections the Conservative Alliance won six seats in the House of Representatives, compared to the prime minister's party's thirty-two seats and the Labour Party's twenty-seven seats. Thus, as in earlier elections, the emblematically "religious" political party did not fare particularly well. Kanailagi himself, however, was appointed to the senate by the prime minister, even though the Church's former president, Koroi, disagreed with the choice, claiming that Kanailagi wanted Methodism to be "a nationalist religion" (199). The VLV drifted into irrelevance, and Fiji's elections supervisor officially deregistered the party in February 2004 (Fijilive 2004).[15]

Texts of Recuperation

I was not in Kadavu during Rabuka's coups of 1987 or Speight's coup of 2000. However, based on conversations I had in 2003, I believe that the majority of people in Tavuki supported the stated aims of the three coups. In this section I attempt to give readers a sense of Kadavuan perspectives on political turmoil, analyzing two texts of recuperation, two examples of Kadavuans expressing desires for new strength and unity: a Fijian chant and a Methodist sermon. Although they take different stances on violence, both are hopeful visions of a better Fiji that suggest why the coups seemed to local observers to be the positive moral acts of good Christians.

A *meke* is a Fijian ceremonial chant and dance. The dancers and the band, who beat drums and sing, are separate groups. In some *meke,* dancers hold clubs; in others, fans; and in some varieties, the dancers hold nothing but move their hands in coordinated patterns and add the occasional percussive clap. They are generally held on formal occasions

FIGURE 11. A Tavuki *meke* troop performs at a Kadavuan festival in Suva, 1998.

in front of large crowds. Composers often create both the lyrics and the dance forms (Fison and Gatschet 1885: 197). Lyrics sometimes come to the composer in a dream (Mahoney 1993: 29), and in the old days composers could earn fame—and a fortune in whales' teeth—for their creations (Fison and Gatschet 1885). *Meke* lyrics sometimes commemorate real personalities and events, as in the example given below about Rabuka's coups, but sometimes they describe mythic events, such as "Wrecked on the Voyage to Lau," a *meke* that tells of a chief's encounter with the shark god Dakuwaqa (Morey 1932). They may also evoke natural events such as waves crashing over coral or fruit bats in a grove of bananas (Derrick 1946: 17; see also Waterhouse 1866: 64–66, 432–435).

Some *meke* conjoin themes of lotu and vanua. Consider these selected verses from the *Meke ni Gone Cidroi* (*Meke* of the Disrespectful Child), which was written around 1980 by a man from Solodamu working at the Nadarivatu forestry station on Vitilevu. His son allowed me to copy the lyrics, which I have reformatted slightly in the translation.

> Please hear me, my kinsfolk
> Please listen so I can make this song
> The meke from the Bible
> Please bear with me if it's too long

You should listen to this book
The gospel is written
In the beginning was the Word
He became God

They gave us four gospels
The information about Jesus
Who became a human in the world
Who was born for our sake

[Chorus:]
Please be so kind and listen
We should love each other and be united
You should follow His path
Like the first preaching [i.e., follow Jesus as his disciples did]

Besides referring to the Bible and paraphrasing a Bible verse (John 1:1, "In the beginning was the Word," which the author amends slightly in its Fijian version), the author makes a proud declaration of his local identity. He says in an early verse that he is "a child of Solodamu," adding, "My drifting island / Its true name is Kadavu." "My drifting island [in the south]" (*Ciri koto [e na ceva], noqu yanuyanu*) is a popular phrase referring to Kadavu. My purpose in presenting these verses is simply to show how this traditional chant form can be used for an explicitly Christian message. The author roots himself in his vanua but appeals to cross-culturally dominant Christian emblems: the Bible, God as "the Word," and Jesus' earthly humanity (see also Dickhardt 2005).

The *meke* that I want to analyze more closely is untitled. I believe it was also composed in Kadavu, although I do not know the identity of the author; I obtained a copy during research in 1998–1999. The verses display a deft weave of religious and martial themes in their celebration of Sitiveni Rabuka's two coups of 1987. Here I present five of the verses, plus the chorus:

Before, Fiji was a despised land
God's judgment lifted [us] up
I am a Jerusalemite
I was raised as a child of Israel
The holy land of Emmanuel
Jesus, the son of Mary

My poem is turning around, I want to tell
About the man, Rabuka
Courageous and strong

He didn't fear or apologize
It was the soul of a man that entered

Suva was stirring
At ten o'clock [A.M.], no mistake
He entered the parliament house
All the people were surprised
The cock of war was leading

The decisions of the Council were too slow
The landowners were anxious
Troubles were increasing
Breaking into shops, breaking into banks
Our vanua was making a mistake

It was cut in the month of September
On the twenty-fifth day, it was clear
Four o'clock [P.M.], a good time
To hear the messenger
Tell our governor
Government is mine, again.

[Chorus:]
Oh dear, oh, dear me
It is very proper that we rejoice
Our war club has returned
"Robe of the Queen of Bau."

The text is remarkable for many reasons, especially its theme of masculine recuperation counterposed to a theme of encroaching social chaos. Indo-Fijians are not mentioned. In fact, it is restless indigenous Fijians who are blamed, referred to in the phrase "Suva was stirring." This claim came straight from Rabuka himself, who, besides describing his May coup as a divine mission, argued that he needed to act as he did because of increasing urban unrest.

The first stanza refers to Fiji as a "despised land," alluding to the canonical narrative of Fiji's heathen days before the coming of the Wesleyan missionaries. The author juxtaposes his reference to heathen darkness with a claim to being one of God's chosen people: he is a Jerusalemite, a true child of Israel. In the second stanza, Rabuka's martial strength is celebrated. He is truly a man, the author claims, his masculinity emphasized by the word *tagane*, denoting male gender. Bold, strong, unapologetic, Rabuka is a virtuous warrior. But the narrative of engulfing chaos appears again, now in the description of turmoil in Suva after the coup: "Breaking into shops, breaking into banks." What began with a decisive, promising moment was degenerating into disorder, un-raveling rapidly. And it was indigenous Fijians who were creating this chaos: "Our vanua was making a mistake." So Rabuka stepped in again, repossessing government in his own Second Coming.

As the chorus suggests, indigenous Fijians have reclaimed—and wielded—their old war club, named "Robe of the Queen of Bau" (cf. Tuwere 2002: 110). This is the club that was owned by precolonial Fiji's paramount chief, Ratu Cakobau. When Fiji was ceded to Queen Victoria in 1874, Ratu Cakobau handed over the club as a symbol of submission. As this *meke* implies, Rabuka symbolically took it back. (The actual artifact was returned by the government of Britain decades earlier.) In doing so, he serves as a Christian figure of redemption: "The holy land of Emmanuel" is Fiji itself. He also serves as the figure of an old Fijian warrior, a mana actor, someone who moves decisively and violently for his land and people. For this composer, Rabuka is a paradigmatically effective actor in all three major domains: lotu, vanua, and matanitu.

Rabuka's reputation has never been very good among Western scholars, not surprisingly, but it is particularly intriguing to consider the ways that his exploits have been folded into new narratives of decline. Marshall Sahlins picks up on this theme at the end of his oft-cited essay "The Return of the Event, Again" (1991). Referring to Georges Duby's *Le Dimanche de Bouvines,* Sahlins writes, "There is a passage in Duby's text about the difference between the medieval trials of sovereignty by battle and the methods of the modern-day tinhorn totalitarians" (84). After analyzing the great mid-nineteenth-century Bau-Rewa war, he dismisses Rabuka's 1987 coup as a weak echo of what real warriors did in the past. From golden past to tinhorn present: in Sahlins's version of the story Rabuka is subject to the narrative of decline—political violence just ain't what it used to be. Rabuka has also been subject to the narrative of decline by indigenous Fijians, who became frustrated at the political compromises he made as prime minister in the 1990s and punished him by voting out his SVT Party in 1999. Rabuka will ultimately benefit from the standardized narrative, however, as he recedes into ancestry and becomes another unmatchable warrior. The revalorization has probably already begun: after all, George Speight is no Sitiveni Rabuka.

In contrast to the *meke*'s image of recuperation through military coups, the catechist Tomasi Laveasiga delivered a sermon in May 1999 that addressed villagers' dissatisfaction with the government but urged unity on the model of Jesus' disciples. The national elections had begun on May 8; it was nine days later, on May 17, when the results were clear, that I first heard Tavukians explicitly discuss the possibility of a coup in reaction to Labour's win. As I described in chapter 4, a joking debate in Tavuki eventually helped dissipate people's tensions. More than a week before the joking debate took place, however, Laveasiga delivered his sermon in the Tavuki Methodist church. It was Pentecost Sunday, May 23, 1999. Pentecost, the fiftieth day after Easter Sunday, commemorates the events described in chapter 2 of the Book of Acts, when Jesus' disciples began speaking in tongues. Fijian Methodists do not speak in tongues. Laveasiga used the story adeptly, however, to comment on indigenous Fijians' anxieties and dissatisfaction with the election results.

Early in his sermon, after referring briefly to the Pentecost story, the catechist summarized the Church calendar's topic for the day: "Only those who are entered by the Holy Spirit, take Jesus to be their Lord, to be their savior, only they will have the Kingdom of God." Then he preached:

I have prepared this sermon which will tell us about observing the progress, the situation that our vanua finds itself in. A time has arrived, a new government has been chosen. There are very many rumors, very many frightening actions have happened now that the new government is in place to lead our vanua. A government I will want to talk about this morning: I believe that we own this government, and we say that the government of the land of Fiji is ours. It will stir up [people] because it is led by people.

In this early stretch of his sermon, Laveasiga refers openly to the ongoing disquiet: "Very many frightening actions have happened." Rumors had circulated about social breakdown on Vitilevu: on May 19 I had written matter-of-factly in my field notes, "Chaudhry was sworn in, and the [prime minister's] office was promptly burned down." No such thing had happened, it turned out, but rumors flew as people contemplated Labour's victory and the prospect of Fiji's first Indo-Fijian leader. The catechist then mentions an apparently different government, one that "we own," by which he is likely referring to the Kingdom of God (*Matanitu ni Kalou*). But after saying this, he immediately refers once more to the government of Fiji itself and comments critically that it will inevitably "stir up" people because it is a human institution. Thus at the beginning of his sermon Laveasiga counterposes divine government against fragile and fractured human government.

After this he refers again to the fact that it is Pentecost Sunday, explaining that "pentecost" means "fifty" in Greek. He claims that Pentecost was "a day the prophet Joel promised a few hundred years before Jesus was born," apparently a reference to Joel 2:28, "And it shall come to pass afterward, that I will pour out my spirit upon all flesh; and your sons and your daughters shall prophesy, your old men shall dream dreams, your young men shall see visions." "The Holy Spirit isn't merely some new thing in the Bible," Laveasiga continues, using a common Fijian rhetorical strategy of asserting that something is "not new," implying that it is therefore legitimate.

Then, turning to the first chapter of Genesis, he quotes the second half of verse 2: "And the Spirit of God moved upon the face of the waters." He explains that "God's spirit is the Holy Spirit," and he repeats his assertion that the Holy Spirit is not "something new." He adds that the Holy Spirit is manifest as wind and breath, and then moves to the next chapter in Genesis:

Genesis chapter 2. It's said that the creation of the first human was made from soil and was then laid down. The soil was not yet humanity. Then when God breathed into it, it was human. And the person moved because the spirit of life was in him. Then he was called human because he was given the Holy Spirit. Breath makes us able to stir, move, speak, go, work. Our sermon this noon, I want to emphasize that the Holy Spirit causes unity. The Holy Spirit causes unity. Luke testifies in his book the first of two lines of thought: our Bible reading tells us "they were all with one accord in one place" [Acts 2:1]. Opinion is divided on this newly elected government. One big division of—we landowners [indigenous Fijians], they're saying that an Indian can't be the prime minister. Difference and division is happening. I want to confirm to us this Sunday, Pentecost Sunday has only one purpose: for us to be united. All united.

In this passage, Laveasiga ties together several major cultural themes. He begins with the soil from which the first human was made. As the preacher tells his audience, "the soil was not yet humanity" and needed God's breath to bring it to life. Note how the five verbs he lays down in a row end with the ace card "work." As described in chapter 2, indigenous Fijian visions of the strong past valorize work—the strong efforts of the ancestors—in contrast to a literal reading of the Genesis story, which describes work as a curse.

Having summarized the Holy Spirit's role in humanity's creation, Laveasiga then compares this original state with the fractious social collectivity of modern indigenous Fiji. Twice he says that "the Holy Spirit causes unity." But, he notes, a large group of indigenous Fijians are angry at the possibility of having an Indo-Fijian prime minister. Laveasiga does not criticize their contempt, but rather criticizes all indigenous

Fijians for not being united. "Difference and division is happening," he laments, and his nine-word phrase (*Sa yaco mai na duidui vata kei na tatawasewase*) can serve as a condensed summary of indigenous Fijian histories of decline and loss. In this sermon, however, Laveasiga does not only lament. He also offers the possibility of recuperation; after all, he reasons, if the Holy Spirit causes unity, then indigenous Fijian dis-unity is a problem that can be fixed by Christianity.

The Holy Spirit, I can tell you, is poured forth this noon. Why? Because we are united. There is only one purpose, for us to serve God, [who] created heaven and earth. It's also the thought of the landowners' [indigenous Fijians'] way of life, our traditional life. The Holy Spirit can be poured forth if we are united. It's a deep thought: our landowners' way of life is to be united. Being united is evident, sprouts there, or the thought is born there of mutual love, working to-gether, unity, hands together, so we are legs together [i.e., going together]. Nothing is possible [nor] will be fulfilled in our traditional life if we are differ-ent. Difference exists: spiritual difference, different thoughts, different judg-ments. It's impossible to build a good Nacolase [clan] or a good Nukunawa [clan] for tomorrow. The early Church was starting up and then the Holy Spirit was poured forth in Jerusalem, poured forth because the people were united. . . . God wants to tell this to the world: the Holy Spirit is poured forth only when people are united.

In this section, Laveasiga begins with the assertion, "The Holy Spirit . . . is poured forth this noon. Why? Because we are united." He seems to mean that everyone in church is united, and that their worshipping to-gether is evidence of the Holy Spirit at work in the world. The preacher then makes a familiar move, asserting that if Fijians will only follow their traditional lives built on the vanua's foundation, they will be united. He spins out a short series of parallel construction, each phrase ending with "together" (*vata*): "working together, unity [lit., "one to-gether"], hands together, so we are legs together." He returns to the theme of social decline, as characterized by disorder, using a new paral-lel construction based on the word "difference" or "different" (*duidui*): "Difference exists: spiritual difference, different thoughts, different judg-ments." The gap between traditional indigenous Fijian lives and present-day lives, he is arguing, is wide but not unbridgeable. He shows a muted optimism that the Holy Spirit can be "poured forth," and maybe is actually being poured forth in the church service.

In the next part of his sermon, the catechist compares the Holy Spirit's presence to a flame and notes the double-edged meaning: Hell "has only one thing there, fire," but fire is also a refining force: it purifies gold. He is apparently alluding to various Bible verses on this subject, such as Zechariah 13:9 ("And I will bring the third part through the fire, and will refine them as silver is refined, and will try them as gold is tried"), although he does not cite or quote them directly. He mentions that Peter, who three times on Good Friday denied knowing Jesus, was the same man who "stood up" at the Pentecost. As the story is told in Acts, the crowd who saw the twelve disciples speaking in tongues asked what was going on, with some observers jeering, "These men are full of new wine" (Acts 2:13). Peter stood up and defended his fellow disciples, arguing that they were not drunk but were fulfilling Joel's prophecy. His speech made the crowd "pricked in their heart" (Acts 2:37) and led thousands to convert (2:41). Laveasiga declares that the Holy Spirit can lead to faith in Jesus and can create unity for Fijians as for the disciples.

At this point he apologizes for the length of the sermon so far and announces that he wants to present "a few short thoughts." He then marches through a succession of condensed statements and arguments: Fijians should energetically study the apostles' teachings, just as the apostles themselves were energetic; "kindly love" (*vilomani*) is urgently needed; people should pray and "break bread" and "fight for the Kingdom of God on earth"; people should not be stingy or selfish; and not enough people are coming together to worship at the same time. He mentions once again the Holy Spirit's pouring forth on Pentecost for Jesus' disciples, and then remarks:

For us, the lotu congregation, on this noon, Pentecost Sunday 1999 will not return. We will await Pentecost Sunday of the year 2000, another new century. What will our vanua look like, our lotu look like, our government look like? [I] want to propose just one government this day. I already told of the path to it. The Kingdom of God will only be theirs who have had the Holy Spirit enter their lives, those who have taken Jesus to be their Lord, to be their savior. There is a lot of stirring up, noisemaking, the rumors we heard when this week came, the things happening are bound up . . . in our human lives, in the world of creation which we are living in. . . . I want to finish the short thought: something is very impoverished in our traditional life, village life: dearth of kindly love, dearth of unity, dearth of working together. . . . The Holy Spirit does not cause division or difference. The purpose of the Holy Spirit's pouring forth is to unite. People are united. Then the spirit of God is poured forth. The Holy Spirit should work in our human lives.

Here the preacher returns to his distinction between the Kingdom of God and the governments of humankind. The Kingdom of God is a unified domain for all Christian believers, with Jesus as the warp and the

Holy Spirit as the weft. In contrast, indigenous Fijians are torn over the newly elected government, and there is "stirring up, noisemaking . . . rumors." The catechist does not argue that indigenous Fijians' anxieties are misguided, but that division is ruinous. He suggests that the rumblings heard over the election results are symptomatic of deeper problems: a "dearth of kindly love, dearth of unity, dearth of working together." (The word I am translating as "dearth," *dravudravua,* can also be translated as "covered with ashes" or "poverty"; see Capell 1991: 58.) Recuperation is possible, however, through the Holy Spirit, whose presence is described as both a cause and a sign of earthly social unity.

Laveasiga's complete sermon was twenty minutes long. As shown in the excerpts I have presented here, it was a relatively straightforward commentary on indigenous Fijian dissatisfactions with the election results. The catechist consistently distinguished between the Kingdom of God and the governments of humans, and faulted indigenous Fijians for being divided against themselves. At certain moments his sermon was a paradigmatic statement of indigenous Fijian themes of loss. At other moments, however, he held out hope for something newer and better. His view of a better future was a distinctly Fijian Christian view, in which indigenous Fijians might be able to recapture their lost unity and strength through faith in Jesus, the help of the Holy Spirit, and insistence on social cohesion framed in the traditionalist terms of the vanua.

During tumultuous times not all preachers have been as balanced as Laveasiga was. Recall the experience of the Rotuman scholar Vilsoni Hereniko (2003: 78) during the upheavals of 1987, quoted in the introduction: "I was shocked to hear the Fijian minister at the pulpit refer to the Indians as evil heathens who needed steering to the Light, and proclaim that until they converted, they deserved to be treated as second-class citizens." I must note that in my fieldwork I have never heard such overt sentiments from the pulpit; many Kadavuans sympathize with the claims of ethnonationalism, but in church services the discourse is considerably more polite than that heard by Hereniko, as shown in sermons such as Laveasiga's. Between Laveasiga's preaching and Hereniko's anecdote, however, there is common ground in the sense of urgency.

The Christian influence in modern Fijian politics is twofold, conjoining the sense of lost mana with the motivation to reclaim it. For indigenous Fijians fear and lament have become the fuel for political action. Having an Indo-Fijian prime minister crystallized the loss of power for many indigenous Fijians: it was a sign of falling *too* far from a golden age.

Months before the 1999 elections, when I asked Rev. Serewai about the possibility of coups, he said he did not think they would happen again (as in 1987), but he expressed the common indigenous Fijian displeasure at the thought of Indo-Fijian leadership by using a telling metaphor: Fijians would not be able to look to the top of the kava circle, he said, and see an Indian (instead of an indigenous Fijian chief) sitting there.

In overthrowing the government, Rabuka presented his actions as divinely led and ordained, and himself as a Christian warrior. In his own coup, Speight referred to Christianity only when it was convenient, but his supporters recirculated discourse about the need for Fiji to be a Christian nation. The national Methodist Church leaders, with the notable exception of certain individual ministers, then supported and legitimized the coups after the fact. All of these actions may seem shortsighted, even self-destructive, from an analytical distance; to some writers they have seemed disturbingly antithetical to broad moral imperatives in Christianity (e.g., Barr 2004). Seen in the light of indigenous Fijian themes of loss, however, such actions make a kind of emotional and practical sense. Support for coups can be seen as sympathy for efforts to recuperate mana.

CHAPTER 7

The Road to Damascus Runs through Waisomo Village

Hirokazu Miyazaki (2004: III) has written that for Suvavou people, the original owners of land on the Suva peninsula, now the site of Fiji's capital city, Psalms 127:1 is a frequently recited verse. It reads, "Except the LORD build the house, they labour in vain that build it," and Miyazaki notes that Suvavou people at the time of his fieldwork were, literally, trying to build a house, or rather, an office building. He argues that the verse helps generate a "discourse on the importance of prayer in all aspects of Fijian social life" (119). That is, if God's power is almighty, the only hope humans have for achieving anything is to communicate with God.

But not all humans are equally adept or authorized communicators. Miyazaki is worth quoting at length for his nuanced argument on Fijian Christian strategies of power and the creation of hope:

The conceptual slippage entailed in the extension and translation of Psalms 127:1 into a discourse on the importance of prayer in all aspects of Fijian social life is one manifestation of a pervasive shift from an emphasis on God's agency to an emphasis on the importance of human agency in Fijian Christian discourse. The shift in turn allows Fijian Christians to present themselves with a model to emulate in order to achieve a state where, as they say, "everything [they want] is possible." Hope therefore follows self-aggrandizing proclamations of faith in humans' work. In other words, in Fijian Christian discourse, the production of hope is paradoxically predicated on the backgrounding of God's agency. This process renders the truthfulness of Biblical texts simultaneously both self-evident and emergent. The source of hope lies in extending the Biblical example to social and political action and foregrounding human agency. (119–120)

By "hope" Miyazaki does not mean the content of desire, but rather "prospective momentum" (4). Drawing on the work of the German philosopher Ernst Bloch, he describes hope as a "method," a generation of momentum. How, he asks, can anthropologists understand the forward-looking perspective of ritual action through an after-the-fact analysis?

In this final chapter I address Miyazaki's concern with hope by analyzing a Methodist catechist's life story. His story unites voice and mana as he learns to speak effectively by choosing the path of the Church. In doing so, he challenges the prominent fall-from-a-golden-age theme by presenting a model of recuperation and growing effectiveness. The way he learns to speak—in prayers, legal pleas, apologies, and then sermons—generates a kind of prospective momentum and displays the "shift from an emphasis on God's agency to an emphasis on the importance of human agency" described by Miyazaki. The narrator's model for his life is the story of Saul of Tarsus, who became Saint Paul.

In the biblical story, Saul was a Jewish persecutor of early Christian communities. Traveling to Damascus one day, "breathing out threatenings and slaughter against the disciples of the Lord" (Acts 9:1), Saul experienced a miracle:

And as he journeyed, he came near Damascus: and suddenly there shined round about him a light from heaven: And he fell to the earth, and heard a voice saying unto him, Saul, Saul, why persecutest thou me? And he said, Who art thou, Lord? And the Lord said, I am Jesus whom thou persecutest: it is hard for thee to kick against the pricks. And he trembling and astonished said, Lord, what wilt thou have me to do? And the Lord said unto him, Arise, and go into the city, and it shall be told thee what thou must do. And the men which journeyed with him stood speechless, hearing a voice, but seeing no man. And Saul arose from the earth; and when his eyes were opened, he saw no man: but they led him by the hand, and brought him into Damascus. And he was three days without sight, and neither did eat nor drink. And there was a certain disciple at Damascus, named Ananias; and to him said the Lord in a vision . . . Arise, and go into the street which is called Straight and inquire in the house of Judas for one called Saul, of Tarsus: for, behold, he prayeth, and hath seen in a vision a man named Ananias coming in, and putting his hand on him, that he might receive his sight. . . . And Ananias went his way, and entered into the house; and putting his hands on him said, Brother Saul, the Lord, even Jesus, that appeared unto thee in the way as thou camest, hath sent me, that thou mightest receive thy sight, and be filled with the Holy Ghost. And immediately there fell from his eyes as it had been scales: and he received sight forthwith, and arose, and was baptized. (Acts 9:3–18)

Once Saul had become Paul, the Christian evangelist, he worked energetically to develop the young Church. Many popularly known verses

FIGURE 12. Sevanaia F. Takotavuki.

in the New Testament come from Paul, including "For the wages of sin is death; but the gift of God is eternal life through Jesus Christ our Lord" (Romans 6:23); "When I was a child, I spake as a child, I understood as a child, I thought as a child: but when I became a man, I put away childish things" (1 Corinthians 13:11); "Therefore if any man be in Christ, he is a new creature: old things are passed away; behold, all things are become new" (2 Corinthians 5:17); and "Wives, submit yourselves unto your own husbands, as unto the Lord" (Ephesians 5:22).

The Fijian narrator who described his own life in terms of Paul's journey was Sevanaia F. Takotavuki. In chapter 2 I presented a short anecdote told by Takotavuki in which he compared the power of traditional chiefs with the power of men serving God: "God gives all the mana," he declared. "When there's a person of God, a messenger of God—receive them, take good care of them because they're standing in for God."

When I recorded his life story in 2003 he was the Methodist catechist in Tavuki, serving under superintendent minister Setareki Tuilovoni.

Takotavuki was born on January 10, 1960. He grew up in Lakeba, in the Lau chain of eastern Fiji, his mother's land. His father was from Waisomo, a village in Tavuki Bay. As he mentions in his autobiography, Takotavuki finally came to his "true village" (*koro dina*, i.e., his father's village) when he wanted to escape the lawless path he had been following.

He was an energetic, generous man with a jauntily assertive manner. He had a personal intellectual fascination with biblical symbolism, including numerology. At various times he conducted discussions somewhat akin to the Seventh-day Adventist Bible study sessions described by Miyazaki (2000: 34–35). Men in these sessions compete with each other by posing questions, hectoring those whose responses they deem inadequate, and then proposing their own solutions: "Although rounds of questions and answers begin as contests among elders . . . the person who asks the question usually concludes the round of answers by providing his own answer" (35). Similarly, Takotavuki once asked an assembly of kava drinkers about the significance of the numbers 5 and 2 in the story of Jesus feeding a huge crowd with five loaves of bread and two fish (found in Matthew 14, Mark 6, and Luke 9). He grilled one man from Tailevu, who said offhandedly that people work for five days a week and rest for two. (This, evidently, was a man from an urban background who was familiar with two-day weekends.) Takotavuki explained authoritatively that the number 5 stood for the books of Moses in the Old Testament (Genesis, Exodus, Leviticus, Numbers, Deuteronomy) and the number 2 stood for the Old and New Testaments together; he added that Moses' and Jesus' lives resembled each other in certain ways.

Besides being a creative thinker and a good preacher, he was a strong manual worker, tending his gardens as a traditional farmer. At the time I recorded his story, he had been married to his wife, Sainiana, for more than ten years, and they were raising the daughters of his sister, Sainimeri and Makareta, who were eleven and nine years old, respectively.

I have divided his narrative into five sections, some of the divisions caused by interruptions (people coming to his house while we were recording) and others based on my decision not to include some relatively extraneous material. The first section is the longest, covering his years as a young criminal and prisoner and discussing his early engagements with Christianity. In the second section, Takotavuki discusses his backsliding—his drawing away from the Church after flirting with a more religious life—and then his homecoming to Kadavu, the land of his father. The third and fourth sections are the most compact and dramatic, in which Takotavuki embraces the Church and becomes a preacher, then a pastor, and then a catechist, fulfilling "God's hidden plans." The fifth and final section is a coda in which Takotavuki brings us back to the present and offers a humorous suggestion that he will become famous in America because of my representations of him.

This story is both a confession and a claim to authority. Most significantly, in a personalized and detailed way it is a counternarrative to the fall from a golden age. Takotavuki tells of how he has become an effective actor, and a more moral subject, through speaking the words of God. This is, perhaps necessarily, an individualistic story, and Takotavuki goes so far as to discuss what it means to be the "true me" (*au dina*).

Unlike the sermons analyzed in chapters 3 and 6, which were crisply delivered in coherent segments, this is a pleasantly meandering story of a life's journey. Accordingly, I stand back a bit, editorially speaking, and let Takotavuki take his time in explaining how Saul became Paul. The reader may find certain moments to be a bit confusing, but, like most good storytellers, Takotavuki keeps weaving his strands together until, at a reflective distance, the general pattern emerges and the larger image becomes distinct.[1]

Catechist Sevanaia F. Takotavuki, July 18, 2003: Narrative of His Life

PART I: A MURDER AND A PLEA

> *Takotavuki:* In 1976, '76, I was in Lakeba, in Lau. That's where it [prison life] all began for me. I was accused of burning one of Ratu Sir Kamisese Mara's pine plantations. He was president, now he's the retired president, eh? Lord Tui Nayau. I'm *vasu* to his island [i.e., Takotavuki's mother is from there]. Lakeba [Island], Waciwaci [village]. We went, we went to burn my grandfather's garden, a yam garden, eh? There was some dried grass there. . . . It was burning and then the wind came strongly, and spread it to the other side. We had made a firebreak . . . we had made one. After that, when we were burning in the interior, then the wind came strongly and [the fire] jumped to the other side. It was burning away for three nights, three days it burned, the island of

Lakeba was on fire. We didn't think it would burn the pine. I didn't light the match, it was someone else. But I was—because I was an outsider, I was accused of having burned Ratu Mara's pine. The fire came and spread, and Ratu Mara's pine really burned. That pine was still new, it had just started to be planted in Lakeba, eh? And it burned, it burned completely.

I was tried in court. Me and a young guy, not a young guy from Lakeba, a young guy from Moce [Island], also in Lau. We went together, eh? With two of my uncles [mother's brothers]. My uncles were Waciwacians, Lakebans. When we all went there, me and the young guy from Moce were charged, eh? Meaning, [because] we were both outsiders. We were charged, then tried, and I got three months in prison. Taken to Suva. Tried in Lakeba. Tried, probably because it was Ratu Mara's pine, because he's a famous person, then I was given [my sentence] because that was my first offense. . . . That wasn't a big offense. That was unintentional, eh? Then I waited, and the boat came, [I was] put on the boat. We, we were both taken to Suva. We boarded, I forget which boat. The boat came from there, then had a long trip around [the outer islands]. Prisoners were on the boat. [We] arrived in Suva, boarded the—disembarked at the wharf in Walu [Bay]. The Black Mariah was there, the old police wagon. Black Mariah was its name, a big black truck, and—y'know? A big truck like this, opens from the back. Go inside and stay there, it's dark.

M. T.: Mm, I understand.

Takotavuki: The door is small, it's a small door, eh? [We were] inside, then taken to Korovou [Prison]. [We were] then taken to RTC.

M. T.: What's the RTC?

Takotavuki: Reformative Training Centre, at Nasinu. It was a new prison that opened there in '76. We were the second group of kids, prisoners, to—a group went before [us], we were the second to go begin the prison there, it's in Nasinu. There were soldiers there. They were above [us] there in the prison. [I] was there three months, cut off at two months, one month cut, with two months [served]—after that, I got out [i.e., he served two months of a three-month sentence and was then released].

Got out, was staying at home, in Nadonumai. I was, lots of times as a young guy, there were lots of things I wanted to buy, but I'd gotten out of prison and there wasn't any work [for me], [I] could look for a job, so I went to town. Then I was sleeping in town, stealing in town, was eating in town. I was sleeping on the verandah, me with lots of my friends who had gotten out of prison. Me, my family, dad, my mom, they didn't kick me out. I just left because they couldn't give me the things they should,

I wanted, because I was a young guy, eh? To buy my clothes, my shoes, radio, cigarettes; they were pursuing their own lives, [and] my brothers were studying. My dad's salary was small. Eh? So I went to town, went to live in town.

I stole, pickpocketed, fought, broke into restaurants, stole money, everything. Stealing. [I would] go to the store on a day like this, go, steal some stuff, take it, put it in a pawnshop, and take the money. That's what my life was like every day. Getting drunk, buying the—stealing every day so I could eat, eating the stuff I stole. No work. Because they didn't like people who had been to prison.

M. T.: It was difficult for you to get work?

Takotavuki: Yes. Because I was, I could only go to the village, eh? But I was—

M. T.: You didn't want to go . . . to Kadavu?

Takotavuki: Didn't want to go to Kadavu. There was lots of new stuff in Suva then, eh? Lots of new things [I would] see, the life in town was sweet, [I] came to live in town. [I] was sleeping in town, sleeping, [on] the, the verandah, there were lots of girls I went with [i.e., had sex with]. Lay down, slept. I, when I was going around, I was, I have a daughter.

M. T.: Oh! [Takotavuki laughs.] Is that so?

Takotavuki: A girl. She's in Raiwaqa now, but I haven't met her again, eh? Right. Going along, then, once again I went to prison, [for] trespass. Back again. Another time in prison, shopbreaking. Back again. Another time in prison, [I] went to Naboro.

M. T.: Ooh, Naboro Prison.

Takotavuki: Shopbreaking, eh? . . . Back again. After that, there were a few more times that I was in prison, [then] the last time I was in prison I was charged with murder. Eh? The murder, I didn't do it, we were going as a gang to steal from a place, eh? And it happened that an Indian died.

M. T.: The garage. [I had heard him refer to this incident before.]

Takotavuki: Right. Dead, eh? When he died, we all were charged. Because we were in a gang. But we just went for a look-see, the money was in the office, eh? We were chosen [i.e., the gang members chose who would carry out the crime]. When the time came, we didn't know because we, [we] drank beer, drank rum, drank some more, smoked marijuana, when we went. [When we] went [we] were doped, wasted, really wasted. [We] mixed everything, when the murder happened. Because we didn't think that, that the young guy who struck the Indian was striking a person, eh?

M. T.: Mm. You were really drunk.

Takotavuki: Right—it was too much marijuana, everything, all together. Then we, at the side of a village, we fled separately, we didn't know that the Indian was dead. We went away, we were staying at a place on Moti Street, next to Rewa Street . . . Moti Street, eh? We were in a house there. And the police came, and raided the house, and—the purpose was to take us all for questioning, because of the murder. An Indian was dead. We were, we were shocked, now we were scared, eh? We hadn't yet done anything where a person died. We just stole, ran away.

We were all taken in for questioning, the girls, the guys. And it was known that we had been out that night. We had drunk, smoked marijuana, then we had said [to each other] that we were going to do a "job." That means going to steal. We're going on a job, that's work, eh? Yeah, that's how [we] would say it in town: "I'm going on a 'job' there is. Here it is." And go, and steal. Because your "job," your work, is stealing. . . . Okay, then I went there and was charged, there were five of us put in prison.

M. T.: [The] year [was] '80—

Takotavuki: 1984. We were in prison, tried, there were five of us in prison. I was the fifth. We were put in the, the, in Korovou [Prison] to wait there for the trial, for another year. . . . August '85, then came the sentence. We waited, were tried. Waited, the trial was going on, for a whole year the trial went on, until it came then, next August '85, I got eight years, we three; those two, who did the killing: life sentence [i.e., Takotavuki and two others got eight-year sentences for manslaughter, and two others got life sentences for murder]. Prison. But a life sentence in Fiji, it's, it's just ten years, then your time in prison is reviewed, it's evident [if you] should go back, eh? "Oh, you ran away once, once you assaulted a guard, another time you were rebellious." If not, you can get out. Ten years solid, eh?

Then we finally went to prison. In prison for eight years. Then I, we appealed. Court appeal, eh? . . . The punishment was too harsh. . . . But when it was written I didn't, didn't write, I was beginning to lotu. The sentence was for eight years. I didn't smoke tobacco, didn't smoke tobacco.

M. T.: [You] began to lotu [i.e., engage in Christian worship] again in prison?

Takotavuki: The lotu begins slowly, eh? Because we Fijians, raised in families, are raised in Sunday school, Sunday school, we're raised there. That's where we get to know the lotu. We're raised up, if there's a Fijian just going around, he or she knows the lotu. Because he or she was already raised in Sunday school. From there, he or she knows God. When that time [in prison] came, my thoughts returned to the things I had learned there, from my parents, the pastors, Sunday school, because there is a God. Then I, we appealed, they had lawyers, I didn't have a lawyer. I didn't have a lawyer for my appeal. I just prayed to God. I just prayed, "Lord, I'm not going to use anyone else. Because I know that there is a God." But then I sinned, because of evil desires, eh? If Paul said, who can free me from the bonds of death, Paul said, said, evil has long been inside me.[2] That's it, it wasn't the true me. The true me, the true me was when I changed because God made you, to be like and resemble God. That was the true you. But at that time, [I] was sinning, it wasn't really me. It wasn't the true me. Evil is just inside me, because Satan put it there, eh?

There I was, praying, praying, when there were a few days left until our appeal would be heard, we were worshipping together, y'know, in prison, some people come here and mock us. [When] someone wants to lotu, [someone else says] "Why do you want to pray now that you're in prison, eh?" When . . . the time came for us to pray, I would pray. They would be laughing, talking, talking. I was kneeling [in prayer], a young prisoner questioned me. "What are you praying for?" I said, "I'm praying because, because of my appeal. I'm appealing. I'm in the Methodist Church, I'm a Methodist." Then he said, "Right. That's good, good for your God to help you." He doubted. He was a Fijian too.

M. T.: . . . He didn't believe.

Takotavuki: Didn't believe. We went to appeal. I was, was pissed off, eh? I was really angry at being questioned, because I could have whipped that guy. The guy who spoke to me, I could have whipped him, because it so happens that I was a strong guy in prison. I'm saying this because I was religious, I forgave his mocking me.

And then I went, I continued with the life in there, and prayed. And the praying went slowly, [I] said to God, "My appeal, I would like for [my sentence] to be commuted." When we went there, went to appeal, those eight years, all of us. They [the court officers] asked, "Okay. First accused." I was fifth accused. The last person. "First accused, second accused." His [*sic*] lawyer stood up. "Third accused, fourth accused," their lawyer stood up. "Fifth accused," something was to be said, and I stood up. Without a lawyer. I just spoke Fijian. . . . "If you reduce my sentence, for the rest of this life that God has given me, I will use it to the best of my ability." I sat down again.

M. T.: The judge, was he a Fijian, a Fijian man?

Takotavuki: It was translated into English.

M. T.: Oh, oh, oh.

Takotavuki: This was the appeal, the high court. Court of appeal. The justices sit there. The high judges, eh? He thanked [me], and answered, translated, there was a translation, there was a man to translate, because I didn't have a lawyer. I sat down again, I believed that it would be reduced, only my sentence would be reduced. Because I didn't depend on any other person. I sat down and then left. Then . . . they found out that their sentence was reduced, those who'd had eight years, three years were cut off. Three years were taken off. One of them [i.e., one of the lucky appealers] was me. The two with a lawyer, and me without a lawyer, cut together.

M. T.: Oh. Is that so?

Takotavuki: There, that's the power of God. When we returned, we heard that it was reduced, those two [others] were not reduced. Their life sentence stuck.

M. T.: Those two were the people who—

Takotavuki: Right. They were the ones who did it, because God could see that thing [i.e., what had really happened during the murder].

There I was. Went back to prison, went to serve five years. I would get out in 1991. . . . January, eh? Another—from the '80s to the '90s [i.e., when he got out it would be a different decade than when he got in].

It was reduced, it came down in '80–, sometime [trying to recall the date], '89. It was reduced in '89. A few more months were cut off [the sentence], after that, [I] was in prison, studying to learn a trade, joinery. I was in joinery until the time I left, our pews in the church in my village, if you go to my village, you'll see them in the church there, [they were] made in prison, I was one of them who made them. I made the—the pews in that church.

M. T.: Getting ready for your return.

Takotavuki: Right.

M. T.: Were you thinking then that you would . . . go to Kadavu?

Takotavuki: No. I didn't know I would come back here. I only knew I would get out, I was studying the guitar.

In this first section, Takotavuki's story has many notable features, including various structural parallels with other well-known narratives.

His journey from Lau to Kadavu can be read as an echo of Fijian migration stories; his claims to being wrongly imprisoned are a common complaint of inmates in many cultures. In addition, like the Christian prisoners in Papua New Guinea described by Adam Reed (2003: 147), Takotavuki presents "God or Satan . . . as the ultimate cause of every action."

Takotavuki's story, like many narratives, is notable for its gaps and elisions—for what it evidently does not say. Specifically, the crime that sent him to prison for his longest stretch, the murder of an Indo-Fijian, is sketched quickly as the product of confusion, drunkenness, and drug abuse, and then dismissed. There are probably several reasons for his cursory treatment of this event, including the fact that he had told me about it on an earlier occasion, and also the fact that the overall trajectory of this story is to show his development as a Christian authority, which could be knocked off course by too much emphasis on such a heinous crime.[3] However, Takotavuki's treatment of the murder is complicated somewhat by the fact that he was not the only churchman said to have killed someone. During the beginning of my fieldwork project in 1998–1999, a lay preacher from Tailevu province lived in Rev. Serewai's house (as did I) because he wanted to become a minister, and he thought he could learn from Rev. Serewai and pass the entrance exam for the Methodist theological college. This man also claimed to have killed an Indo-Fijian (see Tomlinson 2007). For present purposes, my point is simply that Takotavuki's terse treatment of the murder is probably the product of various influences that are not intrinsically related.

Perhaps the most striking feature of the first part of his story is Takotavuki's expression of an individually grounded divine calling. As Reed (2003: 141) describes Papua New Guinean inmates, "Prisoners define Christian faith as the recognition of a certain kind of relation. The tie to God is presented as different in kind, marked out in opposition to other states of connection." Takotavuki displays such an understanding of faith by claiming that while in prison he "didn't smoke tobacco, didn't smoke tobacco." He explained to me that in prison, tobacco is a "part of your life" (*tiki ni nomu bula*). In other words, by denying himself tobacco, Takotavuki was signaling his difference from all of the other prisoners. Cut off from friends and family by his incarceration, he was now cut off from his fellow prisoners by rejecting this vital social product. But he does not deny a communal influence in his life, explaining in an explicitly metacultural passage, "We Fijians, raised in families, are raised in Sunday school, Sunday school, we're raised there. That's where we get to know the lotu. We're raised up, if there's a Fijian just going around, he or she knows the lotu." In other words, being an indigenous Fijian means one is a Christian from his or her earliest days.

However, one needs to rediscover this inheritance individually. Once he was in prison, Takotavuki recalls, "My thoughts returned to the things I had learned . . . from my parents, the pastors, Sunday school, because there is a God. . . . I didn't have a lawyer for my appeal. I just prayed to God. I just prayed, 'Lord, I'm not going to use anyone else. Because I know that there is a God.' " Asserting his knowledge of God's existence, Takotavuki presents his situation as an individual deviation from God's plan for him. In a remarkable passage, he refers to Saint Paul's claim that evil or sinfulness is inherent, and he interprets this as Satanic influence. Like many Protestants worldwide, but contrary to much indigenous Fijian discourse, Takotavuki presents an individual locus of his being, referring to "the true me."

In this singular moment of his narrative, Takotavuki reclaims Genesis 1:26, "And God said, Let us make man in our image, after our likeness." In contrast to the speakers quoted earlier in this book—for whom the verse means that humans have fallen from a divine origin— Takotavuki paraphrases the verse for its hopeful potential. Instead of reading Genesis 1:26 as a lament, he sees it as a promise, something he will both rely on and fulfill: he claims that he was "changed because God made you, to be like and resemble God." In Miyazaki's terms, the verse now has prospective momentum, looking toward a future in which one can be "like God" rather than looking at a perfect past and lamenting its loss.

After this section, he mentions that he wanted to be a musician playing in luxury hotels with a prison friend from Nadroga. He also describes being in prison around the time of Rabuka's first coup in 1987, when inmates were allowed to escape. As Takotavuki tells it, he decided not to take the chance to escape, and was then transferred to a minimum security prison. As we were recording his story, a visitor arrived, and I turned the tape off at that point. When I turned it back on, Takotavuki resumed.

PART 2: BACKSLIDING AND COMING HOME

Takotavuki: After minimum [security prison], I was told that I would have one year outside, eh? Working outside. There was one year left until I would be released. I was a good kid, well prepared, I could see that I would be able to work outside. One year. I was taken, I was free, freed, my freedom was given to me. Went outside, then went to—its name is EP, Extramural Prisoner [the program under whose auspices he got his rehabilitation job].

M. T.: Oh. This means, you slept in prison . . . and went outside during the day.

Takotavuki: No. I slept at home, but I went to work at, at a station in Lami. It was just half days, eh? Half day of rest. Then I was at home, I was studying . . . playing the guitar, I had an aim, one day my friend would get out [of prison], we would go together to, to Nadroga, or wherever—Western Side, go to find a hotel, play the guitar, eh? Because that was what [I] was studying.

Yes, I was lotu'ing [i.e., going to church, worshipping]. When I got out, my friends were waiting, beer was waiting, rum, waiting for me. I came out here, and forgot the lotu again. I went and drank a whole lot. Went dancing. Went to a dance hall, got in another fight at the dance, wanted to steal again. One time, I was out [of prison], the EP [program] was over, I was outside at home, that time, [I] stole from a store, I was back on the old road [i.e., of bad behavior]. Got the goods, was getting ready to put them in a pawnshop, a cop was following us. There were two of us. [We] were going, dumping [the goods] like this, we saw the cop like this, because we had just gotten out, we didn't know some of the new cops, eh? They were in plain-clothes, CID [Criminal Investigation Department] probably. They were following us. I took off then, we took off on a big chase. Hot pursuit. We ran—

M. T.: You ran away.

Takotavuki: We ran away together, we knew we would go to prison. We were running, and a CID officer was chasing us, they didn't catch us.

Coming from there, I humbly requested of my father that I wanted to come here, to Kadavu. . . . I knew I was close to going back to prison. Then I humbly requested, I'm from Kadavu, I finally came here. We came here with an, an elder from Baidamudamu. He was the father of Lepani the elder? He's the Takala [a title], eh? His "big father" [father's older brother], Masi, Aisake Masi. We came here together, we came here, I went to Baidamudamu. And I went to stay in Baidamudamu.

M. T.: Oh. Why did you go to Baidamudamu?

Takotavuki: Because we came here with the Takala. We came here together, Baidamudamu, stayed there a little while. A ceremony was performed, eh? [The ceremony was in regard to his traveling companions' previous absence, not his own arrival.] Were there a little while, then they took me to Waisomo. My house, the, my "small father" [father's younger brother]—who is he? [We] met him that day.

M. T.: Oh oh oh, ah—

Takotavuki: My "small father."

M. T.: Yeah yeah yeah. Jone Jini.

Takotavuki: Right. That's it. Then [I] was there. Was there, and settled in, went to the gardens, planted, was with those people, they had a lot of, ah, brought me back to—another kind of drink here, drinking homebrew, eh? Drinking homebrew was going on there again, marijuana was beginning to be smoked again.

M. T.: In Tavuki Bay?

Takotavuki: Yes. So I came here . . . and then a time came, I was caught, I was planting marijuana in Waisomo. A story about that time. The Waisomoans didn't know yet that marijuana was being grown in Waisomo. They only found out when I was there. My habits were getting bad again there, eh? Then I told the chiefs of Waisomo about it. The meeting hall. A village meeting was held there. They asked us young guys, "It's apparent that there's marijuana in our village. Which of you young men is planting it?" And I said, "I'm growing marijuana." I said it. And they requested of me—they, because they're just my [classificatory] fathers, my grandfathers, eh? Talking about it was easy. They just requested gently, "We ask that you please stop planting it." That was the last time I planted it.

M. T.: Oh. They just requested that you not—

Takotavuki: Because of the planting. They didn't turn me in to the police. Just a Fijian conversation [i.e., mutually respectful and within the in-group]. Then I told them, "Yes. I request, I will not plant it again." I quit.

I began then to come back to the lotu that I had begun in prison, when I was appealing [the sentence], [I] began again. I lotu'ed, I finally married Radini Vakatawa [the respectful title for a catechist's wife], such a young girl, my wife, Radini Vakatawa, a pretty redheaded girl.

M. T.: [Laughs] Phat![4]

Takotavuki: Right. [I] liked her, she was my cousin, right next door, and I stole her. I stole again. Because my father, my mother were in Suva [i.e., he could not ask them to help him request her hand in marriage formally].

> *M. T.:* But that's good stealing.
>
> *Takotavuki:* Right. I stole her, and it happened that our—we almost fought with my "small fathers," because they didn't—he [unclear whom] was back in Suva. Only my "small mother" [mother's younger sister] was around, she rejected it. And [we] said to—it's, we're just married. If not [i.e., if any relatives disapprove], we're just married [anyway]. Never mind, it's nothing. They finally accepted us when the fourth-night ceremonies were performed.

This section of Takotavuki's narrative oscillates between spiritual progress and backsliding. "I was lotu'ing," he recalls, but "When I got out [of prison], my friends were waiting, beer was waiting, rum, waiting for me. I came out here, and forgot the lotu again." In attempting to sell stolen goods to a pawnshop, he and an accomplice are almost caught, running away from the undercover police in a dramatic chase. Takotavuki runs, as it were, all the way back to Kadavu, his father's homeland. For the first time in his life, he is back on the foundation, back in the village where he will always have permanent belonging.

But problems surface again, as he begins drinking locally brewed beer and growing and smoking marijuana. When village elders ask who has been growing the drug, Takotavuki confesses, and in this moment he appeals again to communal dynamics: "Talking about it was easy. They just requested gently, 'We ask that you please stop planting it.' That was the last time I planted it. . . . Just a Fijian conversation." By "Just a Fijian conversation" he means that the discussion was mutually respectful and held within the in-group; the elders did not censure him, but asked him politely to stop growing marijuana, and he was obliged to honor their request. Back in the village he was relearning how to behave in proper Fijian style.

Nothing indicates his "conversion" to village life better than his marriage to his cousin, followed by the appropriate ritual celebrations. This is the right kind of transgression—"good stealing," as I joke to him— the sort of thing a young man ought to do, daring and successful, but also conservative in a way. His "theft," after all, creates a new family. At this point in the storytelling another visitor showed up, and the tape recorder was turned off again. When he resumed his narration, Takotavuki mentioned his marriage again, and then turned to a discussion of his troubles with marijuana, his deeply felt moment of spiritual rebirth, and how he became a preacher, then a pastor, then a catechist. This is the part of his life in which Saul becomes Paul. For Takotavuki, the road to Damascus runs through the middle of Waisomo village.

PART 3: SAUL TO PAUL

Takotavuki: And we were living a life, trying really hard, we didn't have our own house, [but] we were okay, her house was in Waisomo, my house too, Waisomo, eh? It was a difficult life [we] encountered. We finally moved into her house, their house. We were taken care of there. The time came, I started to work hard. I told my father in Suva to come build our house. A Fijian-style house, the one I showed [you] in the photo.

M. T.: Right. Oh, you built that house.

Takotavuki: Me and my father.

M. T.: Oh, Jone Jini.

Takotavuki: No. Apisalome Takotavuki. He's the eldest [of the brothers]. At that time, when the Fijian-style house was built, we moved up, we really began my lotu'ing. And she helped me with the lotu, eh?

M. T.: Your father.

Takotavuki: My, my wife. My wife. Radini Vakatawa helped, said that we should lotu. When it began, I smoked marijuana, and [I] said — and I prayed to God, "If you gave [us] marijuana, you know its usefulness in my life, you make it grow, you made it. If not [i.e., if marijuana is not good to use], take it away." Going on then, we were surprised, eh, Matthew, the time came, its [taste] was gone — because that's what [I] prayed for. God said, it has no use in your life, [so] then it was gone.

M. T.: How did you know [i.e., how did he know God had told him that marijuana was useless]?

Takotavuki: It was finished because I — time was, Matthew, my family knows, when I would get ready to eat, [I] would have two puffs, then I'd eat. If I didn't, I wouldn't enjoy the food. Also when I was getting ready to go to sleep. That's the thing — the level that marijuana got me to. That's what I prayed about. . . . Thereafter, I had no desire to drink or smoke marijuana; my prayers had been answered. We began to lotu then, began strongly [while we were] at the house — the Fijian-style house. Pray, pray. Lotu every day. The drum beats, go to church. Afternoon — morning, noon, afternoon, every Sunday. Whenever there was a church service, [we would] go.

Going along, then [I] knew it was beginning — being born again [lit., "made again"]. Hearing preaching, going [to church]. Then in 1994, I began to preach, to be heard. I was preaching. I was listened to in Waisomo. I was heard by Reverend — oh, catechist Isireli?

M. T.: [Isikeli] Rarasea?

Takotavuki: No, Isireli.

M. T.: Isireli.

Takotavuki: The retired catechist who's in Baidamudamu. Mo's father, and Joeli Leqete's, also a retired catechist. Then I, then they heard me, preaching, and approved it. [Catechists have to approve of trial preachers' performance so that they can become full preachers.] I was confirmed. I was a preacher.

When I was preaching, Waisomoans loved it. Because I spoke straight, sometimes I saw I was about to cry, I was touched, because I am a, I am a, I was showing [them] there the image of Saul—from Saul to Paul. It was plain to see. The story of Saul and Paul was my story. Every time I stood up it was like that. They would cry, they were emotional, that was how the vanua moved.

Then one day Apete Toko came to hold services and to teach. Apete Toko taught here [in Kadavu], at Namalata, then held a service and preached. And he was preaching, we, we were sitting in the meeting house. That was it, I was really nailed by the preaching of Apete Toko. That was evident. My tears were falling. Just falling. It was clear to me that I should be a preacher. I should—I knew that God was calling me. My tears were falling, eh? Because of the preaching, that preaching was sweet, and—it really got to us, eh? It was really affecting for those of us with crushed and broken spirits, you could be like that if you were really pierced by a sermon. Your teardrops will come, signs of the Holy Spirit, or the things that touch you. Speaking like that makes your spirit feel pained, eh?

Then I began to preach, praying about it. Fasting, fasting, fasting on the first day of the week—each Sunday, eh? Praying, because there I was growing, like—y'know? Fasting so I could grow strong, [be a] strong person. . . . Eventually Radini Vakatawa said to me, "Don't you want to study to be a catechist?" When I was a preacher, eh? "You—you should go study to be a catechist." Because they saw the big change, and when I was preaching, some of them would tell me, "You're preaching just like a minister." Some of them told me that, eh? . . . Then I told Radini Vakatawa, "Radini Vakatawa, if the place that God is calling us is Waisomo, I'm just a preacher, but that's enough." We—. After that, some—maybe two or three years in Waisomo. [I was a] pastor, eh? I began to be called to be a pastor. I was the pastor at Waisomo. We were called, some of us young people, in [Tavuki] Bay. There were six of us who sat for the catechist exam. Trial catechist [i.e., the test was to become a trial catechist, who could later become a full catechist]. Me and them [he gives the names of the others]. We all failed, only I and Tu Nai passed it that first year. Our first year of sitting for the exam and we two passed it. That would be the call [to take the exam] from the leader of this division, Setareki Tuilovoni [the superintendent minister]. Choosing us to sit for it.

M. T.: You didn't sit . . . [for the] exam when Rev. Serewai was here?

Takotavuki: No. It was his call [Rev. Tuilovoni's]. But another, I know that lots of [other] ministers helped me a lot, my growth, my preaching. Rev. Isikeli Koroi, hearing his preaching was good for me. Because he was an older man, eh? His preaching touched me a lot, because he was older, it's like it confirmed things because he was an older man, being a preacher has brought maturity to my life, eh? His theology, everything he said was good for me. His preaching touched me a lot, Isikeli Koroi. Then Isikeli Serewai reinforced [me], good older man.

In this part of his story, effective action is almost entirely verbal. Unable to give up marijuana completely, Takotavuki prays, and God miraculously takes away the drug's appeal. Freed from this bond, he begins worshipping fervently: "Pray, pray. Lotu every day." He also begins to preach: "Waisomoans loved it. Because I spoke straight. . . . I was showing [them] there the image of Saul—from Saul to Paul. It was plain to see. The story of Saul and Paul was my story." Among his own people, Takotavuki is suggesting, the enormous changes wrought in his life by Christianity were dramatically evident.

Yet more verbal sparks were to fly. Apete Toko, who was mentioned in chapter 5 as the author of the Fijian Methodist Church's annual calendar, came as a visiting preacher and teacher to Namalata village, a twenty-minute boat ride from Tavuki. Toko's performance "nailed" Takotavuki, whose "tears were falling. Just falling." He was now completely sure that God wanted him to be a preacher, to speak divine words: "It was clear to me that I should be a preacher. I should—I knew that God was calling me. My tears were falling, eh? Because of the preaching, that preaching was sweet, and—it really got to us, eh? It was really affecting for those of us with crushed and broken spirits." He was changing from being "under conviction" to being "saved," that is, developing from a listener to religious discourse into a speaker of it (Harding 2000: 59). After he heard Rev. Toko's performances, Takotavuki's new sense of salvation propelled him forward, and other people's appreciation of his skills led to talk that he might advance within the Church hierarchy: "Because they [his fellow villagers] saw the big change, and when I was preaching, some of them would tell me, 'You're preaching just like a minister.' "

In quick narrative order, Takotavuki becomes the Waisomo village pastor (*qase*) and then, under the superintendency of Rev. Tuilovoni, sits for the catechists' examination. He and another young man, Ratu Alipate Naivolivoli from Nagonedau, are the only two to pass. He mentions (in a section I am not including here) that a former minister knew Takotavuki had been a prisoner. Next comes a remarkable segment of the story in which he skips backward a few years, explaining how, before he became the Tavuki catechist, God was preparing him for the position.

PART 4: ONLY GOD KNOWS THE PLANS

> *Takotavuki:* When he gave the call here, [Rev.] Serewai was here taking care of things, I was still a preacher. The church leaders' meetings were called, the pastors were [told] to come and work, I would come. I wasn't supposed to come, [but] I came, I just knew, because I was lotu'ing, I had given my life to God. I didn't care for—everything is God's, I believe that. But I didn't know it had begun, God was preparing me, in the church compound,[5] that one day I would be in charge there, [in the] small circuit of Tavuki. Those are the things we don't know; only God knows the plans.

Although God is presented here as the driving force of events, Takotavuki repeatedly characterizes himself as an effective actor who is gaining authority: "I would come . . . I came, I just knew, because I was lotu'ing, I had given my life to God." In these few sentences, Takotavuki illuminates the process described by Miyazaki (2004: 119–120), in which Christian speakers foreground their own agency and place God's agency in the background—all while prominently referring to God as the ultimate agent. As in his earlier paraphrase of Genesis 1:26, here too Takotavuki is drawing himself and God into closer alignment, presenting himself as the active fulfillment of a divine plan.

At this point he mentions that he had joked that Tavuki would be his first assignment as a catechist, although he had not known this would really happen. Indeed, as he explains below, it should not happen, according to Church policy. But when the Tavuki position opened up, the circuit leaders' meeting appointed him. After saying that he had joked about such an event, Takotavuki claims that he "wasn't surprised" (*au sa sega ni kurabui*) because he knew God approved the choice. This leads to the final part of his autobiography, the coda in which Takotavuki summarizes his progress to the present and ends the story with a quip about fame.

PART 5: THE MIRACLE OF GOD

> *Takotavuki:* Finally I, we were appointed here, appointed here, I shouldn't have been here because this is [the place for] a full catechist, but I was still a trial catechist, [the] first step. But that's the miracle of God. Then [we] came and were here, and the minister said, the lessons for the exam for the full catechists are a bit difficult. We prayed, and PowerHouse prayed, prayed for me, [for] us who were sitting [for the exam]. I sat with Isimeli Wawaisoro, [who is] my steward now, we both became full catechists at this time. It was confirmed.
>
> *M. T.:* He also became a full catechist?
>
> *Takotavuki:* Yes. Full catechist. He became a full catechist.
>
> *M. T.:* But he's not . . . isn't yet—
>
> *Takotavuki:* He's still waiting for his appointment, eh? Waiting for his appointment. And here we are. It's a great blessing that you're able to record my story, my friend, my friend Matthew, coming all the way from America to be a witness, in case, some day God's calling is not heard around the world, my picture will be out there.

In this concluding section, Takotavuki explains that as a beginning catechist he should not have been eligible to serve on the Tavuki circuit, but he was appointed anyway: "That's the miracle of God." Then, fulfilling God's plans for him—with the help of PowerHouse, the Tavuki women's prayer group (see chapter 1, note 22)—he passes the examination to become a fully accredited catechist. The other man passing the test was, at the time of this story's telling, the village steward for Tavuki, still waiting for an appointment as a catechist somewhere else. Takotavuki finishes his story by joking that he might become famous because of my photographs of him.

Perhaps the most remarkable thing about Takotavuki's narrative is how his relationship to language defines his progress as a religious authority. For him, becoming a Christian authority means learning to speak in new ways. His life story is ultimately a story about finding a voice: first he learns to pray, then to preach; he pleads his legal case without a lawyer and eventually gains his freedom; he successfully passes institutional examinations as both a preacher and a catechist. Now, at the end, he jokes that I have come "all the way from America" to hear him and see his influence—and perhaps to propagate his influence by circulating his image.

Takotavuki's story reverses the golden age theme. His golden age is right now: a life of crime over and finished, a life of religious authority proceeding and progressing. At other moments, in other narratives, he was as adept at telling tales of lost mana as any other person in Tavuki Bay. In his autobiography, however, Takotavuki is attempting to reclaim mana through learning to speak for God.

In the mid-nineteenth century, a Fijian man complained bitterly to the missionary Joseph Waterhouse about the deep and irreversible changes that Methodists had caused. "Will you leave me without a god?" he asked in melancholy and anger. "Is this your religion of love? You talk of benevolence and of love. It is a veil with which you would conceal your cruelty. Missionary, you are cruel! You deprive us of all our gods; you take from us our best deities . . . and you make us forlorn wanderers on earth without a solitary god to comfort us!" (quoted in Thornley 2002: 69). The man's despair is moving. But an intriguing thing happened to the sense of loss that he expressed: once it became a standardized narrative, it became detachable from its original context. That is, once it became a story about the fall from a golden age, in which the past was a time of mana and the present is relatively powerless, it became generic and highly recontextualizable. Once this metacultural talk of decline and loss began to circulate, it circulated with remarkable vigor. In fact, it circulated so well that it was soon used to prove the very opposite of this man's dismal vision of a depleted Fijian spiritual world. The Fijian spirits were still around. Indeed, they still had effectiveness in the world, in contrast to fallen humanity.

The Methodists had triumphed in Fiji, but one of the most significant and lasting developments they brought to the islands was a sense of loss and diminution. Yet Methodism also offers the recuperation of mana to people like Takotavuki. His autobiography is a performance in which his life's trajectory—a coming-into-power—is the mirror image of Fijian history in discourse about the golden age.

Whether the nation of Fiji will experience its own redemption after the violence of coups remains to be seen. Anthropologically speaking,

the most evident fact is that Fiji's immediate future, for many indigenous Fijians, is an inherently and consequentially Christian one. The
most intriguing question, then, is how visions of power and possibility
will change in the coming years. What happens when promised lands
suffer broken trust? How does a sense of divine mission move from violence to new kinds of salvation? Finally, when does the painful certainty of loss become a sense of luminous potential?

Notes

Introduction

1. Will Swanton, "Let's Do It Again," *The Age,* special section on the Commonwealth Games, March 17, 2006.

2. Beliefs about Fijians' descent from the tribes of Israel began forming in the late nineteenth century, elaborated in stories about an ancestral journey from Tehran via Iraq and Ethiopia. The widespread acceptance of this legend was spurred by Methodist missionaries' teachings, which were partly based on incorrect beliefs about racial origins (Thornley 2002: 479). The story gained national prominence through a newspaper contest in 1892, when the government publication *Na Mata* held a competition "in order to select and preserve a definitive version of the legendary history of the people" (France 1966: 112). In the 1960s, Ratu Kitione Vesikula, a high chief of Verata, told the tale in a series of radio addresses, giving the narrative "its final irreproachable authority" (Tuwere 2002: 22; see also Geraghty 1977, Sahlins 1962: 229).

3. Christianity is not the only cultural force that generates irresolvable tensions, certainties of loss, and ongoing attempts at recuperation. A work such as Marilyn Ivy's 1995 *Discourses of the Vanishing* provides a useful point of comparison. Ivy examines Japanese anxieties about modernity's "losses" and "remainders," which are manifest in practical-nostalgia projects: folklore, tourism in which one discovers a "homeland," commodified séances in lands associated with spirits of the dead, and so forth. As Ivy describes it, "Japanese of all generations seek a recognition of continuity that is coterminous with its negation" (10); modernity forges new desires for the emblematically old. Her term *vanishing* applies well to Fijian *mana:* "The vanishing . . . (dis)embodies in its gerund form the movement of something passing away, gone but not quite, suspended between presence and absence, located at a point that both is and is not here in the repetitive process of absenting" (20).

4. In this book, I use the term *discourse* in the linguistic sense expressed by Émile Benveniste (1971: 208–209): "Discourse must be understood in its widest sense: every utterance assuming a speaker and a hearer, and in the speaker, the intention of influencing the other in some way. It is primarily every variety of oral discourse of every nature and every level, from trivial conversation to the most elaborate oration. But it is also the mass of writing that reproduces oral discourse or that borrows its manner of expression and its purposes."

5. Andrew Arno (2003, 2005) has developed detailed analyses of the non-verbal generation of meaning in Fijian ritual performances. For example, in a *dranukilikili* ritual that Arno observed in Lau (Fiji's eastern group of islands), women rub stones with perfumed oil and place them on a relative's gravesite, later wrapping the stones in bark cloth and giving the packages to female kin; the participants are unable to explain the meaning of these actions, but, Arno (2003: 808–809) argues, this is "precisely because a verbal expression of the stones' meaning was not necessary to the communicative functions of the ritual acts. Their essential, deeper meaning did not reside in language and would have been inadequately represented in language." Their meaning emerges instead from the way their manipulation resonates with patterns of routine practice, such as oiling one's own body, massaging other people's bodies when they are in pain, and wrapping honored people's bodies in bark cloth on special occasions. The actions in *dranukilikili* are meaningful because of their practical, nonverbal expression of *veilomani,* acts of love and caring (815). I agree with Arno's argument that "all ritual elements . . . [have] a considerable component of meaning in the doing that does not depend on the symbolic representation of explicit, verbalized ideas" (2005: 49), but I also argue that Fijian Methodist ritual is dominated by talking *as* doing: the act of worship is embodied most effectively in the generation of utterances.

6. On this paraphrase of Genesis 1:26, see the prologue to part 2.

Chapter 1. Situating Kadavu

1. On this distinction and its consequences, see especially Arno (1993), Kaplan (1990a, 1990b, 1995); Lawson (1997); Ryle (2005); Sahlins (1962, 1985, 2004); Tuwere (2002); cf. Toren (1999).

2. "Tukutuku Lekaleka me Baleti Baidamudamu" (Short Information about Baidamudamu), in *Ai Tuvatuva ni Soqo ni Kena Curumi ka Vakatabui ni Valenilotu "Kenisareti"* (Program for the Opening and Consecration of Kenisareti [Gennesaret] Church), April 3, 1999, unpublished document in author's possession.

3. I was told during fieldwork that the Nephew-to-Naceva's name was Naidusidodonu; however, a version of the story published in a Fijian-language newspaper in 2007 gives his identity as Ratu Dausigavakawalu. See Alipate Driu, "Tutu Vaka Tui Tavuki e Kadavu" (The Position of Tui Tavuki in Kadavu), *Na i Volasiga* (Morning Star), May 22, 2007, available at http://www.fijidailypost.com/print.php?type=volasiga&index=184.

4. Toren (1999: 166–167), working in Gau Island, notes a somewhat similar situation there with "a putative paramount . . . often named and never installed. . . . This was also the case in the past." She adds, "When I asked people why this was so I received one of two answers: one gave particular reasons to account for particular instances and usually referred to the unfitness of a particular person to take office; the other was contained in the explanation that 'there . . . is too much *veiqati*' (lit., rivalry)" (see also Arno 1993: 54–56).

5. In contrast to Hocart's version of the Nephew-to-Naceva story, in Nayacakalou's version the office of Tui Tavuki predated the war, and the victory simply caused the transfer of the title between subclans. Nayacakalou traced the present situation to around 1917, when, according to this version of the story, Nacolase tried to claim Nukunawa's traditional role as installers of the paramount chief when they informed a government commission about hereditary roles in the village. "The Nukunawa were thereupon divested of these functions, but the Nacolase dared not carry them out themselves for fear of supernatural punishment and no *Tui* Tavuki has been installed to this day" (Nayacakalou 1975: 40).

6. The population fluctuates as people leave for education or work elsewhere. The figure of 166 church congregants in Tavuki listed in table 3 is several dozen higher than I counted in 1999, but had I surveyed households at Christmastime I would have counted a higher number.

7. For a survey of various translations of *yavusa,* see Nayacakalou (1975: 13–14). Fijian kin groups do not always nest neatly because they are partly the invention of colonial administrators, as shown by scholars such as Clammer (1973), France (1969), Kelly and Kaplan (2001), and Nayacakalou (1975). That is, different regions of Fiji used different systems with different terminologies, and British bureaucrats jammed disparate systems together into an unwieldy—and for some Fijians, unrecognizable—jumble. One of the main reasons the Crown insisted on neatly logical units was to settle issues of landownership, but their efforts only complicated matters. Indeed, disagreements persist within Tavuki about whether the three main patrilineal groups of Nacolase—Nadurusolo, Naocovonu, and Vunikarawa—are properly *mataqali* or are instead *itokatoka,* the unit below the *mataqali* (cf. Nayacakalou 1961, 1975). Such disagreements reinforce the local sense that social order is now chaotic.

8. The social unit above the *yavusa* is the vanua, and although vanua can be translated in this regard as "chiefdom," *yavusa* and *mataqali* have their own leading chiefs as well. Depending on which criteria are used, one can count four, nine, or fourteen vanua within Kadavu. The four paramount vanua of Kadavu, ceremonially recognized as the island's most powerful chiefdoms, are Tavuki, Nabukelevu, Naceva, and Nakasaleka. Kadavu is divided into nine government districts, each headed by a chief, and these nine chiefdoms-cum-districts include Ravitaki, Sanima, Yale, Yawe, and Ono. Finally, at present there are fourteen polities officially recognized as vanua by Fijian Affairs: Tavuki, Nabukelevu, Nakasaleka, Nasegai, Ravitaki, Sanima, Koroisoso, Tabanivonolevu, Vadraivakaruru, Nakaugasele, Lomanikoro, Yale, Yawe, and Ono (Seruvakula 2000: 138–139).

9. Thornley (2000: 179 n. 116) mentions that the phrase "walking in the mouths of sharks" might refer to the activities of Qaraniqio, a notoriously anti-Christian chief whose name means "shark's cave." Presumably, the teacher might also have been implying the presence of Dakuwaqa, the shark god with the "tattooed belly" (Tuwere 2002: 142; see also Sahlins 2004: 217 n. 18; Toren 1999: 174; Wall 1918, 1919).

10. One Tahitian and two Moorean Christian teachers had begun working in Fiji several years earlier, but their impact was slight (Thornley 1995; Wood 1978: 21).

11. Page references are included for all quotations where possible. In cases where the pages of the original source are unnumbered, no page reference is given.

12. Because of these Bible translation efforts, what was called Bauan later became the standardized national language called Fijian, although biblical Fijian and modern standard Fijian diverge considerably. Drawing a connection between dialectal forms in the Bible and eastern Fijians' reputations as "papaw [papaya] eaters," one of Floyd Cammack's informants complained that the language of Methodism "smells of papaw" (1962: 14). Geraghty (1989: 385) describes the language of the Fijian Bible as a creation of the missionaries: "The language this small band of well-intentioned amateur language-planners . . . forged was far from native; it even verged on the pidgin in some respects, yet the Bible was written in it, and, wholly or partially, most Fijian literature since."

13. For lists of mission-introduced loanwords in Fijian, including many of the examples I have given here, see Clammer (1976: 40, 48–50) and Schütz (1985, 2004).

14. Buatava (1996: 182), citing an earlier source, describes the persecution of Catholics in Kadavu and mentions an incident in Tavuki in which "a local chief traditionally presented mats and food with a tabua (whale's tooth) to some Catholics asking them to give up the faith." Unfortunately, he does not give the date of the occurrence, but it seems to have been in the late nineteenth century.

15. Paul Geraghty (personal communication, July 2008) confirms that this phrase is used generally in Fiji, not only in Kadavu.

16. Robson's "verified" figures, as quoted by Tippett (1974b: 30), were 697 men, 458 women, and 546 children. However, this should add up to a total of 1,701 fatalities, not 1,811. Moreover, in his 1875 Kadavu Circuit Report, Robson reported 1,273 deaths. Thus the actual figure is difficult to determine. But whatever the amount, it was a devastating total for an island of 10,000 people. One writer reports that an estimated 28 percent of Fiji's entire population succumbed to the disease that year (Wood 1978: 205).

17. In 1855 control of the Fiji mission had shifted from London to Sydney, and the Methodist Church in Fiji became a district of the New South Wales and Queensland Conference of Australia's Methodist Church (Wood 1978: vii). Various organizational changes took place over the next century, including the creation of the Methodist Church of Australasia, which included Fiji, in 1902 (vii).

18. Karen Brison (2007: 50, 46) writes that "church structure, in some ways, gave women more obvious prominence than did vanua occasions," but allows that "in practice . . . rank within the church reflected fairly closely rank outside the church." Taking a historical perspective, Christina Toren (1988: 707–708) notes, "In pre-Christian Fiji, women . . . had access to the *mana* of the ancestors only through their menfolk (father, brother or husband)"; with the coming of the Church, women could approach divinity without the mediation of a man— through prayer, for example. Thus Methodism allows women greater opportunity for public authority and responsibility than the vanua does, but it is important not to overdraw the comparison, as some vanua-related events are conducted by women only (see, e.g., Arno 1993: 61) and Methodism does maintain many constraints on women's actions.

Toren observes that women's differential status within the lotu and the vanua are marked by seating patterns at church services and kava-drinking sessions, respectively. In church services, women and men sit on separate sides— in Tavuki, women on the left, men on the right—which are hierarchically equivalent to each other, although the seating within each section varies hierarchically. (Those of higher status sit closer to the front of the church, although children and the choir also have their separate sections at the front; high chiefs sometimes sit in special chairs at the very "top" end of the church, behind or to the side of the pulpit.) Spatially, then, the lotu allows for a kind of equivalence between male and female. In mixed-sex kava-drinking sessions, by contrast, women almost always sit lower than men, often in a separate group by themselves; thus the vanua consistently keeps women in a lower place.

19. Thornley (2005: 148) argues that the official creation of the position of *vakatawa*, which took place in 1876, was a strategy by which European and Australian missionaries intended to limit the number of indigenous Fijians who became ordained ministers.

20. In April 2002 the Tavuki catechist listed a total of nineteen preachers in Tavuki and Nagonedau (out of 171 congregants); the superintendent minister's statistics for 2003 counted fourteen preachers in Tavuki and Nagonedau and a total of 110 preachers for the entire circuit of Tavuki.

21. In formal presentations, representatives often act on behalf of the main parties (see, e.g., Arno 1985: 130).

22. In 2003 I learned that a group of women in Tavuki had formed their own prayer group, dubbed "PowerHouse." Their meetings were held in the Methodist church independently of regular Methodist prayer meetings and services, but PowerHouse was not a dissident group. At the meeting I attended, the prayer topics were the lotu, the vanua, and the provincial office (i.e., the government). In other words, the topics were the same as those at many regular prayer services.

23. Another obligation is to provide the morning service's preacher with lunch. This particular responsibility is assigned to a different household each week.

24. The catechist evidently made a small mathematical error here.

Chapter 2. Signs of the Golden Age

1. The story of a fall is seen not only in the Bible, but also in the writings of early Christian theologians such as Origen, who posited "the fall of rational creatures from an original unity with God, a fall that, in his opinion, accounted for the very existence of the material world" (Trigg 1983: 105). Similarly, Cyprian asked in A.D. 250, "Who cannot see that the world is already in its decline, and no longer has the strength and vigor of former times?" (quoted in Boyer 1992: 231). These writers built on a foundation laid in Greek and Roman mythology, wherein Kronos and Saturn, respectively, ruled a superior past. Once established, the story was of course open to parody: Telecleides joked about "rivers of soup and self-frying fish" in the old days (Baldry 1952: 86).

2. Although I am treating Christianity and colonialism separately, their practical interplay is vital in constructing a sense of loss, diminution, and disorder. Joel Robbins (2005: 47), extending a suggestion of Marshall Sahlins (1992), argues persuasively that "Christianity becomes something of a clearinghouse for processing colonial humiliation and sending it out to local people as something they themselves have ordered."

3. Myths of prehistoric Kadavu include stories of massive giants, superhuman beings who bent the world to their will. "They . . . have in [Kadavu] a number of legendary or fabulous accounts concerning giants, &c.," wrote one seafarer in the mid-nineteenth century. "One of these is of a wonderfully large man who arrived there in a canoe about a hundred times as big as the biggest ship they ever saw" (Jackson 1999: 7). Another tale describes fighting between the giants Tautaumolau from Nabukelevu and Tanovo from Ono, and the effects their battles wrought upon the landscape (Beauclerc 1999: 26–29; Deane 1999: 30–35). One well-known story from Naceva, on the south coast, concerns the octopus god Bakaliceva, who fought the famous shark god Dakuwaqa. (Bakaliceva is local to Kadavu, specifically to the Naceva area, but Dakuwaqa is known throughout Fiji.) Although Dakuwaqa had a fierce reputation, the octopus fought resolutely, placing four tentacles on the reef and grabbing the shark with his other four tentacles. As the mighty octopus was winning the battle, he told Dakuwaqa that he would let him go if the shark god promised never to harm Nacevans.

4. The missionary Jesse Carey (1867–1874: 154) reported in 1869 that he had measured fifty students at Rijimodi, Kadavu—apparently all adults—and that their average height was a modest five feet, seven inches. Decades later, A. M. Hocart (1929: 43) measured thirty-nine men in two villages on Lakeba, in Lau, and listed an average height between five feet, six and a half inches and five feet, eight and a half inches. Thus the Fijians of past centuries were giants only in people's imaginations.

5. In an article on the Wiru of Papua New Guinea, Jeffrey Clark (1989) noted the figurative relationship between body size and social vigor. He also analyzed Christianity's role in generating ideologies of diminution: "Christianity, as an ideology stressing obeisance, meekness, non-violence, a wider brotherhood, and so forth, has contributed to this perception [Wiru] men have of their chang-

ing nature, which, although behavioural, is explained in physical terms"—namely, as bodily shrinking (128; see also Clark 2000).

6. It is unclear whether Veibataki meant that life was less precious in those days and that soldiers were therefore more pliable, or if he was making a poetic association between life and a language (*na vosa* can mean "word," "language," or "speak"); that is, everyone spoke (acted) with one voice. When I asked him to explain what he meant, he said that he was comparing people's lives in the past to soldiers' lives: they were quick, disciplined, and didn't make excuses.

7. *[I]taukei* literally means "owners," connoting landownership; it is a term integral to the conceptualization of the vanua. See Kaplan (2005), Srebrnik (2002).

8. Haircuts were not a trivial matter in older Fijian estimations: "It is the heads . . . which excite wonder, and on no other part of his person does the Fijian expend so much time, pains, and skill. . . . One stranger, on seeing their performances in this department, exclaims, 'What astonishing wigs!' another, 'Surely the beau-ideal of hairdressing must reside in Fiji' " (Williams 1982: 157).

9. Dixon includes a third term as a translation for *leqa:* "responsibility"; I have not heard it used in this sense. *Leqa* can also be used as a euphemism for death (see Toren 2004: 234) or mental illness.

10. I am paraphrasing the conversation from memory and field notes.

Chapter 3. Sermons

Epigraph: Cargill (1977: 77).

1. Arno (1993: 82) notes, "The hypocritical churchman . . . represents somewhat of a stock character in village storylines—at least among those who are less than staunch in their support of the church."

2. Sermon notes were circulated early in Fiji's mission history: in 1844 "2000 copies of [John] Hunt's short sermons and lectures" were printed (Thornley 2000: 261; see also Tippett 1974a: 406).

3. Perhaps the most telling statement of the authority of the English language came from a young girl in Tavuki. I asked her in Fijian what subjects she studied at school, and she answered in English, "maths, social studies, health, elemental science, English, writing." I asked a follow-up question: *"O iko vulica na vosa Vaviti?"* (Do you study the Fijian language?). "Mm mm," she replied, again in English, "Fijian."

4. Prayers are formulaic and highly honorific and often given in a register of Standard Fijian. The linguist Robert Dixon writes that he was invited to say a prayer in a Methodist church in Taveuni. He prayed aloud in the local dialect, Bouma, undoubtedly supposing that his efforts would be appreciated. Instead, he remarks, "I received a reprimand—God, the Christian priests had said, only likes to be addressed in [Standard Fijian]" (1997: 105; see also Cammack 1962).

5. See chapter 6 for a fuller analysis of his sermon, including one part in which he seems to suggest that the Holy Spirit was present among the congregation.

6. The question of what the lotu is can be raised in public discourse outside of church services. In a remarkable kava session at Wailevu, on Kadavu's south coast, in June 2003, a group of around forty men heard a friendly debate on this subject. The debate was instigated by the Ravitaki village catechist. He kept asking, *"Na yava na lotu?"* (What is the lotu?), and criticizing the responses he received in a mildly combative but generally genial way. Occasionally he rephrased his question, using lotu as a verb: *"'Au lai lotu.' Na yava na kena ibalebale?"* ([People say] "I'm going to lotu." What does that mean?). At least six members of the audience participated substantially, including the minister of the Ravitaki circuit. The respondents' speaking styles varied. One old man, whom I never identified, sounded peeved at the question; the pastor from Mokoisa village sounded earnest, pleading, almost desperate in his answers. Through it all, the Ravitaki catechist was confident and humorous, thoroughly in charge of the debate and enjoying it. Various answers that he swatted away were "clothing" (*isulu*, i.e., one's dress as a mark of dedication to God); "a Tongan word" (*vosa Vatoga*, not as sarcastic an answer as it sounds, because the speaker was calling attention to the fact that the lotu had come to Fiji from elsewhere); "just people" (*tamata ga*); and "the Gospel, the good news" (*itukutuku vinaka*). On Fijian joking debates, see Arno (1985, 1990, 1993); see also Miyazaki's description of a Seventh-day Adventist Bible study leader whose hectoring tone is reminiscent of the Ravitaki catechist's (2000: 34–35).

7. The translation "pronounce the vanua" (for *cavuta na vanua*) is based on *cavuta*'s meaning "to pronounce a name" (Capell 1991: 28). It sounds awkward in English, but I want to keep the connotation of effective declaration.

8. Here I am translating *itukutuku* as "story," although it has the sense of "news" or "information."

9. The verb used by Veibataki, *vakadodonutaka,* means "to correct" (Dixon 1988: 360); Capell (1991: 54) notes that the root *donu* is used "in church language sometimes for 'holy'; correct, befitting, becoming, true, righteous." I translate it here literally as "straighten out" to convey the sense of correcting a process gone awry.

10. The name Bethlehem is Hebrew for "house of bread" (Cheyne and Black 1899: 560), and Jesus calls himself the "bread of life" in John 6, suggesting the relevance of these lines to Veibataki's sermon. However, I too neglected to ask Rev. Serewai for his own statement of what he meant. It may be that Veibataki knew the etymology but preferred to defer my question to a higher Church authority.

11. By making the noun *itosotoso* the object of the verb *vabacia,* "to harm," Veibataki casts movement as something positive but threatened; thus I translate it as "progress."

12. Karen Brison's 2007 interviews with indigenous Fijian women in Ra province are revealing. Despite their widely divergent ages, socioeconomic positions, religious orientations, and personalities, the women consistently represent themselves as truly adhering to tradition, in contrast to others who fail to do so. Whatever their circumstances, the women—even the self-conscious

modernizers—frame their narratives in terms of their own success at upholding traditional values of the vanua.

13. *Sucu me lewai kia na ivunau* can be translated as either "made under the law" or "born under the law." *Sucu* means "born." Galatians 4:4 ("But when the fulness of the time was come, God sent forth his Son, made of a woman, made under the law") was translated into Fijian with the word *sucu* for "made," and I am following that example here.

Chapter 4. Kava

1. An Australian pharmacological study suggests that kava may "produce impairment in the more complex tests of cognitive function. . . . The most pronounced effects were in the [reaction time] component of the divided attention task" (Prescott, Jamieson, Emdur, and Duffield 1993: 56).

2. Sometimes kava is drunk "raw," that is, when the roots are still fresh and not sun-dried. Traditionally, the roots were not pounded into powder, but chewed.

3. Some matanivanua inherit the role, but at casual kava-drinking sessions with no hereditary matanivanua present, someone simply chooses to fill the role. In a pinch, when there are very few people present, it can even be the foreign anthropologist who plays the role. The missionary Thomas Williams (1982: 27) wrote that matanivanua were "the legitimate medium of communication between the Chiefs and their dependencies, and form a complete and effective agency" (see also Hocart 1936: 105). Ilaitia Tuwere (2002: 72, 106), noting that the herald is "a go-between or mediator," refers to Jesus as a "supreme *matanivanua* who has come not only to affirm but also to challenge and redeem and to set a new order."

4. At casual drinking sessions the mixer claps with hands cupped and held crosswise for a deep, resonant sound. On formal occasions, he coils the wet bark strainer tightly and holds it, slightly concave, in his left palm, clapping against the strainer with his right hand for a thudding sound.

5. As noted earlier, women often drink kava in mixed-sex groups, but it is acceptable for a woman to decline to drink, whereas a man can almost never do this. At informal kava sessions men and women may flirt by carrying cups of kava to each other; this is called *somi suka* (drinking sugar). Children may hang around kava sessions, but they are only rarely offered a sip and never join in regular drinking. I was told that young men begin drinking kava regularly around the time they stop attending school.

6. For example, one middle-aged woman in Tavuki noted that the job of a *turaga* (often translated "chief" but denoting the head of any kin-based social unit; see Nayacakalou 1975: 153 n. 1) was to "just sit [and] lead" (*dabe ga, vakatulewa*). She complained that the head of her subclan sometimes had to pound and mix his own kava, as well as sit high in the kava circle; in other words, he was both high and low, served and server. In disapproval, she said that this was

"erroneous" (*cala*). On chiefs' obligation to "just sit," see Sahlins (1985: 91; 2004: 60).

7. Smoking tobacco and drinking kava go together for many adult men. Some men roll their own natural tobacco in thin strips of newspaper for smoking, but many purchase and smoke Benson & Hedges Special Filter "king size" packs of ten. In the mid-nineteenth century, Thomas Williams (1982: 161) wrote, "Tobacco, though known only for about thirty years, is in such high favour, that its use is all but universal, children as well as adults indulging in it freely."

8. As it happened, Tavuki already had two relevant village laws: "Drinking kava on Sunday [is forbidden] (until the afternoon church service is finished)," and "Cutting down the overconsumption of Fijian kava [is a goal]." "Lawa ni Koro ko Tavuki" (Tavuki Village Laws), photocopy in author's possession.

9. The loss of meaning (*ibalebale*) is another kind of loss marking the fall from a golden age. Speakers who criticize contemporary kava drinking as meaningless are evidently judging meaningfulness in terms of intention and function and evaluating its loss morally. In a similar vein, Fiji's military commander turned coup leader and prime minister, Voreqe Bainimarama, said about Fiji's national insignia, "Mottos such as 'Fear God and Honour the King' are no longer meaningful. We do things that are not supposed to be done in a Christian country. The values are gone" (quoted in Kaplan 2004: 179–180). See also Engelke and Tomlinson (2006); Tomlinson (2006a).

10. Penny Baba, "Yaqona: Is It Getting the Nation Doped?" *Weekend: Fiji Times Magazine,* April 6, 1996.

11. During my period of fieldwork in Kadavu, kava was usually not bought for an evening's consumption because so much was grown locally.

12. Baba, "Yaqona."

13. Turner (1986: 209) writes, "In Fiji it is believed that a person's *mana* can be nurtured or enhanced by the drinking of *yaqona,* for *yaqona* is itself *mana.* Informants stated this to me explicitly" (see also Toren 1988: 704). Such claims are predicated on drinking the "proper" amount, however, not overconsuming. In Tavuki I was occasionally told that kava was good medicine (*wai ni mate*), but when people felt sick, they sometimes refrained from drinking kava for a few nights until the "coldness" they felt inside them dissipated (cf. Turner 1986: 210; Turner 1995). Kava is considered a "cold" beverage and alcohol a "hot" beverage for several reasons, including the sensations they generate in a drinker's body.

14. People sometimes described how a Chinese storekeeper had sold methylated spirits in Tavuki twenty years earlier, and how this had led to undesirable amounts of alcoholic drunkenness. After the sale of spirits was banned in the village, I was told, people drank more kava. A middle-aged man from Waisomo village, near Tavuki, told me that Kadavuans drank more kava in the late 1990s than when he was twenty years old (around 1963). He attributed the increased consumption to the growth of the market for selling kava. Sofer (1985: 418) recorded an increase in Kadavuan kava cultivation over a ten-year period: in 1968, 73 percent of Kadavuan farmers in his study grew the crop, but this increased to 92 percent in 1978 (see also Ward 1964).

15. Quoted in Paul Geraghty, "'When I Was a Lad . . .': Thoughts on Our National Drink," *Fiji's Daily Post,* April 28, 1996.

16. "Women Highlight Social Problem," *Fiji Times,* January 21, 1999.

17. "Ratu Mara Warns over Kava Abuse," *Fiji's Daily Post,* August 13, 1999.

18. Ravuvu (1987: 25) writes, "It is through the medium of *yaqona* that direct communication with the spirit world can be achieved." See also Brewster (1922: 20); Brunton (1989); Deane (1921: 30); Deihl (1932: 66); Hocart (1952: 12); Kaplan (1995: 106–107); Ravuvu (1983: 92–93); Spencer (1941: 12); Toren (1999: 34); Turner (1986: 209). On seers using kava as a physical medium—that is, seeing past or future events on the surface of the liquid—see Kaplan (1995: 209); Katz (1993: 284); Spencer (1941: 54–55).

19. "Devil Told Me to, Says Molester," *Fiji Times,* January 27, 1999.

20. In pre-Christian Fiji, tossing kava into the sea was an act of spiritual pacification: "Canoes have been lost because the crew, instead of exerting themselves in a storm, have quitted their posts to *soro* [humble themselves] to their god, and throw yaqona and whales' teeth at the waves to propitiate them" (Williams 1982: 89).

21. Irene Manueli, "Drunk Youths Bash Old Man," *Fiji Times,* March 8, 1999.

22. Kava can be the solution as well as the problem: "In cases of witchcraft-induced illness, an effective cure requires [kava] to be drunk in a ceremony where the *dauvagunu* 'giver of drink' . . . prepares the [kava] and calls on the winds to beg the ancestor God to remove the curse," according to Toren (1999: 155). She adds, "Sometimes he or she places a *tabua* (whale's tooth) on a Bible and calls on Jesus Christ as well as on the ancestor God; but whatever the specific form of the ceremony, the tributary offering of *yaqona* is essential."

23. One man in Tavuki occasionally attended kava-drinking sessions but did not drink because he belonged to an evangelical sect that forbade it. Despite his Church's ban on consumption, which he faithfully observed, when he attended kava sessions he voiced his approval of the proceedings (cf. Thomas 1997: 50).

24. "Women Highlight Social Problem"; see also "Stay Off the Grog, Clergy Told," *Fiji Times,* August 25, 1998.

Chapter 5. Sacred Land and the Power of Prayer

1. The authors circulated versions in both Fijian and English, but the English translation (which they apparently did themselves) is somewhat misleading. For example, the parenthetical gloss of *veivakaturagataki* should be "chiefs, heads of households, warriors and other traditional roles" and not simply "chiefly system." Also, the "other peoples" concluding the English paragraph is not in the Fijian version.

2. "Tauri kei na Kena Soli na Lewa kei Viti" (Deed of Sovereignty), 2000, unpublished document in author's possession.

3. *Tevoro* is a loanword from the English "devil" (Dixon 1988: 369). Ravuvu (1983: 93) translates *tevoro* as "devil or spirits," eliding the issue of whether or

not they are ancestral. Capell's *Fijian Dictionary* (1991) defines *tevoro* as "an evil spirit, a demon." The slippage between devils as nonhuman and devils as human ancestors is evident in Hocart (1929). First he translates *tevoro* as "devil" (185), but then he quotes an informant: "[He] once asked me if I had ever seen *tevoro* in Europe, 'the souls of the dead you know' " (187; see also Hocart 1912b).

4. "Landowners Up in Arms over Outlets," *Fiji's Daily Post,* March 3, 2003, available at http://www.fijilive.com/news/show/news/2003/03/03/03f.htm.

5. In a previously published account of this chain prayer (in *American Anthropologist* 106(1) [2004]: 6–16), I described Rev. Serewai's mentioning the leaf remedy after the chain prayer of July 31, but this is incorrect; he told me this on July 24.

6. In a later retelling of these events, I was told that Venina claimed that the agent possessing her was a relative (whom she named) who was still alive. To this day I have been unable to learn more about this claim, and I have not heard any similar claims made about people being possessed by living relatives.

7. In late 1990s Tavuki, millennialism evinced itself in fleeting ways. A few people asked me about the "Y2K Bug" they had read about in the *Fiji Times.* A friend told me he had dreamed of Judgment Day and its fireballs from the sky, blood soaking the earth, and a man in white reclining in the heavens above. One chief was told by a woman in Suva that an earthquake, causing a big tidal wave, would hit Kadavu in July 1999. Rev. Serewai himself became interested for a while in the prophecies of Nostradamus (as interpreted by a Japanese man and reported by the *Fiji Times*), specifically the prediction that the "King of Terror" would fall from the sky on July 24, 1999. The Methodist Church's official position on the year 2000, however, was a calmly moderate one, and people's thoughts thus seemed to tend toward mild apprehension rather than panic.

8. Listed households came from Tavuki and Nagonedau, plus the school near Tavuki, but since there were only twenty-four time slots for prayer giving at each event (six hours of ritual action divided into fifteen-minute intervals) and there were thirty-five households at the time, eleven households did not participate in any given month.

9. See also Newland (2004), who argues that Fijian Methodists have appropriated Pentecostal practices of spiritual cleansing—which Fijian Pentecostals use because of their concerns about close ties between the Methodist Church and the vanua.

10. After removing the Bibles and the bag of soil, Rev. Serewai shook hands with most of the assembly. The chain prayer was over, but the kava drinking continued. After the final bowl was finished, we went home. The minister placed the bag of soil on his bookshelf next to two wooden trays of communion glasses. The bag remained there for a week or so, after which he emptied it.

11. If chain prayers have been influenced by American evangelical "spiritual warfare" practices, as suggested earlier, the Fijian Methodist use of ambiguity in confronting demons is a unique detail. Jorgensen (2005: 453) observes, "In spiritual warfare, as with exorcisms, names are essential ingredients" (see also De-

Bernardi 1999: 76). In the Vale chain prayer, by contrast, it seemed important that no specific name be given and no particular spirit be identified definitively.

Chapter 6. Onward Christian Soldiers

1. Many indigenous Fijians do not endorse coups, and neither do I, as will become clear throughout this chapter. But it is also the case that many indigenous Fijians did approve of Rabuka's and Speight's coups, whether they were listening appreciatively to radio updates during village kava-drinking sessions or actively participating by heading into Suva and occupying the parliamentary grounds. As an ethnographer, I consider it a primary task to understand why violence can seem, to its participants and local observers, to be a positive moral act of good Christians. Thus I treat people's statements seriously and sympathetically even if I disagree with them intellectually. Many scholars have provided excellent general analyses of Fiji's politics of violence from diverse perspectives; key texts are Halapua (2003); Howard (1991); Kaplan (1988, 1990a, 1990b, 1995, 1998, 2004, 2005); Kaplan and Kelly (1999); Kelly (1991, 1995, 2004, 2005); Kelly and Kaplan (1994, 2001); B. Lal (1992, 2000, 2001, 2004, 2006); B. Lal and Pretes (2001); V. Lal (1990); Lawson (1990, 1991, 1997); Norton (1977); Rutz (1995); and Srebrnik (2002); see also Field, Baba, and Nabobo-Baba (2005) and Robertson and Sutherland (2001). For ethnographies of the 2000 coup, see Trnka (2002).

2. Quoted in Nicholas D. Kristof, "In a South Seas Eden, a First Taste of Race Strife," *New York Times,* May 1, 1987.

3. According to Winston Halapua (2003: 120), the Taukei Movement held its initial public meeting in July, opening the event with the words "God is with us," a fragment of John Wesley's famous deathbed utterance, which echoes Romans 8:31.

4. Tuwere (2002: 101–102) describes Fijian Christians' confusion during the political upheavals of 1987 and 2000: "The bulk of Fijian Christians of all denominations were unprepared for the moment, not knowing what to say or where to stand in relation to the crisis. The difficulty was also bolstered through interpretation of certain biblical texts in relation to the station of chiefs. This is particularly true of Romans 13:1–2, where reference is made to 'supreme authorities' and unmistakably relates to chiefs in the Fijian social system: . . . Those who already are chiefs are appointed by God. Whoever rebels against the chief is rebelling against what God has instituted." The intellectual élite were as confused as anyone. Winston Halapua (2003: 35 n. 1), who was the Anglican Church's vicar-general in 1987, recalls that during the turmoil he "became keenly aware of the deficiency within the theological community in handling militarism."

5. See Riles (2000: 31) for the story of a Taiwanese minister who became "the only 'nonindigenous person' ministering to the indigenous Fijian [Methodist] community" but lost her high-level position because of postcoup Church politics.

6. In 1996 Rabuka annulled the Sunday ban, provoking hostility from religious ethnonationalists (Srebrnik 2002: 194). On the Sunday ban and the Church coup, see also Dropsy (1993); Garrett (1990: 100–104); Halapua (2003: 76–79).

7. Ethnonationalists had succeeded in getting a new national constitution in 1990, a "pro-ethnic Fijian and racially discriminatory" document (Kaplan 2004: 154). In 1997, following the research and recommendations of the Constitutional Review Commission, "a well-crafted, far more democratic constitution" was promulgated (154; see also Lal 2001, 2004: 274), but it became a lightning rod for criticism from conservative indigenous Fijians.

8. Bernadette Hussein, "Christian Party Principles," *Fiji Times,* October 26, 1998.

9. Sainimili Lewa and Matelita Ragogo, "Methodists Face Division," *Fiji Times,* October 20, 1998.

10. Ruci Mafi, "Chaudhry Tells of Coup Abuse," *Fiji Times,* November 29, 2002.

11. Speight occasionally used religion as an after-the-fact justification. For example, describing the day of the coup, he said, "The story behind how the coup took place and how we met — all the players — is quite miraculous in and of itself. It's nothing short of providential influence. And yet, I'm not a religious man. I haven't been to church in 15 years. And yet having said that, I think all of us in our hearts, you know, have a quiet resolve and respect for the Almighty, in our own way" (quoted in Robertson and Sutherland 2001: 14). Later, when soldiers shot at Speight's car, "an angry Speight claimed divine intervention saved him from assassination" (28).

12. Akuila Yabaki, letter from Fiji Citizens' Constitutional Forum, May 19, 2000, distributed electronically by the Pacific People's Partnership. See also Lal (2004: 276); Robertson and Sutherland (2001: 46, 48, 118).

13. Michael Field, "Mongooses Scamper as Fiji's Hostage Drama Drags On," Agence France-Presse, July 2, 2000.

14. Asha Lakhan, "Fiji's Indigenous Parties in Unity Talks in Lead Up to Elections," Agence France-Presse, July 2, 2000.

15. "In 2003, the [Methodist] church was pleading for the pardoning of the soldiers involved in the 2000 mutiny, as a part of the reconciliation process" (Lal 2004: 275). Thus the work of retroactive legitimation continues. The subject of pardoning the 2000 coup leaders was one of the justifications Voreqe Bainimarama used for his own coup of December 2006. Bainimarama's coup is, in my opinion, still too fresh for analysis in this book.

Chapter 7. The Road to Damascus Runs through Waisomo Village

1. The version of Fijian that Takotavuki speaks in this narrative is not fully idiomatic; it is marked by occasional pidginization, reflecting the fact that he was

telling the story to me, a Westerner whose skills in Fijian are not those of an indigenous speaker.

2. This is apparently a reference to such verses as Romans 7:20–21: "Now if I do that I would not, it is no more I that do it, but sin that dwelleth in me. I find then a law, that, when I would do good, evil is present with me."

3. However, as Susan Harding (2000) has argued, scandals can enhance a preacher's reputation when they force listeners to "harmonize" gaps and conflicts in stories. Writing of Jerry Falwell, Harding claims that "what makes Falwell's scandalous actions productive is that they also bound people to him"; their acceptance of him "was the outcome of continuous interpretive labor, of wrestling with the doubts and qualms Falwell generated, of overcoming them, of having—of making—faith in spite of them" (100). A sinful past also makes a captivating story and a great contrast to present-day moral behavior.

4. The term I used, *uro,* literally means "animal fat" and was used in the early 2000s as slang for an attractive person; see Tent (2004: 315). Here I use the 1990s American English slang *phat* because it works as a homonym, although a more resonant translation might be "Juicy!"

5. The term I am translating as "church compound" is *lomanibai,* which literally means "inside the fence" and designates the church grounds within the village. During my time in Tavuki there was no longer a fence around the grounds, but the term remains.

References

Abramson, Allen. 2000. Bounding the Unbounded: Ancestral Land and Jural Relations in the Interior of Eastern Fiji. In *Land, Law and Environment: Mythical Land, Legal Boundaries,* ed. A. Abramson and D. Theodossopoulos, 191–210. London: Pluto Press.

Allen, William. 1887. Kadavu Circuit Annual Report. Methodist Missionary Society of Australia Collection, National Archives of Fiji.

Arendt, Hannah. 1969. Reflections on Violence. *New York Review of Books* 12(4), February 27. http://www.nybooks.com/articles/11395.

Arms, D. G. 1984. The Church and the Vernacular. In *Duivosavosa: Fiji's Languages—Their Use and Their Future,* ed. G. B. Milner, D. G. Arms, and P. Geraghty, 17–31. Suva, Fiji: Oceania Printers.

Arno, Andrew. 1985. Impressive Speeches and Persuasive Talk: Traditional Patterns of Political Communication in Fiji's Lau Group from the Perspective of Pacific Ideal Types. *Oceania* 56(2): 124–137.

———. 1990. Disentangling Indirectly: The Joking Debate in Fijian Social Control. In *Disentangling: Conflict Discourse in Pacific Societies,* ed. K. A. Watson-Gegeo and G. M. White, 241–289. Stanford: Stanford University Press.

———. 1993. *The World of Talk on a Fijian Island: An Ethnography of Law and Communicative Causation.* Norwood, NJ: Ablex.

———. 2003. Aesthetics, Intuition, and Reference in Fijian Ritual Communication: Modularity in and out of Language. *American Anthropologist* 105(4): 807–819.

———. 2005. *Cobo* and *Tabua* in Fiji: Two Forms of Cultural Currency in an Economy of Sentiment. *American Ethnologist* 32(1): 46–62.

Austin, J. L. 1962. *How to Do Things with Words.* 2nd ed. Ed. J. O. Urmson and M. Sbisà. Cambridge, MA: Harvard University Press.

Bakhtin, Mikhail. 1981. Discourse in the Novel. In *The Dialogic Imagination: Four Essays by M. M. Bakhtin.* Ed. M. Holquist. Trans. C. Emerson and M. Holquist, 259–422. Austin: University of Texas Press.

Baldry, H. C. 1952. Who Invented the Golden Age? *Classical Quarterly* (n.s.) 2(1–2): 83–92.

Barr, Kevin J. 2004. *The Church and Fijian Ethnocentrism: An Adventure in Religious History and Sociology*. Suva, Fiji: Ecumenical Centre for Research Education and Advocacy.

Bauman, Richard. 1983. *Let Your Words Be Few: Symbolism of Speaking and Silence among Seventeenth-Century Quakers*. Cambridge, UK: Cambridge University Press.

Beauclerc, G. A. F. W. 1999. Legend of the Elevation of Mount Washington, Kadavu. *Domodomo* (Masthead) 12(1): 26–29.

Becker, Anne E. 1995. *Body, Self, and Society: The View from Fiji*. Philadelphia: University of Pennsylvania Press.

Benveniste, Émile. 1971. *Problems in General Linguistics*. Trans. M. E. Meek. Coral Gables, FL: University of Miami Press.

Besnier, Niko. 1995. *Literacy, Emotion, and Authority: Reading and Writing on a Polynesian Atoll*. Cambridge, UK: Cambridge University Press.

Birtwhistle, Allen. 1983. Methodist Missions. In *A History of the Methodist Church in Great Britain*, vol. 3, ed. R. Davies, A. R. George, and G. Rupp, 1–116. London: Epworth Press.

Boyer, Paul. 1992. *When Time Shall Be No More: Prophecy Belief in Modern American Culture*. Cambridge, MA: Belknap Press.

Brenneis, Donald. 1984a. Grog and Gossip in Bhatgaon: Style and Substance in Fiji Indian Conversation. *American Ethnologist* 11(3): 487–506.

———. 1984b. Straight Talk and Sweet Talk: Political Discourse in an Occasionally Egalitarian Community. In *Dangerous Words: Language and Politics in the Pacific*, ed. D. L. Brenneis and F. R. Myers, 69–84. New York: New York University Press.

———. 1990. Dramatic Gestures: The Fiji Indian *Pancayat* as Therapeutic Event. In *Disentangling: Conflict Discourse in Pacific Societies*, ed. K. A. Watson-Gegeo and G. White, 214–238. Stanford: Stanford University Press.

Brewster, A. B. 1922. *The Hill Tribes of Fiji*. Philadelphia: J. P. Lippincott.

Brison, Karen J. 2007. *Our Wealth Is Loving Each Other: Self and Society in Fiji*. Lanham, MD: Lexington Books.

Brunton, Ron. 1989. *The Abandoned Narcotic: Kava and Cultural Instability in Melanesia*. Cambridge, UK: Cambridge University Press.

Buatava, Vitori. 1996. In the Footsteps of Mosese: The Foundation Years of Roman Catholic Catechists in Fiji, 1842–1893. In *The Covenant Makers: Islander Missionaries in the Pacific*, ed. D. Munro and A. Thornley, 173–185. Suva, Fiji: Pacific Theological College and the Institute of Pacific Studies at the University of the South Pacific.

Burns, Alan, T. Y. Watson, and A. T. Peacock. 1960. *Report of the Commission of Enquiry into the Natural Resources and Population Trends of the Colony of Fiji 1959*. London: Crown Agents for Oversea Governments and Administrations.

Cammack, Floyd McKee. 1962. Bauan Grammar. Ph.D. diss., Cornell University.

Cannell, Fenella, ed. 2006. *The Anthropology of Christianity.* Durham, NC: Duke University Press.

Capell, A. 1991. *A New Fijian Dictionary.* 3rd ed. Suva, Fiji: Government Printer.

Carey, Jesse. 1867–1874. Letterbook. Methodist Overseas Mission Collection, CY Reel 452, Mitchell Library, Sydney.

Cargill, David. 1977. *The Diaries and Correspondence of David Cargill, 1832–1843.* Ed. A. J. Schütz. Canberra: Australian National University Press.

Cato, A. C. 1947. A New Religious Cult in Fiji. *Oceania* 18(1): 146–156.

Cheyne, T. K., and J. Sutherland Black, eds. 1899. *Encyclopædia Biblica,* vol. 1. New York: Macmillan.

Clammer, John R. 1973. Colonialism and the Perception of Tradition in Fiji. In *Anthropology and the Colonial Encounter,* ed. T. Asad, 199–220. New York: Humanities Press.

———. 1976. *Literacy and Social Change: A Case Study of Fiji.* Leiden, Netherlands: E. J. Brill.

Clark, Jeffrey. 1989. The Incredible Shrinking Men: Male Ideology and Development in a Southern Highlands Society. *Canberra Anthropology* 12(1–2): 120–143.

———. 2000. *Steel to Stone: A Chronicle of Colonialism in the Southern Highlands of Papua New Guinea.* Oxford: Oxford University Press.

Clunie, Fergus. 1986. *Yalo i Viti: Shades of Viti: A Fiji Museum Catalogue.* Suva: Fiji Museum.

Codrington, R. H. 1957. *The Melanesians: Studies in Their Anthropology and Folk-Lore.* New Haven, CT: HRAF Press.

Colchester, Chloe. 2005. Objects of Conversion: Concerning the Transfer of *Sulu* to Fiji. In *The Art of Clothing: A Pacific Experience,* ed. S. Küchler and G. Were, 33–46. London: UCL Press.

Coleman, Simon. 2000. *The Globalisation of Charismatic Christianity: Spreading the Gospel of Prosperity.* Cambridge, UK: Cambridge University Press.

Collocott, Alfred J. 1884. Kadavu Annual Circuit Report. Methodist Missionary Society of Australia Collection, National Archives of Fiji.

Colony of Fiji. 1896. *Report of the Commission Appointed to Inquire into the Decrease of the Native Population.* Suva, Fiji: Edward John March, Government Printer.

Cook, Barbara Ellen. 1975. Na Kai Kandavu: A Study of Bilingualism, Acculturation, and Kinship in the Fiji Islands. Ph.D. diss., Stanford University.

Cook, C. O. Leigh, ed. 1996. *Fijian Diary, May Cook, 1904–1906: A Young Australian Woman's Account of Village Life in Fiji.* Mount Martha, Australia: Pen-Folk Publishing.

Cronheim, Georg E., Joseph P. Buckley, Clellan S. Ford, Carleton Gajdusek, Lowell D. Holmes, Murle W. Klohs, Hans J. Meyer, and Carl C. Pfeiffer. 1967. Discussion. In *Ethnopharmacologic Search for Psychoactive Drugs,* ed. D. H. Efron, B. Holmstedt, and N. S. Kline, 174–181. Washington, DC: U.S. Department of Health, Education, and Welfare.

Csordas, Thomas J. 1997. *Language, Charisma, and Creativity: The Ritual Life of a Religious Movement.* Berkeley: University of California Press.

Dean, Eddie, and Stan Ritova. 1988. *Rabuka: No Other Way.* Sydney: Double-day.

Deane, W. 1921. Fijian Society: Or the Sociology and Psychology of the Fijians. London: Macmillan.

———. 1999. Tanovo—The God of Ono. *Domodomo* 12(1): 30–35.

DeBernardi, Jean. 1999. Spiritual Warfare and Territorial Spirits: The Globalization and Localisation of a "Practical Theology." *Religious Studies and Theology* 18(2): 66–96.

Deihl, Joseph R. 1932. Kava and Kava-Drinking. *Primitive Man* 5(4): 61–68.

Derrick, R. A. 1946. *A History of Fiji,* vol. 1. Suva, Fiji: Printing and Stationery Department.

———. 1957. *The Fiji Islands: A Geographical Handbook.* Suva, Fiji: Government Printer.

Dickhardt, Michael. 2000. Das Land, die Ahnen, die Dämonen, die Kirche und der Gott in der Höhe Formen religiöser Räumlichkeit in Fiji (Land, Ancestors, Demons, the Church, and God on High: Forms of Religious Space in Fiji). In *Cartografia Religiosa—Religiöse Kartographie—Cartographie Religieuse* (Religious Cartography) (Studia Religiosa Helvetica Series Altera 4), ed. D. Pezzoli-Olgiati and F. Stolz, 253–288. Bern, Switzerland: Peter Lang.

———. 2005. *Viti,* the Soil from Eden: On Historical Praxis as a Mode of Connecting in Kadavu. *Oceania* 75(4): 342–353.

Dixon, R. M. W. 1988. *A Grammar of Boumaa Fijian.* Chicago: University of Chicago Press.

———. 1997. *The Rise and Fall of Languages.* Cambridge, UK: Cambridge University Press.

Dropsy, Audrey. 1993. The Church and the Coup: The Fijian Methodist Church Coup of 1989. *Review* (Fiji) 13(20): 43–57.

Dundon, Colin George. 2000. Raicakacaka: "Walking the Road" from Colonial to Post-Colonial Mission. Ph.D. diss., Australian Defence Force Academy, University of New South Wales.

Dureau, Christine. 2001. Recounting and Remembering "First Contact" on Simbo. In *Cultural Memory: Reconfiguring History and Identity in the Postcolonial Pacific,* ed. J. M. Mageo, 130–162. Honolulu: University of Hawai'i Press.

Edwards, Maldwyn. 1955. *John Wesley and the Eighteenth Century: A Study of His Social and Political Influence.* Rev. ed. London: Epworth Press.

Emberson-Bain, 'Atu. 1994. *Labour and Gold in Fiji.* Cambridge, UK: Cambridge University Press.

Endicott, William. 1923. *Wrecked among Cannibals in the Fijis: A Narrative of Shipwreck and Adventure in the South Seas.* Salem, MA: Marine Research Society.

Engelke, Matthew. 2007. *A Problem of Presence: Beyond Scripture in an African Church.* Berkeley: University of California Press.

Engelke, Matthew, and Matt Tomlinson, eds. 2006. *The Limits of Meaning: Case Studies in the Anthropology of Christianity.* New York: Berghahn.

Ernst, Manfred. 1994. *Winds of Change: Rapidly Growing Religious Groups in the Pacific Islands.* Suva, Fiji: Pacific Conference of Churches.

Evans-Pritchard, E. E. 1965. *Theories of Primitive Religion.* Oxford: Clarendon Press.

Ferguson, James. 1999. *Expectations of Modernity: Myths and Meanings of Urban Life on the Zambian Copperbelt.* Berkeley: University of California Press.

Field, Michael, Tupeni Baba, and Unaisi Nabobo-Baba. 2005. *Speight of Violence: Inside Fiji's 2000 Coup.* Canberra, Australia: Pandanus Books.

Fiji Islands Bureau of Statistics. 1998. *1996 Fiji Census of Population and Housing: General Tables.* Parliamentary Paper no. 43 of 1998. Suva: Fiji Islands Bureau of Statistics.

Fijilive. 2004. Christian Democrats Deregistered. http://www.fijilive.com, February 25.

———. 2005. Catholics Dedicate Mass to Sick Pope. http://www.fijilive.com, April 2.

Fiji Visitors Bureau. 1983. *Annual Reports for the Years 1979–1981.* Parliament of Fiji, Parliamentary Paper no. 71 of 1983.

Firth, Stewart. 1997. Colonial Administration and the Invention of the Native. In *The Cambridge History of the Pacific Islanders,* ed. D. Denoon, S. Firth, J. Linnekin, M. Meleisea, and K. Nero, 253–288. Cambridge, UK: Cambridge University Press.

Fison, Lorimer, and A. S. Gatschet. 1885. Specimens of Fijian Dialects. *Internationale Zeitschrift für Allgemeine Sprachwissenschaft* 2: 193–208.

Ford, Clellan S. 1967. Ethnographical Aspects of Kava. In *Ethnopharmacologic Search for Psychoactive Drugs,* ed. D. H. Efron, B. Holmstedt, and N. S. Kline, 162–173. Washington, DC: U.S. Department of Health, Education, and Welfare.

France, Peter. 1966. The Kaunitoni Migration: Notes on the Genesis of a Fijian Tradition. *Journal of Pacific History* 1: 107–113.

———. 1969. *The Charter of the Land: Custom and Colonization in Fiji.* Melbourne, Australia: Oxford University Press.

Gajdusek, D. Carleton. 1967. Recent Observations on the Use of Kava in the New Hebrides. In *Ethnopharmacologic Search for Psychoactive Drugs,* ed. D. H. Efron, B. Holmstedt, and N. S. Kline, 119–125. Washington, DC: U.S. Department of Health, Education, and Welfare.

Garrett, John. 1982. *To Live among the Stars: Christian Origins in Oceania.* Geneva, Switzerland: World Council of Churches.

———. 1990. Uncertain Sequel: The Social and Religious Scene in Fiji since the Coups. *Contemporary Pacific* 2(1): 87–111.

———. 1992. *Footsteps in the Sea: Christianity in Oceania to World War II.* Geneva, Switzerland: World Council of Churches.

Geraghty, Paul. 1977. How a Myth Is Born—The Story of the Kaunitoni Story. *Mana* 2(1): 25–29.

———. 1989. Language Reform: History and Future of Fijian. In *Language Reform: History and Future,* vol. 4, ed. I. Fodor and C. Hagège, 377–395. Hamburg, Germany: Helmut Buske Verlag.

Government of Fiji. 1995. Provincial Profile Report, 1994–1995: Kadavu. Unpublished document in author's possession.

Graham, Laura R. 1993. A Public Sphere in Amazonia? The Depersonalized Collaborative Construction of Discourse in Xavante. *American Ethnologist* 20(4): 717–741.

Groves, Murray. 1963. The Nature of Fijian Society. *Journal of the Polynesian Society* 72: 272–291.

Gunson, Niel. 1966. On the Incidence of Alcoholism and Intemperance in Early Pacific Missions. *Journal of Pacific History* 1: 43–62.

Halapua, Winston. 2003. *Tradition, Lotu and Militarism in Fiji.* Lautoka: Fiji Institute of Applied Studies.

Halèvy, Elie. 1971. *The Birth of Methodism in England.* Chicago: University of Chicago Press.

Hanns Seidel Foundation. 1999. Na Vuli ni Veituberi ni "Duavata" kei na Mata ni Tikina kei na Yasana—Yawe [Kadavu] (The "Duavata" Program Workshop and the District Representatives and the Province—Yawe [Kadavu]). Unpublished document in author's possession.

Harding, Susan Friend. 1991. Representing Fundamentalism: The Problem of the Repugnant Cultural Other. *Social Research* 58(2): 373–393.

———. 2000. *The Book of Jerry Falwell: Fundamentalist Language and Politics.* Princeton, NJ: Princeton University Press.

Hashimoto, Kazuya. 1989. Fijian Christianization: A Multidimensional Approach to Third World Christianity. *Man and Culture in Oceania* 5: 1–19.

Hau'ofa, Epeli. 1993. Our Sea of Islands. In *A New Oceania: Rediscovering Our Sea of Islands,* ed. E. Waddell, V. Naidu, and E. Hau'ofa, 2–16. Suva, Fiji: University of the South Pacific.

Hefner, Robert W, ed. 1993. *Conversion to Christianity: Historical and Anthropological Perspectives on a Great Transformation.* Berkeley: University of California Press.

Heighway family. 1932. *"Not as Men Build": The Story of William Aitken Heighway of Fiji.* Sydney, Australia: Robert Dey, Son & Co.

Heinz, Donald. 1993. The Sabbath in Fiji as Guerrilla Theatre. *Journal of the American Academy of Religion* 61(3): 415–442.

Hereniko, Vilsoni. 2003. Interdisciplinary Approaches in Pacific Studies: Understanding the Fiji Coup of 19 May 2000. *Contemporary Pacific* 15(1): 75–90.

Hobsbawm, E. J. 1964. *Labouring Men: Studies in the History of Labour.* London: Weidenfeld and Nicolson.

Hocart, A. M. 1912a. A Native Fijian on the Decline of His Race. *Hibbert Journal* 11(1): 85–98.

———. 1912b. On the Meaning of Kalou and the Origin of Fijian Temples. *Journal of the Royal Anthropological Institute* 42: 437–449.

———. 1929. *Lau Islands, Fiji.* Honolulu: Bernice P. Bishop Museum, Bulletin 62.

———. 1936. *Kings and Councillors: An Essay in the Comparative Anatomy of Human Society.* Cairo: Printing Office Paul Barbey.

———. 1952. *The Northern States of Fiji.* London: Royal Anthropological Institute of Great Britain and Ireland.

———. n.d. Heart of Fiji. Unpublished manuscript, Turnbull Library, Wellington, New Zealand.

Hooper, Steven. 2003. Cannibals Talk. *Anthropology Today* 19(6): 20.

Howard, Michael C. 1991. *Fiji: Race and Politics in an Island State.* Vancouver: University of British Columbia Press.

ICL [International Constitutional Law]. 2000. Fiji Constitution. http://www.oefre.unibe.ch/law/icl/fj00000_.html.

Irvine, Judith. 1979. Formality and Informality in Communicative Events. *American Anthropologist* 81(4): 773–789.

Ivy, Marilyn. 1995. *Discourses of the Vanishing: Modernity, Phantasm, Japan.* Chicago: University of Chicago Press.

Jackson, John. 1999. Feejeean Islands. *Domodomo* 12(1): 7–8.

Jolly, Margaret. 1992. Custom and the Way of the Land: Past and Present in Vanuatu and Fiji. *Oceania* 62(4): 330–354.

———. 1998. Other Mothers: Maternal "Insouciance" and the Depopulation Debate in Fiji and Vanuatu, 1890–1930. In *Maternities and Modernities: Colonial and Postcolonial Experiences in Asia and the Pacific,* ed. K. Ram and M. Jolly, 177–212. Cambridge, UK: Cambridge University Press.

Jorgensen, Dan. 1981. Taro and Arrows: Order, Entropy, and Religion among the Telefolmin. Ph.D. diss., University of British Columbia.

———. 2005. Third Wave Evangelism and the Politics of the Global in Papua New Guinea: Spiritual Warfare and the Recreation of Place in Telefolmin. *Oceania* 75(4): 444–461.

Kaplan, Martha. 1988. The Coups in Fiji: Colonial Contradictions and the Post-Colonial Crisis. *Critique of Anthropology* 8(3): 93–116.

———. 1989. Luve ni Wai as the British Saw It: Constructions of Custom and Disorder in Colonial Fiji. *Ethnohistory* 36(4): 349–371.

———. 1990a. Christianity, People of the Land, and Chiefs in Fiji. In *Christianity in Oceania: Ethnographic Perspectives,* ed. J. Barker, 127–147. Lanham, MD: University Press of America.

———. 1990b. Meaning, Agency, and Colonial History: Navosavakadua and the *Tuka* Movement in Fiji. *American Ethnologist* 17(1): 3–22.

———. 1995. *Neither Cargo nor Cult: Ritual Politics and the Colonial Imagination in Fiji.* Durham, NC: Duke University Press.

———. 1998. When 8,870−850=1: Discourses against Democracy in Fiji, Past and Present. In *Making Majorities: Constituting the Nation in Japan, Korea, China, Malaysia, Fiji, Turkey, and the United States,* ed. D. C. Gladney, 198–214. Stanford: Stanford University Press.

———. 2004. Promised Lands: From Colonial Lawgiving to Postcolonial Takeovers in Fiji. In *Law and Empire in the Pacific: Fiji and Hawai'i,* ed. S. E. Merry and D. Brenneis, 153–186. Santa Fe, NM: School of American Research Press.

———. 2005. The *Hau* of Other Peoples' Gifts: Land Owning and Taking in Turn-of-the-Millennium Fiji. *Ethnohistory* 52(1): 29–46.

Kaplan, Martha, and John D. Kelly. 1999. On Discourse and Power: "Cults" and "Orientals" in Fiji. *American Ethnologist* 26(4): 843–863.

Katz, Richard. 1993. *The Straight Path: A Story of Healing and Transformation in Fiji*. Reading, MA: Addison-Wesley.

Keane, Webb. 1991. Delegated Voice: Ritual Speech, Risk, and the Making of Marriage Alliances in Anakalang. *American Ethnologist* 18(2): 311–330.

———. 1995. The Spoken House: Text, Act, and Object in Eastern Indonesia. *American Ethnologist* 22(1): 102–124.

———. 1997a. From Fetishism to Sincerity: On Agency, the Speaking Subject, and Their Historicity in the Context of Religious Conversion. *Comparative Studies in Society and History* 39(4): 674–693.

———. 1997b. Religious Language. *Annual Review of Anthropology* 26: 47–71.

———. 1997c. *Signs of Recognition: Powers and Hazards of Representation in an Indonesian Society*. Berkeley: University of California Press.

———. 2002. Sincerity, "Modernity," and the Protestants. *Cultural Anthropology* 17(1): 65–92.

———. 2006. Anxious Transcendence. In *The Anthropology of Christianity*, ed. F. Cannell, 308–323. Durham, NC: Duke University Press.

———. 2007. *Christian Moderns: Freedom and Fetish in the Mission Encounter*. Berkeley: University of California Press.

Keesing, Roger M. 1984. Rethinking *Mana*. *Journal of Anthropological Research* 40(1): 137–156.

———. 1985. Conventional Metaphors and Anthropological Metaphysics: The Problematic of Cultural Translation. *Journal of Anthropological Research* 41(2): 201–217.

Keesing-Styles, Esther, and William Keesing-Styles, eds. 1988. *Unto the Perfect Day: The Journal of Thomas James Jaggar, Feejee, 1838–1845*. Auckland, New Zealand: Solent Publishing.

Keller, Eva. 2005. *The Road to Clarity: Seventh-Day Adventism in Madagascar*. New York: Palgrave Macmillan.

Kelly, John D. 1991. *A Politics of Virtue: Hinduism, Sexuality, and Countercolonial Discourse in Fiji*. Chicago: University of Chicago Press.

———. 1995. *Bhakti* and Postcolonial Politics: Hindu Missions to Fiji. In *Nation and Migration: The Politics of Space in the South Asian Diaspora*, ed. P. van der Veer, 43–72. Philadelphia: University of Pennsylvania Press.

———. 2004. Gordon Was No Amateur: Imperial Legal Strategies in the Colonization of Fiji. In *Law and Empire in the Pacific: Fiji and Hawai'i*, ed. S. E. Merry and D. Brenneis, 61–100. Santa Fe, NM: School of American Research Press.

———. 2005. Boycotts and Coups, *Shanti* and *Mana* in Fiji. *Ethnohistory* 52(1): 13–27.

Kelly, John D., and Martha Kaplan. 1990. History, Structure, and Ritual. *Annual Review of Anthropology* 19: 119–150.

Kelly, John D., and Martha Kaplan. 1994. Rethinking Resistance: Dialogics of "Disaffection" in Colonial Fiji. *American Ethnologist* 21(1): 123–151.

Kelly, John D., and Martha Kaplan. 2001. *Represented Communities: Fiji and World Decolonization*. Chicago: University of Chicago Press.

Kempf, Wolfgang. 1999. Cosmologies, Cities, and Cultural Constructions of Space: Oceanic Enlargements of the World. *Pacific Studies* 22(2): 97–114.

Knauft, Bruce M. 2002. *Exchanging the Past: A Rainforest World of Before and After.* Chicago: University of Chicago Press.

Kuhlken, Robert Thomas. 1994. Agricultural Terracing in the Fiji Islands, vol. 2. Ph.D. diss., Louisiana State University.

Lal, Brij V. 1992. *Broken Waves: A History of the Fiji Islands in the Twentieth Century.* Honolulu: University of Hawai'i Press.

———, ed. 2000. *Fiji before the Storm: Elections and the Politics of Development.* Canberra: Asia Pacific Press at the Australian National University.

———. 2001. *Mr Tulsi's Store: A Fijian Journey.* Canberra: Pandanus Books.

———. 2004. Heartbreak Islands: Reflections on Fiji in Transition. In *Law and Empire in the Pacific: Fiji and Hawai'i,* ed. S. E. Merry and D. Brenneis, 261–280. Santa Fe, NM: School of American Research Press.

———. 2006. *Islands of Turmoil: Elections and Politics in Fiji.* Canberra: Asia Pacific Press and ANU E Press.

Lal, Brij V., and Michael Pretes, eds. 2001. *Coup: Reflections on the Political Crisis in Fiji.* Canberra, Australia: Pandanus Books.

Lal, Victor. 1990. *Fiji: Coups in Paradise.* London: Zed Books.

Latour, Bruno. 1993. *We Have Never Been Modern.* Trans. C. Porter. New York: Harvester Wheatsheaf.

Lawson, Stephanie. 1990. The Myth of Cultural Homogeneity and Its Implications for Chiefly Power and Politics in Fiji. *Comparative Studies in Society and History* 32(4): 795–821.

———. 1991. *The Failure of Democratic Politics in Fiji.* Oxford: Clarendon Press.

———. 1997. Chiefs, Politics, and the Power of Tradition in Contemporary Fiji. In *Chiefs Today: Traditional Pacific Leadership and the Postcolonial State,* ed. G. M. White and L. Lindstrom, 108–118. Stanford: Stanford University Press.

Lebot, Vincent, Mark Merlin, and Lamont Lindstrom. 1997. *Kava: The Pacific Elixir.* Rochester, VT: Healing Arts Press.

Lester, R. H. 1941. Kava Drinking in Vitilevu, Fiji, Part I. *Oceania* 12(2): 97–121.

Lévi-Strauss, Claude. 1987. *Introduction to the Work of Marcel Mauss.* Trans. F. Baker. London: Routledge & Kegan Paul.

Lotu Wesele e Viti kei Rotuma. 1998. *I Vola ni Vula* [calendar]. Suva: Methodist Church in Fiji and Rotuma.

———. 1999. *I Vola ni Vula* [calendar]. Suva: Methodist Church in Fiji and Rotuma.

Macnaught, Timothy J. 1977. "We Seem to Be No Longer Fijians": Some Perceptions of Social Change in Fijian History. *Pacific Studies* 1(1): 15–24.

Mahoney, John. 1993. The Liberation of a Fijian Christian Artist. *Pacific Journal of Theology* 9: 29–36.

Makihara, Miki. 2005. Being Rapa Nui, Speaking Spanish: Children's Voices on Easter Island. *Anthropological Theory* 5(2): 117–134.

Malcomson, Scott L. 1990. *Tuturani: A Political Journey in the Pacific Islands.* New York: Poseidon Press.

Martin, John, ed. 1979. *An Account of the Natives of the Tonga Islands in the South Pacific Ocean*. New York: AMS Press.

Maskarinec, Gregory G. 1995. *The Rulings of the Night: An Ethnography of Nepalese Shaman Oral Texts*. Madison: University of Wisconsin Press.

Mauss, Marcel. 1972. *A General Theory of Magic*. Trans. R. Brain. London: Routledge & Kegan Paul.

McLeod, Hugh. 1996. *Religion and Society in England, 1850–1914*. London: Macmillan.

Methodist Overseas Missions Trust Association. 1981. *Ai Vola ni Sere ni Lotu Wesele e Viti* (Fijian Methodist Hymnbook). Suva, Fiji: Methodist Church Press.

Meyer, Birgit. 1999. *Translating the Devil: Religion and Modernity among the Ewe in Ghana*. Trenton, NJ: Africa World Press.

Michener, James A. 1951. *Return to Paradise*. New York: Random House.

Milner, G. B. 1952. A Study of Two Fijian Texts. *Bulletin of the School of Oriental and African Studies* 14, part 2: 346–377.

Miyazaki, Hirokazu. 2000. Faith and Its Fulfillment: Agency, Exchange, and the Fijian Aesthetics of Completion. *American Ethnologist* 27(1): 31–51.

———. 2004. *The Method of Hope: Anthropology, Philosophy, and Fijian Knowledge*. Stanford: Stanford University Press.

Moore, William. 1868. Letter from Ovalau, January 20. *Wesleyan Missionary Notices* 2(6): 84–86.

Morey, C. J. 1932. Wrecked on the Voyage to Lau. *Journal of the Polynesian Society* 41: 310–311.

Nacagilevu, Ratu Mekemeke. 1996. Yale kei Naikorokoro, Kadavu. In *Mai Kea ki Vei?* [From There to Where?] *Stories of Methodism in Fiji and Rotuma, 1835–1995*, ed. A. Thornley and T. Vulaono, 266–267. Suva: Methodist Church in Fiji and Rotuma.

Nayacakalou, Rusiate R. 1955. The Fijian System of Kinship and Marriage (Part 1). *Journal of the Polynesian Society* 64(1): 44–55.

———. 1957. The Fijian System of Kinship and Marriage (Part 2). *Journal of the Polynesian Society* 66(1): 44–59.

———. 1961. The Bifurcation and Amalgamation of Fijian Lineages over a Period of Fifty Years. *Transactions and Proceedings of the Fiji Society* 8(2): 122–133.

———. 1975. *Leadership in Fiji*. Melbourne, Australia: Oxford University Press.

———. 1978. *Tradition and Change in the Fijian Village*. Suva, Fiji: Institute of Pacific Studies, University of the South Pacific.

Nettleton, Joseph. 1866a. Letter from Kadavu, dated June 27, 1865. *Wesleyan Missionary Notices* 1(34): 540–542.

———. 1866b. Letter from Kadavu, dated July 1, 1865. *Wesleyan Missionary Notices* 1(34): 542.

Newland, Lynda. 2004. Turning the Spirits into Witchcraft: Pentecostalism in Fijian Villages. *Oceania* 75(1): 1–18.

Niukula, Paula. 1994. *The Three Pillars: The Triple Aspect of Fijian Society*. Suva, Fiji: Christian Writing Project.

Norton, Robert. 1977. *Race and Politics in Fiji*. St. Lucia, Australia: University of Queensland Press.

———. 2000. Understanding the Results of the 1999 Fiji Elections. In *Fiji before the Storm: Elections and the Politics of Development,* ed. B. V. Lal, 49–72. Canberra: Asia Pacific Press at the Australian National University.

Nunn, Patrick D. 1999. Early Human Settlement and the Possibility of Contemporaneous Volcanism, Western Kadavu. *Domodomo* 12(1): 36–49.

Pawley, Andrew. 1980. A Sketch Grammar of the Nabukelevu Language of Kadavu. Working Papers in Anthropology, Archaeology, Linguistics, Maori Studies, Paper no. 57. Department of Anthropology, University of Auckland.

Pick, Daniel. 1989. *Faces of Degeneration: A European Disorder, c. 1848–c. 1918.* Cambridge, UK: Cambridge University Press.

Premdas, Ralph R. 1995. *Ethnic Conflict and Development: The Case of Fiji.* Aldershot, UK: Avebury.

Prescott, John, Dana Jamieson, Nicole Emdur, and Pat Duffield. 1993. Acute Effects of Kava on Measures of Cognitive Performance, Physiological Function and Mood. *Drug and Alcohol Review* 12: 49–58.

Qereti, Paula. n.d. Na Ivolavosa Vakaviti [monolingual Fijian dictionary]. Computer files.

Quain, Buell. 1948. *Fijian Village.* Chicago: University of Chicago Press.

Rack, Henry D. 1989. *Reasonable Enthusiast: John Wesley and the Rise of Methodism.* Philadelphia: Trinity Press International.

Rafael, Vicente L. 1988. *Contracting Colonialism: Translation and Christian Conversion in Tagalog Society under Early Spanish Rule.* Ithaca, NY: Cornell University Press.

Rakaseta, Vilimaina. 1999. *Fiji Islands Population Profile Based on 1996 Census: A Guide for Planners and Policy-Makers.* Noumea, New Caledonia: Secretariat of the Pacific Community.

Ratuva, Steven. 2002. God's Will in Paradise: The Politics of Ethnicity and Religion in Fiji. *Development Bulletin* 59: 19–23.

Ravuvu, Asesela D. 1983. *Vaka i Taukei: The Fijian Way of Life.* Suva, Fiji: Institute of Pacific Studies, University of the South Pacific.

———. 1987. *The Fijian Ethos.* Suva, Fiji: Institute of Pacific Studies, University of the South Pacific.

———. 1991. *The Facade of Democracy: Fijian Struggles for Political Control, 1830–1987.* Suva, Fiji: Reader Publishing House.

Reed, Adam. 2003. *Papua New Guinea's Last Place: Experiences of Constraint in a Postcolonial Prison.* New York: Berghahn Books.

Reeves, Edward. 1898. *Brown Men and Women, or, the South Sea Islands in 1895 and 1896.* London: Swan Sonnenschein.

Riles, Annelise. 2000. *The Network Inside Out.* Ann Arbor: University of Michigan Press.

Rivers, W. H. R. 1968. *The History of Melanesian Society,* vol. 1. Oosterhout, Netherlands: Anthropological Publications.

Robbins, Joel. 2001a. God Is Nothing But Talk: Modernity, Language, and Prayer in a Papua New Guinea Society. *American Anthropologist* 103(4): 901–912.

———. 2001b. Ritual Communication and Linguistic Ideology. *Current Anthropology* 42(5): 591–614.

———. 2003. What Is a Christian? Notes toward an Anthropology of Christianity. *Religion* 33(3): 191–199.

———. 2004. *Becoming Sinners: Christianity and Moral Torment in a Papua New Guinea Society.* Berkeley: University of California Press.

———. 2005. The Humiliations of Sin: Christianity and the Modernization of the Subject among the Urapmin. In *The Making of Global and Local Modernities in Melanesia: Humiliation, Transformation and the Nature of Cultural Change,* ed. J. Robbins and H. Wardlow, 43–56. Aldershot, UK: Ashgate.

———. 2006. Anthropology and Theology: An Awkward Relationship? *Anthropological Quarterly* 79(2): 285–294.

Robbins, Joel, and Holly Wardlow, eds. 2005. *The Making of Global and Local Modernities in Melanesia: Humiliation, Transformation, and the Nature of Cultural Change.* Aldershot, UK: Ashgate.

Robertson, Robbie, and William Sutherland. 2001. *Government by the Gun: The Unfinished Business of Fiji's 2000 Coup.* Annandale, New South Wales: Pluto Press Australia.

Robson, John. 1875. Kadavu Circuit Annual Report. Methodist Missionary Society of Australia Collection, National Archives of Fiji.

Rokowaqa, Epeli. 1926. Ai Tukutuku kei Viti (History of Fiji). *Methodist Missionary Magazine,* April, 1–84.

Roth, G. K. 1973. *Fijian Way of Life.* 2nd ed. Melbourne, Australia: Oxford University Press.

Routledge, David. 1985. *Matanitū: The Struggle for Power in Early Fiji.* Suva, Fiji: University of the South Pacific.

Royce, James S. H., and C. J. Baird. 1861. Kadavu Circuit Annual Report. Methodist Missionary Society of Australia Collection, National Archives of Fiji.

Rutherford, Danilyn. 2006. Nationalism and Millenarianism in West Papua: Institutional Power, Interpretive Practice, and the Pursuit of Christian Truth. In *The Limits of Meaning: Case Studies in the Anthropology of Christianity,* ed. M. Engelke and M. Tomlinson, 105–127. New York: Berghahn.

Rutz, Henry J. 1995. Occupying the Headwaters of Tradition: Rhetorical Strategies of Nation Making in Fiji. In *Nation Making: Emergent Identities in Postcolonial Melanesia,* ed. R. J. Foster, 71–93. Ann Arbor: University of Michigan Press.

Rutz, Henry J., and Erol M. Balkan. 1992. Never on Sunday: Time-Discipline and Fijian Nationalism. In *The Politics of Time,* ed. H. J. Rutz, 62–85. Washington, DC: American Anthropological Association.

Ryle, Jacqueline. 2001. "My God, My Land": Interwoven Paths of Christianity and Tradition in Fiji. Ph.D. diss., University of London.

———. 2005. Roots of Land and Church: The Christian State Debate in Fiji. *International Journal for the Study of the Christian Church* 5(1): 58–78.

Sahlins, Marshall D. 1962. *Moala: Culture and Nature on a Fijian Island.* Ann Arbor: University of Michigan Press.

——. 1985. *Islands of History*. Chicago: University of Chicago Press.

——. 1991. The Return of the Event, Again; With Reflections on the Beginnings of the Great Fijian War of 1843 to 1855 between the Kingdoms of Bau and Rewa. In *Clio in Oceania: Toward a Historical Anthropology*, ed. A. Biersack, 37–99. Washington, DC: Smithsonian Institution Press.

——. 1992. The Economics of Develop-Man in the Pacific. *Res* 21: 13–25.

——. 1993. Cery Cery Fuckabede. *American Ethnologist* 20: 848–867.

——. 2004. *Apologies to Thucydides: Understanding History as Culture and Vice Versa*. Chicago: University of Chicago Press.

Sanneh, Lamin. 2003. *Whose Religion Is Christianity?: The Gospel beyond the West*. Grand Rapids, MI: William B. Eerdmans.

Scarr, Deryck. 1984. *Fiji: A Short History*. Sydney: George Allen & Unwin.

Schieffelin, Bambi B. 2000. Introducing Kaluli Literacy: A Chronology of Influences. In *Regimes of Language: Ideologies, Polities, and Identities*, ed. P. V. Kroskrity, 293–327. Santa Fe, NM: School of American Research Press.

Scott, David. 1994. *Formations of Ritual: Colonial and Anthropological Discourses on the Sinhala* Yaktovil. Minneapolis: University of Minnesota Press.

Schütz, Albert J. 1985. *The Fijian Language*. Honolulu: University of Hawai'i Press.

——. 2004. English Loan Words in Fijian. In *Borrowing: A Pacific Perspective*, ed. J. Tent and P. Geraghty, 253–294. Canberra: Pacific Linguistics, Research School of Pacific and Asian Studies, Australian National University.

Seruvakula, Semi B. 2000. *Bula Vakavanua*. Suva, Fiji: Institute of Pacific Studies, University of the South Pacific.

Sharpham, John. 2000. *Rabuka of Fiji: The Authorised Biography of Major-General Sitiveni Rabuka*. Rockhampton, Australia: Central Queensland University Press.

Siegel, Jeff. 1995. How to Get a Laugh in Fijian: Code-Switching and Humor. *Language in Society* 24: 95–110.

Sofer, Michael. 1985. Yaqona and Peripheral Economy. *Pacific Viewpoint* 26(2): 415–436.

Spate, O. H. K. 1959. The Fijian People: Economic Problems and Prospects. Suva, Fiji: Government Press, Legislative Council Paper no. 13.

Spencer, Dorothy M. 1941. *Disease, Religion and Society in the Fiji Islands*. Seattle: University of Washington Press.

Srebrnik, Henry. 2002. Ethnicity, Religion, and the Issue of Aboriginality in a Small Island State: Why Does Fiji Flounder? *Round Table* 364: 187–210.

Steedly, Mary Margaret. 1993. *Hanging without a Rope: Narrative Experience in Colonial and Postcolonial Karoland*. Princeton, NJ: Princeton University Press.

Sukuna, Ratu Sir Lala. 1983. *Fiji: The Three-Legged Stool: Selected Writings of Ratu Sir Lala Sukuna*. Ed. D. Scarr. London: Macmillan Education.

Tambiah, Stanley Jeyaraja. 1985. A Performative Approach to Ritual. In *Culture, Thought, and Social Action: An Anthropological Perspective*, 123–166. Cambridge, MA: Harvard University Press.

Tent, Jan. 2004. Lexical Borrowing in Fiji English. In *Borrowing: A Pacific Perspective,* ed. J. Tent and P. Geraghty, 307–330. Canberra: Pacific Linguistics, Research School of Pacific and Asian Studies, Australian National University.

Theroux, Paul. 1992. *The Happy Isles of Oceania: Paddling the Pacific.* New York: G. P. Putnam's Sons.

Thomas, Nicholas. 1986. *Planets around the Sun: Dynamics and Contradictions of the Fijian* Matanitu. Sydney: University of Sydney.

———. 1990. Sanitation and Seeing: The Creation of State Power in Early Colonial Fiji. *Comparative Studies in Society and History* 32(1): 149–170.

———. 1992. The Inversion of Tradition. *American Ethnologist* 19(2): 213–232.

———. 1997. *In Oceania: Visions, Artifacts, Histories.* Durham, NC: Duke University Press.

Thompson, E. P. 1963. *The Making of the English Working Class.* London: Victor Gollancz.

Thomson, Basil. 1908. *The Fijians: A Study of the Decay of Custom.* London: William Heinemann.

Thornley, Andrew. 1979. Fijian Methodism, 1874–1945: The Emergence of a National Church. Ph.D. diss., Australian National University.

———. 1995. A Letter from Oneata: The First Missionary Report from Fiji. *Pacific Journal of Theology* (series 2), 14: 31–34.

———. 2000. *The Inheritance of Hope: John Hunt, Apostle of Fiji.* Suva, Fiji: Institute of Pacific Studies, University of the South Pacific.

———. 2002. *Exodus of the I Taukei: The Wesleyan Church in Fiji: 1848–74.* Suva, Fiji: Institute of Pacific Studies, University of the South Pacific.

———. 2005. "Through a Glass Darkly": Ownership of Fijian Methodism, 1850–80. In *Vision and Reality in Pacific Religion: Essays in Honour of Niel Gunson,* ed. P. Herda, M. Reilly, and D. Hilliard, 132–153. Christchurch, New Zealand: Macmillan Brown Centre for Pacific Studies.

Tippett, Alan Richard. 1944. The Snake in Early Fijian Belief (with Special Reference to the Cult which Survived until Recently at Naikorokoro, Kadavu). *Transactions and Proceedings of the Fiji Society* 2: 279–296.

———. 1945. General Statement on the Type of School Represented by the Two I Have Managed: Tavuki (Cuvu, Nadroga) and Richmond (Kadavu). Report addressed to the Secretary, Commission Examining Mission Education, Fiji, June 20. Methodist Missionary Society of Australasia collection, National Archives of Fiji.

———. 1947. Co-Partners with God. In Historical Writing: Fiji, 1947–1967, 59–70. Unpublished manuscript, Tippett Collection, St. Mark's National Theological Centre Library, Canberra, Australia.

———. 1955. Anthropological Research and the Fijian People. In Fijian Current Affairs 1941–1965, 67–80. Unpublished manuscript, Tippett Collection, St. Mark's National Theological Centre Library, Canberra, Australia.

———. 1958a. The Integrating Gospel. Unpublished manuscript, Tippett Collection, St. Mark's National Theological Centre Library, Canberra, Australia.

———. 1958b. Shifting Foci of Methodist Witness in Fiji, 1835–1900, with a 20th Century Postscript. In Historical Writing: Fiji, 1947–1967, 1–58. Unpublished manuscript, Tippett Collection, St. Mark's National Theological Centre Library, Canberra, Australia.

———. 1960. Fijian Proverbs, Metaphoric Idioms and Riddles: An Ethnolinguistic Study. *Transactions and Proceedings of the Fiji Society* 8(1): 65–93.

———. 1961. A Historical Survey of the Character and Training of the Fijian Ministry. In Historical Writing: Fiji, 1947–1967, 216–226. Unpublished manuscript, Tippett Collection, St. Mark's National Theological Centre Library, Canberra, Australia.

———. 1971. The Continuity of Sorcery and Magic in Fiji. In Anthropological Writing—1962–1971, 343–387. Unpublished manuscript, Tippett Collection, St. Mark's National Theological Centre Library, Canberra, Australia.

———. 1974a. A Diachronic Study of Religious Innovation in the Fiji Islands. In Research and Writing—1973–74, 382–447. Unpublished manuscript, Tippett Collection, St. Mark's National Theological Centre Library, Canberra, Australia.

———. 1974b. The Ethnopsychology of Depopulation in the Pacific. In Research and Writing—1973–74, 1–72. Unpublished manuscript, Tippett Collection, St. Mark's National Theological Centre Library, Canberra, Australia.

———. 1974c. The Meaning of Meaning. In Research and Writing—1973–74, 306–343. Unpublished manuscript, Tippett Collection, St. Mark's National Theological Centre Library, Canberra, Australia.

———. 1976a. The Metaanthropology of Conversion in Non-Western Society. In The Phenomenology of Cross-Cultural Conversion in Oceania, 83–147. Unpublished manuscript, Tippett Collection, St. Mark's National Theological Centre Library, Canberra. (Originally printed as Research in Progress Pamphlet no. 14, Fuller Theological Seminary, Pasadena, CA, 1976)

———. 1976b. The Role of the Fijian Herald in Negotiations between Persons and Parties at Different Status Levels. In Research and Writing: Sept. 1974–April 1976, 135–177. Unpublished manuscript, Tippett Collection, St. Mark's National Theological Centre Library, Canberra, Australia.

———. 1985. The Role of Christianity in the Emergence of the Fijian Nation. In Missiological Essays 1982–1985, 17–24. Unpublished manuscript, Tippett Collection, St. Mark's National Theological Centre Library, Canberra, Australia.

Tomlinson, Matt. 2002. Voice and Earth: Making Religious Meaning and Power in Christian Fiji. Ph.D. diss., University of Pennsylvania.

———. 2006a. The Limits of Meaning in Fijian Methodist Preaching. In *The Limits of Meaning: Case Studies in the Anthropology of Christianity*, ed. M. Engelke and M. Tomlinson, 129–146. New York: Berghahn.

———. 2006b. Retheorizing Mana: Bible Translation and Discourse of Loss in Fiji. *Oceania* 76(2): 173–185.

———. 2007. Mana in Christian Fiji: The Interconversion of Intelligibility and Palpability. *Journal of the American Academy of Religion* 75(3): 524–553.

Toren, Christina. 1988. Making the Present, Revealing the Past: The Mutability and Continuity of Tradition as Process. *Man,* n.s. 23(4): 696–717.

———. 1990. *Making Sense of Hierarchy: Cognition as Social Process in Fiji.* London: Athlone Press.

———. 1994. The Drinker as Chief or Rebel: Kava and Alcohol in Fiji. In *Gender, Drink and Drugs,* ed. M. McDonald, 153–173. Oxford: Berg.

———. 1999. *Mind, Materiality, and History: Explorations in Fijian Ethnography.* London: Routledge.

———. 2004. Becoming a Christian in Fiji: An Ethnographic Study of Ontogeny. *Journal of the Royal Anthropological Institute* 10(1): 221–240.

Trawick, Margaret. 1988. Ambiguity in the Oral Exegesis of a Sacred Text. *Cultural Anthropology* 3(3): 316–351.

Trigg, Joseph Wilson. 1983. *Origen: The Bible and Philosophy in the Third-Century Church.* Atlanta, GA: John Knox.

Trnka, Susanna, ed. 2002. Ethnographies of the May 2000 Fiji Coup. Special issue of *Pacific Studies* 25(4).

Turner, James W. 1986. "The Water of Life": Kava Ritual and the Logic of Sacrifice. *Ethnology* 25(3): 203–214.

———. 1988. A Sense of Place: Locus and Identity in Matailobau, Fiji. *Anthropos* 83: 421–431.

———. 1995. Substance, Symbol, and Practice: The Power of Kava in Fijian Society. *Canberra Anthropology* 18 (1–2): 97–118.

Tuwere, Ilaitia S. 1998. Nai Talatala kei na Politiki (Ministers and Politics). *Domodra* 2(4): 13–14.

———. 2002. *Vanua: Towards a Fijian Theology of Place.* Suva, Fiji: Institute of Pacific Studies at the University of the South Pacific.

Urban, Greg. 1991. *A Discourse-Centered Approach to Culture: Native South American Myths and Rituals.* Austin: University of Texas Press.

———. 1996. *Metaphysical Community: The Interplay of the Senses and the Intellect.* Austin: University of Texas Press.

———. 2001. *Metaculture: How Culture Moves through the World.* Minneapolis: University of Minnesota Press.

Vale ni Volavola ni Yasana ko Kadavu. 1995. *Taro* (Questions), questionnaire for Provincial Profile Project. Copy in provincial office at Tavuki.

Vitebsky, Piers. 1993. *Dialogues with the Dead: The Discussion of Mortality among the Sora of Eastern India.* Cambridge, UK: Cambridge University Press.

Von Hoerschelmann, Dorothee. 1995. The Religious Meaning of the Samoan Kava Ceremony. *Anthropos* 90: 193–195.

Wall, Colman. 1918. Dakuwaqa. *Transactions of the Fijian Society for the Year 1917,* 39–46.

———. 1919. [Untitled response to comments on "Dakuwaqa."] *Transactions of the Fijian Society for the Year 1918,* 10–12.

Wallis, Mary. 1851. *Life in Feejee, or, Five Years among the Cannibals.* Boston: William Heath.

Walsh, Crosbie. 2006. *Fiji: An Encyclopaedic Atlas.* Suva, Fiji: University of the South Pacific.

Ward, R. Gerard. 1961. Internal Migration in Fiji. *Journal of the Polynesian Society* 70: 257–71.

———. 1964. Cash Cropping and the Fijian Village. *Geographical Journal* 130(4): 484–500.

Waterhouse, Joseph. 1866. *The King and People of Fiji.* London: Wesley Conference Office.

Watters, R. F. 1969. *Koro: Economic Development and Social Change in Fiji.* Oxford: Clarendon Press.

Webb, A. J. 1870. Letter from Kadavu, dated July 30, 1870. *Wesleyan Missionary Notices* 2(15): 212–214.

White, Geoffrey M. 1991. *Identity through History: Living Stories in a Solomon Islands Society.* Cambridge, UK: Cambridge University Press.

Williams, Raymond. 1973. *The Country and the City.* London: Chatto & Windus.

Williams, Thomas. 1982. *Fiji and the Fijians,* vol. 1. Ed. G. S. Rowe. Suva: Fiji Museum.

Williksen-Bakker, Solrun. 1990. Vanua—A Symbol with Many Ramifications in Fijian Culture. *Ethnos* 55 (3–4): 232–247.

Wood, A. Harold. 1978. *Overseas Missions of the Australian Methodist Church,* vol. 2: *Fiji.* Melbourne, Australia: Aldersgate Press.

Young, Raymond. 2001. A Land with a Tangled Soul: Lakeban Traditions and the Native Lands Commission. *Journal of the Polynesian Society* 110(4): 347–376.

Index

Adam, 67, 85, 99–102, 104, 138
alcohol, 26, 109, 124–25, 216n13; crime and, 190–91, 194, 196, 198; drunkenness, 63, 68, 216n14; homebrewed, 197–98; introduction of, 44
ambiguity, 142–43, 151–55, 218n11
Ananias, 185
ancestors: deified, 36, 116, 159–61; Israelites and, 10, 92, 107, 207n2; kava drinking habits, 121, 125–26; missionary views of, 36, 45–46; owners of land, 136; recently deceased, 71–72; size and strength of, 5, 9–10, 73–75, 151–52, 212n4; spirits of, 3, 5, 10, 26, 80, 142–56, 204; spiritual presence in soil, 137–40, 142, 145, 151–56. *See also* curses; demonization
Anglicans, 7, 219n4
Arendt, Hannah, 94–95
Arno, Andrew, 68, 114, 118, 208n5, 213n1
Assemblies of God, 7, 9*table*, 48, 48*table*, 128
Australian Baptist Mission, 15

Ba, 51, 132
Baidamudamu, 32–33, 57, 196; church opening, 130–31; church statistics, 48*table*; people from, 49, 88, 101, 200; preachers' meeting, 86
Bainimarama, Voreqe, 171–72, 216n9, 220n15
Baird, C. J., 38
Bakaliceva, 212n3
Baker, Thomas, 81–82

Bakhtin, M. M., 16
Balkan, Erol, 165
baptism, 42, 51, 58, 127
bark cloth, 208n5
Bau, 36, 51, 177; dialect of, 38–40, 210n12
Bavadra, Timoci, 163–64
Becker, Anne, 147
Benjamin, 102
Benveniste, Émile, 208n4
Bethlehem, 100–103, 108, 214n10
Bible, 85, 147; application to life, 91, 100–108; knowledge of, 86; law in, 104–5, 215n13; materiality of, 13, 16–17, 145, 153, 217n22; popular passages, 63–64; readings in chain prayers, 150–51; readings in church services, 56, 58, 93–94, 96, 98–99, 105, 107; translation, 18, 38–41, 39*table*, 126, 210n12; violence and, 168
Bible Society of the South Pacific, 165, 169
Bloch, Ernst, 185
Bonnke, Reinhard, 7
Brison, Karen, 68, 211n18, 214n12
British and Foreign Bible Society, 39–40
Buatava, Vitori, 210n14
Bunyan, John, 38
Burebasaga confederacy, 36
Buretu, 51
Busa, 52
Butadroka, Sakeasi, 169

Cakaudrove, 36
Cakobau, Ratu Seru, 132, 177

Text:	10/13 Galliard
Display:	Galliard
Compositor:	Binghamton Valley Composition
Printer and binder:	Maple-Vail Book Manufacturing Group